D1109558

THE BRITANNICA GUIDE TO

EXPLORERS AND EXPLORATIONS

THAT CHANGED THE MODERN WORLD

TURNING POINTS IN HISTORY

THE BRITANNICA GUIDE TO
EXPLORERS AND EXPLORATIONS
THAT CHANGED THE MODERN WORLD

EDITED BY KENNETH PLETCHER, SENIOR EDITOR, GEOGRAPHY AND HISTORY

Britannica®
Educational Publishing

IN ASSOCIATION WITH

ROSEN
EDUCATIONAL SERVICES

Published in 2010 by Britannica Educational Publishing
(a trademark of Encyclopædia Britannica, Inc.)
in association with Rosen Educational Services, LLC
29 East 21st Street, New York, NY 10010.

First Edition

Britannica Educational Publishing
Michael I. Levy: Executive Editor
Marilyn L. Barton: Senior Coordinator, Production Control
Steven Bosco: Director, Editorial Technologies
Lisa S. Braucher: Senior Producer and Data Editor
Yvette Charboneau: Senior Copy Editor
Kathy Nakamura: Manager, Media Acquisition
Kenneth Pletcher: Senior Editor, Geography and History

Rosen Educational Services
Jeanne Nagle: Senior Editor
Nelson Sá: Art Director
Matthew Cauli: Designer
Introduction by Jeri Freedman

Library of Congress Cataloging-in-Publication Data

The Britannica guide to explorers and explorations that changed the modern world /
edited by Kenneth Pletcher.
    p. cm. — (Turning points in history)
"In association with Britannica Educational Publishing, Rosen Educational Services."
ISBN 978-1-61530-028-0 (library binding)
1. Discoveries in geography — History. 2. Explorers — History. 3. Explorers — Biography.
I. Pletcher, Larry, 1946–
G80.B85 2010
910.9 — dc22

                                                                2009037672

Manufactured in the United States of America

CONTENTS

49

110

114

149

188

302

317

*I*ntroduction

Few things have changed the world as much as exploration. The discoveries made by explorers through the ages have altered the culture, commerce, and geopolitical landscape of nations. Exploration has opened markets to new products and led to the cross-fertilization of philosophies and ideas. By climbing the highest mountains and fathoming ocean depths explorers have increased our knowledge of the natural world. Venturing into uncharted territory, they have opened the door to new possibilities and paved the way for progress.

All facets of exploration are examined in this book. A trek through its pages takes readers along on journeys of discovery, introducing them to the men and women who have led expeditions in the name of national glory, unrelenting inquisitiveness, or personal vindication.

Generally, exploration is undertaken for one of three primary reasons. The first revolves around conquest. Throughout history governments have sought the acquisition of land to fortify or expand their domains, thus enhancing their power and gaining prestige in the world view. Explorers traditionally have been the emissaries regarding such ventures, representing the interests of various emperors, kings, queens, and other rulers, and laying claim to land in their name.

The second reason for exploration is commerce. Into this category fall endeavours funded by groups of businessmen to bolster profits, such as the Hudson's Bay Company of England in the 17th century. Such companies often paid for expeditions to distant lands. Their goal was to find new sources of materials and goods they could sell back home. New territories provided much-needed funds if valuable resources such as gold were found. Even if precious metals were not forthcoming, the natural resources such as wood for shipbuilding, furs, and other materials provided valuable income. Explorers also have sought new markets and trade routes. Thus they might bring tea and spices from the Far East to Europe, or transport manufactured goods from Europe for sale in distant lands. A company's bottom line could broaden considerably with greater access to new and existing markets.

The third major category that defines exploration is scientific investigation. There are many different types of scientific expeditions. Some explorers have sought to unlock the mysteries of ancient civilizations; for example, Lord Carnavon's expedition, led by Howard Carter, in search of King Tutankhamen's tomb. Others have sought to accomplish what no one had done before, as was the case with Sir Edmund Hillary's ascent of Mount Everest and Roald Amundsen's expedition to the South Pole. Still others are designed to prove or disprove a hypothesis or theory. For instance, Charles Darwin's around-the-world expedition aboard the *Beagle* had been part of a trend toward explorers taking naturalists with them on their journeys. The trip allowed Darwin to conduct research on creatures and plant life from far-off, exotic locales, which he used in an attempt to reveal the origin of species—and the crux of life itself.

No matter what the rationale for exploration, there is little doubt that plenty of explorers have been motivated by a desire for adventure and fame, as well as practical reward. One reason people are captivated by the exploits of explorers is the inherent mystery and romance of searching for something hitherto unknown, often in the face of risk and peril.

People have always wanted to know what lies beyond the boundaries of their own lands. From the times that people first constructed ships that could sail on the open sea they've set out to explore. One of the earliest known explorers is Pytheas. Sailing from Greece in the 4th century BCE, he explored the Atlantic coast of Europe, reaching as far as Britain.

Although Pytheas most likely traveled by following the European coastline, wanderlust would eventually lead explorers farther afield. Some of the earliest recorded explorers were the Vikings. By the end of the first millennium the Vikings had built ships capable of sailing across the ocean. The son of the founder of the Norse colony of Greenland, Lief Eriksson traveled all the way to North America.

Explorers often brought more than resources or trade goods back from their travels. Marco Polo was a member of an Italian family that traded between Italy and the Mideast. As such, he traveled extensively throughout Eastern Europe and the Far East, venturing as far as China. Along the way he met with dignitaries, a circumstance that eventually led him to provide diplomatic services to the emperor of China. When he returned to Italy after spending years in China Polo brought knowledge of the Far East back to Europe. His experiences, captured in the books he wrote, expanded Europeans' knowledge of the world outside their geographic boundaries and fostered understanding of other cultures, paving the way for fruitful relationships between people previously unknown to each other.

Such early expeditions led to more widespread exploration. The Age of Discovery began in the 15th century as European explorers set out to find new sources of valuable resources to enrich the kingdoms of Europe. Sometimes they found more than they had expected. While searching for a Western route to the East Indies for access to the spice trade Christopher Columbus (1451–1506) discovered a new land. Ferdinand Magellan (1480–1521), an explorer who, like Columbus, had been retained by the regency of Spain, succeeded in going completely around the world.

In 1580 Sir Francis Drake (1540–96), sailing under the auspices of Queen Elizabeth I of England, also had completed a circuit around the globe. Their explorations not only provided the opportunity to claim resource-rich lands but added to human knowledge by, among other things, demonstrating that the world was indeed round, not flat as previously believed.

By the late 17th century ships were large and sturdy enough to carry adventurous souls anywhere in the world. Dutch explorer Abel Jansoon Tasman (1603–1659) traveled to the islands off the coast of Australia, now known as Tasmania and New Zealand. Jean François de Galaup, comte de La Pérouse (1741–c. 1788), Rear Adm. Jules Sébastien César Dumont d'Urville (1790–1842), and Capt. James Cook (1728–79) explored the South Pacific. When Scottish missionary David Livingstone (1813–73) delved deep into the heart of Africa, he became the first European to see the magnificent wonder of a waterfall he subsequently named in honor of England's Queen Victoria.

By the mid-18th century, when the Age of Discovery was nearing an end, exploration had begun to take on a more scientific bent. Instead of merely seeking riches, explorers sought knowledge. German naturalist Friedrich Wilhelm Heinrich Alexander Freiherr von Humboldt (1769–1859) explored South America, looking not for gold but for scientific knowledge. He kept detailed notes and published his findings to share what he'd learned of the botany and geography of the lands he explored. Sir Richard Burton, known for translating *The Arabian Nights*, traveled throughout the African continent, seeking the source of the Nile River.

Despite the many positive aspects of this period, the Age of Discovery also had a dark side. The search for resources led European rulers to claim massive tracts of land throughout the hitherto unexplored world as their own. Throughout the 17th century, English, French, Spanish, and Portuguese explorers carved up North and South America, largely ignoring the claims of native inhabitants, whom they considered inferior. Traders along the coast of Africa began the slave trade, bringing goods such as rum to the tribes along the coast and trading them for human cargo.

By the 19th century, European explorers had reached every corner of the inhabited world. New frontiers were becoming harder to find. Explorers set out to conquer the extreme ends of the Earth--the North and South Poles, the highest mountains, and the depths of the sea. Thus the period between the late 19th and early 20th centuries came to be known as the Heroic Age of Exploration.

The race to reach the North Pole culminated in 1909 with the expedition of Adm. Robert Peary (1856–1920). Although there has been controversy over his claim, Peary is generally considered the first man ever to reach the top of the world. The spirit of competition that marked this time period was further exemplified by the race to reach Antarctica. British, Belgian, Norwegian, Japanese, Swedish, German, French, and Australian explorers, all eager to gain renown, competed to be the first to reach the South Pole and explore the nearly inaccessible, frozen continent. Successful expeditions led by Roald Amundsen and Richard Byrd, and especially Ernest Shackleton and Robert Falcon Scott's ill-fated attempts, provide some of the most dramatic accounts in the annals of exploration.

Explorers have plumbed the depths of time as well as the far reaches of geography. Fueled by the romanticism of the 19th century and an increased interest in scientific investigation as the 20th century dawned, explorers began to find new frontiers by delving into the past. At the same time, several European countries had established major empires, holding vast parts of the Near East and Africa as colonies. Armed with an unassailable sense of right and even duty, these nations sent in explorers to unearth the secrets and artifacts of ancient civilizations of their holdings.

German archaeologist Heinrich Schliemann (1822–90) established the location of the ancient city of Troy in the 1870s. In 1911, Hiram Bingham III (1875–1956) discovered the Incan settlement of Machu Picchu. Howard Carter (1874–1939) unearthed King Tutankhamen's long-hidden tomb during a 1923 archaeological dig in Egypt's Valley of Kings. Arthur Evans (1851–1941) located the Palace of Knossos on the island of Crete, shedding light on the ancient Minoan civilization. Louis Leakey (1903–72) and Mary Leakey (1913–96) did pioneering work in evolution, discovering fossilized remains of prehistoric people in Africa. All of these discoveries shed light on the physical and cultural past of the human race.

No locale is too remote or too inhospitable for explorers. Even the frozen peaks of Mount Everest, the highest mountain in the world, have not proved to be a barrier to human exploration. Attempt after attempt had been made to reach Everest's summit. The goal was finally achieved by Sir Edmund Hillary (1919–2008) and Tenzing Norgay (1914–86) in 1953. Japanese climber Tabei Junko completed the first successful ascent to the summit by a woman in 1975. Expeditions meant to conquer those mighty slopes continue to the present day.

Indeed, as long as there are mountains to climb, challenges to meet, gains to be made, and information to be learned, there will be men and women who engage in explorations of all types and on all scales. In the process, who can tell how these future explorers may change the world, in ways big and small.

Chapter 1: Early Explorers

The motives that spur human beings to examine their environment are many. Strong among them are the satisfaction of curiosity, the pursuit of trade, the spread of religion, and the desire for security and political power. At various times and in distinct places, different motives are dominant. Sometimes one motive inspires discovery, and another motive may inspire the individuals who carry out the search.

The threads of geographical exploration are continuous and, being entwined one with another, are difficult to separate. Three major phases of investigation may nevertheless be distinguished. The first phase is the exploration of the Old World centred on the Mediterranean Sea. The second is the so-called Age of Discovery, during which, in the search for sea routes to Cathay (the name by which China was known to medieval Europe), a New World was found. The third is the establishment of the political, social, and commercial relationships of the New World to the Old and the elucidation of the major physical features of the continental interiors—in short, the delineation of the modern world.

However, as the general parameters of the physical world became known, interest grew in scientific inquiry. As the voyages to claim territory or secure trading rights were completed, people increasingly sought to systematically study the natural world—its physical attributes, flora, and fauna—and, ultimately, humanity's past. This human curiosity has always led individuals to seek Earth's extremes, be they its remote polar regions, its highest mountains, or its greatest ocean depths.

From the time of the earliest recorded history to the beginning of the 15th century, Western knowledge of the world widened from a river valley surrounded by mountains or desert (the views of Babylonia and Egypt) to a Mediterranean world with hinterlands extending from the Sahara to the Gobi deserts and from the Atlantic to the Indian oceans (the views of Greece and Rome). It later expanded again to include the far northern lands beyond the Baltic and another and dazzling civilization in the Far East (the medieval view).

EXPLORATION OF THE ATLANTIC COASTLINES

Beyond the Pillars of Heracles (the Strait of Gibraltar), the Carthaginians (from the Phoenician city of Carthage in what is now Tunisia), holding both shores of the strait, early ventured out into the Atlantic Ocean. A Greek translation of a Punic (Carthaginian) inscription states that Hanno, a Carthaginian, was sent forth "to found cities." Even allowing for a possible great exaggeration of numbers, this expedition, if it occurred, can hardly have been the first exploratory voyage along the coast of West Africa; indeed, Herodotus reports that Phoenicians circumnavigated the continent about 600 BCE. Some scholars think that Hanno reached only the desert edge south of the Atlas; other scholars identify the "deep river infested with crocodiles and hippopotamuses" with the Sénégal River; and still others believe that the island where men "scampered up steep rocks and pelted us with stones" was an island off the coast of Sierra Leone. There is no record that Hanno's voyage was followed up before the era of Henry the Navigator, a Portuguese prince of the 15th century.

About the same time, Himilco, another Carthaginian, set forth on a voyage northward. He explored the coast of Spain, reached Brittany, and in his four-month cruise may have visited Britain. Two centuries later, about 300 BCE,

HANNO

The Carthaginian Hanno conducted a voyage of exploration and colonization to the west coast of Africa sometime
during the 5th century BCE. Setting sail with 60 vessels
holding 30,000 men and women, Hanno founded
Thymiaterion (now Kenitra, Mor.) and built a temple at
Soloeis (Cape Cantin, now Cape Meddouza). He then
founded five additional cities in and around present
Morocco, including Carian Fortress (Greek: Karikon
Teichos) and Acra (Agadir). The Carian Fortress is perhaps
to be identified with Essaouira on the Moroccan coast,
where archaeological remains of Punic settlers have been
found. Farther south he founded Cerne, possibly on the
Río de Oro, as a trading post. He evidently reached the
coast of present Gambia or of Sierra Leone and may have
ventured as far as Cameroon. An account of his voyage was
written in the temple of Baal at Carthage and survives in a
10th-century-CE Greek manuscript known as *Periplus of
Hannon*, which claims to be an ancient Greek translation
from the Punic inscription. Modern scholars doubt whether
Hanno actually continued beyond Morocco.

Carthaginian power at the gate of the Mediterranean temporarily slackened as a result of squabbles with the Greek
city of Syracuse on the island of Sicily, so Pytheas, a
Greek explorer of Massilia (Marseille), sailed through.

It was not Mediterranean folk but Northmen from
Scandinavia, emigrating from their difficult lands centuries
later, who carried exploration farther in the North Atlantic.
From the 8th to the 11th century, bands of Northmen,
mainly Swedish, trading southeastward across the Russian
plains, were active under the name of Varangians in the

PYTHEAS

The navigator, geographer, and astronomer Pytheas (fl. 300
BCE) was the first Greek to visit and describe the British
Isles and the Atlantic coast of Europe. Though his principal work, *On the Ocean*, is lost, something is known of his
ventures through the Greek historian Polybius (*c.* 200–*c.*
118 BCE).

Sailing from the Mediterranean Sea into the Atlantic,
Pytheas stopped at the Phoenician city of Gades (present-
day Cádiz, Spain), probably followed the European
shoreline to the tip of Brittany, and eventually reached
Belerium (Land's End, Cornwall), where he visited the tin
mines, famous in the ancient world. He claimed to have
explored a large part of Britain on foot; he accurately estimated its circumference at 4,000 miles (6,400 km).
Pytheas also estimated the distance from north Britain to
Massalia (Marseille) at 1,050 miles (1,690 km); the actual
distance is 1,120 miles (1,800 km). He visited some northern European countries and may have reached the mouth
of the Vistula River on the Baltic Sea. He also told of
Thule, the northernmost inhabited island, six days' voyage from northern Britain and extending at least to the
Arctic Circle; the region he visited may have been Iceland
or Norway.

Pytheas's comments on small points—e.g., on the
native drinks made of cereals and honey and the use of
threshing barns (contrasted with open-air threshing in
Mediterranean regions)—show acute observation. His scientific interests appear from his calculations made with a
sundial at the summer solstice and from notes on the
lengthening days as he traveled northward. He also observed
that the polestar is not at the true pole and that the Moon
affects tides.

ports of the Black Sea. At the same time other groups, mainly Danish, raiding, trading, and settling along the coasts of the North Sea, arrived in the Mediterranean in the guise of Normans. Neither the Swedes nor the Danes traveling in these regions were exploring lands that were unknown to civilized Europeans, but it is doubtless that contact with them brought to these Europeans new knowledge of the distant northern lands.

It was the Norsemen of Norway who were the true explorers, though since little of their exploits was known to contemporaries and those accounts were soon forgotten, they perhaps added less to the common store of Europe's knowledge than their less adventurous compatriots. About 890 CE, Ohthere of Norway, "desirous to try how far that country extended north," sailed round the North Cape, along the coast of Lapland to the White Sea. But most Norsemen sailing in high latitudes explored not eastward but westward. Sweeping down the outer edge of Britain, settling in Orkney, Shetland, the Hebrides, and Ireland, they then voyaged on to Iceland, where in 870 they settled among Irish colonists who had preceded them by some two centuries. The Norsemen may well have arrived piloted by Irish sailors; and Irish refugees from Iceland, fleeing before the Norsemen, may have been the first discoverers of Greenland and Newfoundland, although this is mere conjecture.

ERIK THE RED

Erik the Red (fl. 10th century), founder of the first European settlement on Greenland (c. 986) and the father of Leif Eriksson, was one of the first Europeans to reach North America. As a child, Erik left his native Norway for western Iceland with his father, Thorvald, who had been exiled for manslaughter. In the Scandinavian style of the time he was known as Erik Thorvaldson and in his youth was nicknamed Erik the Red. When Erik was similarly exiled from Iceland about 980, he decided to explore the land to the west (Greenland). That land, visible in distorted form because of the effect of looming (a type of mirage) from the mountaintops of western Iceland, lay across 175 miles (280 km) of water. It had been skirted by the Norwegian Gunnbjörn Ulfsson earlier in the 10th century. Erik sailed in 982 with his household and livestock but was unable to approach the coast because of drift ice. The party rounded the southern tip of Greenland and settled in an area near present Julianehåb (Qaqortoq). During the three-year period of Erik's exile, the settlers encountered no other people, though they explored to the northwest, discovering Disko Island (now Qeqertarsuaq).

Erik returned to Iceland in 986. His descriptions of the territory, which he named Greenland, convinced many people anxious for more habitable land to join a return expedition. Of the 25 ships that sailed from Iceland, only 14 ships and 350 colonists are believed to have landed safely at an area later known as Eystribygdh (Eastern Colony). By the year 1000 there were an estimated 1,000 Scandinavian settlers in the colony, but an epidemic in 1002 considerably reduced the population. Erik's colony, commemorated in the Icelandic *Eiríks saga* ("Saga of Erik"; translated in the *The Vineland Sagas*), gradually died out; but other Norse settlements in Greenland continued and maintained contact with Norway until the 15th century, when communications stopped for more than 100 years.

LEIF ERIKSSON THE LUCKY

The second of Erik's three sons, Leif Eriksson (fl. 11th century) is widely held to have been the first European to reach the shores of North America. The 13th- and 14th-century Icelandic accounts of his life and additional later evidence show that he was certainly a member of an early Viking voyage to North America, but it remains doubtful whether he led the initial expedition.

Leif sailed from Greenland to Norway in 1000, according to the Icelandic *Eiríks saga*, and was there converted to Christianity by the Norwegian king Olaf I Tryggvason. The following year Leif was commissioned by Olaf to urge Christianity upon the Greenland settlers. He sailed off course on the return voyage and landed on the North American continent, at a region he called Vinland. On returning to Greenland, he proselytized for Christianity and converted his mother, who built the first Christian church in Greenland, at Brattahild.

According to the *Groenlendinga saga* (*Grænlendinga saga*; "Tale of the Greenlanders") in the *Flateyjarbók* ("Songbook"; also translated in *The Vineland Sagas*)— considered more reliable than the *Eiríks saga* by many modern scholars—Leif learned of Vinland from the Icelander Bjarni Herjulfsson, who had been there 14 years earlier. The *Saga* pictures Leif as reaching North America several years after 1000 and visiting Helluland (possibly Labrador) and Markland (possibly Newfoundland) as well as Vinland. Further expeditions to Vinland were then made by Thorvald, Leif's brother, and by the Icelander Thorfinn Karlsefni.

VINLAND

The exact location of the wooded land in North America that was visited and named by Leif Eriksson is not known, but it was probably somewhere along the Atlantic coast-line of what is now eastern or northeastern Canada. As indicated above, the two saga accounts differ somewhat.

According to the *Groenlendinga saga*, Bjarni Herjulfsson's Greenland-bound ship was blown westward off course about 986. He apparently sailed along the Atlantic coastline of eastern Canada and then returned to Greenland. About 1000 a crew of 35 men led by Leif Eriksson set out to try to find the land accidentally sighted by Bjarni. (*Eiríks saga* presents Leif himself as the first to sight Vinland.) Leif's expedition came first to an icy, barren land which they called Helluland ("Flat-Stone Land"); sailing southward, they encountered a flat, wooded land which they named Markland ("Wood Land"). Again they set sail southward, and the warmer, wooded area that they found they named Vinland. There they built some houses and explored the region before returning to Greenland.

In 1003 Leif's brother Thorvald led an expedition to Vinland and spent two years there. In 1004 (or 1010, according to other historians) Thorfinn Karlsefni, encouraged by Thorvald's reports of grapes growing wild in Vinland, led a colonizing expedition of about 130 people (or 65, according to one saga) to Vinland. By the time they had stayed there three years, the colonists' trade with the local Native Americans (First Nations) had turned to warfare, and so the colonists gave up and returned to Greenland. About 1013 Erik the Red's daughter Freydis led an unsuccessful expedition to Vinland and soon afterward returned to Greenland. So ended the Norse visits to the Americas as far as the historical record is concerned.

The Norsemen's name for the land they discovered, Vinland, means "Wine Land." Thorfinn reported that he found "wine berries" growing there, and these were later interpreted to mean grapes, though the Norsemen referred to any berry as a "wine berry," and it is probable that they had actually come upon cranberries. This fruit evidently proved disappointing to Thorfinn's colonists, for when they became disgruntled during the third year of the colonizing expedition, they made a grievance out of not having seen much of the wine banquets that had been promised them.

Nevertheless, the Scandinavians retained the Vinland name. It was as a wine land that the North American continent entered the literature of continental Europe, almost certainly first in 1075 through the *History of the Archbishops of Hamburg-Bremen* written by Adam, head of the cathedral school of Bremen. Adam mentioned Vinland on the authority of King Sweyn II Estridsen of Denmark, who told of Iceland, Greenland, and other lands of the northern Atlantic known to the Scandinavians. Adam says of King Sweyn: "He spoke also of yet another island of the many found in that ocean. It is called Vinland because vines producing excellent wines grow there."

In the 1960s Helge Ingstad adopted the view of the Swedish philologist Sven Söderberg that Vinland did not mean "wine land" but rather "grassland" or "grazing land." Ingstad discovered in 1963 the remains of house sites and other artifacts of a Norse settlement at L'Anse aux Meadows, at the northernmost tip of Newfoundland. Dating techniques have conclusively proved that the remains date from about 1000 CE—i.e., the time of the Norsemen's reputed visits. Further evidence of Viking exploration came in 1965, when the Yale University Press published a medieval map showing the outlines of continental Europe, Iceland, Greenland, and Vinland, the latter being described in a notation on the map as "Island of Vinland, discovered by Bjarni and Leif in company." The authenticity of this map, however, has been sharply debated.

PERSIAN AND ROMAN EXPLORATIONS

Trade, across the land bridges and through the gulfs linking those parts of Asia, Africa, and Europe that lie between the Mediterranean and Arabian seas, was actively pursued from very early times. It is therefore not surprising that exploratory voyages early revealed the coastlines of the Indian Ocean. Herodotus wrote of Necho II, king of Egypt in the late 7th and early 6th centuries BCE, that "when he stopped digging the canal . . . from the Nile to the Arabian Gulf . . . [he] sent forth Phoenician men in ships ordering them to sail back by the Pillars of Hercules." According to the story, they completed the voyage in three years. Upon their return, "they told things . . . unbelievable by me," says Herodotus, "namely that in sailing round Libya they had the sun on the right hand." Whatever he thought of the story of the sun, Herodotus was inclined to believe in the voyage: "Libya, that is Africa, shows that it has sea all round except the part that borders on Asia." Strabo records another story with the same theme: one Eudoxus, returning from a voyage to India about 108 BCE, was blown far to the south of Cape Guardafui. Where he landed he found a wooden prow with a horse carved on it, and he was told by the Africans that it came from a wrecked ship of men from the west.

PILLARS OF HERACLES

The Pillars of Heracles (or Hercules) constitute two promontories at the eastern end of the Strait of Gibraltar. The northern pillar is the Rock of Gibraltar at Gibraltar, and the southern pillar has been identified as one of two peaks: Jebel Moussa (Musa), in Morocco, or Mount Hacho (held by Spain), near the city of Ceuta (the Spanish exclave on the Moroccan coast). The pillars are fabled to have been set there by Heracles as a memorial to his labour of seizing the cattle of the three-bodied giant Geryon.

About 510 BCE Darius the Great, king of Persia, sent one of his officers, Scylax of Caria, to explore the Indus. Scylax traveled overland to the Kabul River, reached the Indus River, followed it to the sea, sailed westward, and, passing by the Persian Gulf (which was already well known), explored the Red Sea, finally arriving at Arsinoë, near modern Suez, Egypt. The greater part of the campaigns of the Macedonian conqueror Alexander the Great were military exploratory journeys. The earlier expeditions through Babylonia and Persia were through regions already familiar to the Greeks, but the later ones through the enormous tract of land from the south of the Caspian Sea to the mountains of the Hindu Kush brought the Greeks a great deal of new geographical knowledge. Alexander and his army crossed the mountains to the Indus Valley and then made a westward march from the lower Indus to Susa through the desolate country along the southern edge of the Iranian plateau; Nearchus, his admiral, in command of the naval forces of the expedition, waited for the favourable monsoon and then sailed from the mouth of the Indus to the mouth of the Euphrates, exploring the northern coast of the Persian Gulf on his way.

As Roman power grew, wealth brought increasing demands for Oriental luxuries; this led to great commercial activity in the eastern seas. As the coasts became well known, the seasonal character of the monsoonal winds was more skillfully used; the southwest monsoon was long known as Hippalus, named for a sailor who was credited with being the first to sail with it direct from the Gulf of Aden to the coast of the Indian peninsula. During the reign of the Roman emperor Hadrian in the 1st century BCE, Western traders reached Siam (now Thailand), Cambodia, Sumatra, and Java; a few also seem to have penetrated northward to the coast of China. In 161 CE, according to Chinese records, an "embassy" came from

the Roman emperor Marcus Aurelius to the emperor
Huandi, bearing goods that Huandi gratefully received
as "tribute." Ptolemy, however, did not know of these
voyages: he swept his peninsula of Colmorgo (Malay)
southwestward to join the eastward trend of his coast of
Africa, thus creating a closed Indian Ocean. He presuma-
bly did not believe the story of the circumnavigation of
Africa. As the 2nd century CE passed and Roman power
declined, trade with the eastern seas did not cease but was
gradually taken over by Ethiopians, Parthians, and Arabs.
The Arabs, most successful of all, dominated eastern sea
routes from the 3rd to the 15th century. In the tales of der-
ring-do of Sindbad the Sailor (a hero of the collection of
Arabian tales called *The Thousand and One Nights*), there
may be found, behind the fiction, the knowledge of these
adventurous Arab sailors and traders, supplying detail to
fill in the outline of the geography of the Indian Ocean.

EAST-WEST CONTACT IN EURASIA

The prelude to the Age of Discovery, however, is to be
found neither in the Norse explorations in the Atlantic
nor in the Arab activities in the Indian Ocean but, rather,
in the land journeys of Italian missionaries and merchants
that linked the Mediterranean coasts to the China Sea.
Cosmas Indicopleustes, an Alexandrian geographer writing in the 6th century, knew that Tzinitza (China) could be
reached by sailing eastward, but he added: "One who
comes by the overland route from Tzinitza to Persia makes
a very short cut." Goods had certainly passed this way
since Roman times, but they usually changed hands at
many a mart, for disorganized and often warring tribes
lived along the routes. In the 13th century the political
geography changed. In 1206 a Mongol chief assumed the
title of Genghis Khan and, after campaigns in China that

gave him control there, turned his conquering armies westward. He and his successors built up an enormous empire until, in the late 13th century, one of them, Kublai Khan, reigned supreme from the Black Sea to the Yellow Sea. Europeans of perspicacity saw the opportunities that friendship with the Mongol power might bring. If Christian Europe could only convert the Mongols, this would at one and the same time heavily tip the scales against Muslim and in favour of Christian power and also give political protection to Christian merchants along the silk routes to the legendary sources of wealth in China. With these opportunities in mind, Pope Innocent IV sent friars to "diligently search out all things that concerned the state of the Tartars" and to exhort them "to give over their bloody slaughter of mankind and to receive the Christian faith." Among others, Giovanni da Pian del Carpini in 1245 and Willem van Ruysbroeck in 1253 went forth to follow these instructions. Traveling the great caravan routes from southern Russia, north of the Caspian and Aral seas and north of the Tien Shan ("Celestial Mountains"), both Carpini and Ruysbroeck eventually reached the court of the emperor at Karakorum. Carpini returned confident that the emperor was about to become a Christian; Ruysbroeck told of the city in Cathay "having walls of silver and towers of gold"; he had not seen it but had been "credibly informed" of it.

Travels of Ibn Baṭṭūṭah

Ibn Baṭṭūṭah (1304–1368/69 or 1377)—in full, Abū ʿAbd Allāh Muḥammad ibn ʿAbd Allāh al-Lawātī al-Ṭanjī ibn Baṭṭūṭah—the greatest medieval Arab traveler, vowed "never to travel any road a second time." Like such Europeans as the members of the Polo family, Ibn Baṭṭūṭah also reached China via the overland route. He was from a family that produced a number of Muslim judges (*qāḍīs*), and he received the traditional juristic and literary education in his native town of Tangier, Mor. In 1325, at the age of 21, he started his travels by undertaking the pilgrimage to Mecca. At first his purpose was to fulfill this religious duty and to broaden his education by studying under famous scholars in the Near East (Egypt, Syria, and the Hejaz). That he achieved his objectives is corroborated by long enumerations of scholars and Sufi (Islamic mystic) saints whom he met and also by a list of diplomas conferred upon him (mainly in Damascus). These studies qualified him for judicial office, whereas the claim of being a former pupil of the then-outstanding authorities in traditional Islamic sciences greatly enhanced his chances and made him thereafter a respected guest at many courts.

But this was to follow later. In Egypt, where he arrived by the land route via Tunis and Tripoli, an irresistible passion for travel was born in his soul, and he decided to visit as many parts of the world as possible. His contemporaries traveled for practical reasons (such as trade, pilgrimage, and education), but Ibn Baṭṭūṭah did it for its own sake, for the joy of learning about new countries and new peoples. He made a living of it, benefitting first from his scholarly status and later from his increasing fame as a traveler. He enjoyed the generosity and benevolence of numerous sultans, governors, and high dignitaries in the countries he visited, thus securing an income that enabled him to continue his wanderings.

From Cairo, Ibn Baṭṭūṭah set out via Upper Egypt to the Red Sea but then returned and visited what is now Syria, there joining a caravan for Mecca. Having finished the pilgrimage in 1326, he crossed the Arabian Desert to regions that are now known as Iraq, southern Iran, Azerbaijan, and Baghdad. There he met the last of the Mongol khans of Iran, Abū Saʿīd (ruled 1316–36), and some lesser rulers. Ibn

Baṭṭūṭah spent the years between 1327 and 1330 in Mecca and Medina leading the quiet life of a devotee, but such a long stay did not suit his temperament.

Embarking on a boat in Jiddah, he sailed with a retinue of followers down both shores of the Red Sea to Yemen, crossed it by land, and set sail again from Aden. This time he navigated along the eastern African coast, visiting the trading city-states as far as Kilwa (Tanzania). His return journey took him to southern Arabia, Oman, Hormuz, southern Persia, and across the Persian Gulf back to Mecca in 1332.

There a new, ambitious plan matured in his mind. Hearing of the sultan of Delhi, Muḥammad ibn Tughluq (ruled 1325–51), and his fabulous generosity to Muslim scholars, he decided to try his luck at the sultan's court. Forced by lack of communications to choose a more indirect route, Ibn Baṭṭūṭah turned northward, again passed Egypt and Syria, and boarded ship for Asia Minor (Anatolia) in Latakia. He crisscrossed this "land of the Turks" in many directions at a time when Anatolia was divided into numerous sultanates. Thus, his narrative provides a valuable source for the history of this country between the end of the Seljuq power and the rise of the house of Ottoman. All local rulers and heads of religious brotherhoods (ākhīs) received Ibn Baṭṭūṭah cordially.

His journey continued across the Black Sea to the Crimea, then to the northern Caucasus and to Saray on the lower Volga River, capital of the khan of the Golden Horde, Muḥammad Özbeg (ruled 1312–41). According to his narrative, he undertook an excursion from Saray to Bulgary on the upper Volga and Kama, but there are reasons to doubt his veracity on this point. On the other hand, the narrative of his visit to Constantinople (modern Istanbul) in the retinue of the khan's wife, a Byzantine princess, seems to be an eyewitness record, although there are some minor chronological discrepancies. Ibn Baṭṭūṭah's description of the Byzantine capital is vivid and, in general, accurate. Although he shared the strong opinions of his fellow Muslims toward unbelievers, his account of the "second Rome" shows him as a rather tolerant man with a lively curiosity. Nevertheless, he always felt happier in the realm of Islam than in non-Muslim lands, whether Christian, Hindu, or pagan.

After his return from Constantinople through the Russian steppes, he continued his journey in the general direction of India. From Saray he traveled with a caravan to Central Asia, visiting the ancient towns of Bukhara, Samarkand, and Balkh, all of these still showing the scars left by the Mongol invasion. He took rather complicated routes through Khorāsān and Afghanistan, and, after crossing the Hindu Kush mountain range, he arrived at the frontiers of India on the Indus River on Sept. 12, 1333, by his own dating. The accuracy of this date is doubtful, as it would have been impossible to cover such enormous distances (from Mecca) in the course of only one year. Because of this discrepancy, his subsequent dating until 1348 is highly uncertain.

At this time he was already a man of some importance and fame, with a large train of attendants and followers and also with his own harem of legal wives and concubines. India and its ruler, Muḥammad ibn Tughluq, lived up to Ibn Baṭṭūṭah's expectations of wealth and generosity, and the traveler was received with honours and gifts and later appointed grand *qāḍī* of Delhi, a sinecure that he held for several years.

Though he had apparently attained an easy life, it soon became clear that his new position was not without danger. Sultan Muḥammad, an extraordinary mixture of generosity and cruelty, held sway over the greater part of India with an iron hand that fell indiscriminately upon high and low, Muslim and Hindu alike. Ibn Baṭṭūṭah witnessed all the glories and setbacks of the sultan and his rule, fearing daily for his life as he saw many friends fall victim to the suspicious despot. His portrait of Muḥammad is an unusually fine piece of psychological insight and mirrors faithfully the author's mixed feelings of terror and sympathy. Notwithstanding all his precautions, Ibn Baṭṭūṭah at last fell into disgrace, and only good fortune saved his life; gaining favour again, he was appointed the sultan's envoy to the Chinese emperor in 1342.

He left Delhi without regrets, but his journey was full of other dangers: not far away from Delhi his party was waylaid by Hindu insurgents, and the traveler barely escaped with his life. On the Malabar Coast he became involved in local wars and was finally shipwrecked near Calicut (now Kozhikode), losing all his property and the gifts for the Chinese emperor. Fearing the wrath of the sultan, Ibn Baṭṭūṭah chose to go to the Maldive Islands, where he spent nearly two years; as a *qāḍī*, he was soon active in politics, married into the ruling family, and apparently even aspired to become sultan.

Finding the situation too dangerous, he set out for Ceylon (Sri Lanka), where he visited the ruler as well as the famous Adam's Peak. After a new shipwreck on the Coromandel Coast, of eastern India, he took part in a war led by his brother-in-law and went again to the Maldives and then to Bengal and Assam. At that time he decided to resume his mission to China and sailed for Sumatra. There he was given a new ship by the Muslim sultan and started for China. His description of that itinerary contains some discrepancies.

Ibn Baṭṭūṭah landed at the great Chinese port Zaytūn (identified as Quanzhou, near Xiamen [Amoy]) and then traveled on inland waterways as far as Beijing and back. This part of his narrative is rather brief, and its chronology

presents many problems and difficulties, not yet sur-
mounted, that cast shadows of doubt on his veracity.

Equally brief is his account of the return voyage via
Sumatra, Malabar, and the Persian Gulf to Baghdad and
Syria. In Syria he witnessed the ravages of the Black Death
of 1348, visited again many towns there and in Egypt, and
in the same year performed his final pilgrimage to Mecca.
At last he decided to return home, sailing from Alexandria
to Tunisia, then to Sardinia and Algiers, finally reaching
Fès, the capital of the Marīnid sultan, Abū 'Inān, in
November 1349.

But there still remained two Muslim countries not yet
known to him. Shortly after his return he went to the kingdom of Granada, the last remnant of Moorish Spain, and
two years later (in 1352) he set out on a journey to the western Sudan. His last journey (across the Sahara to Western
Africa) was taken unwillingly at the command of the sultan.
Crossing the Sahara, he spent a year in the empire of Mali,
then at the height of its power under Mansa Sulaymān; his
account represents one of the most important sources of
that period for the history of that part of Africa.

Toward the end of 1353 Ibn Baṭṭūṭah returned to
Morocco and, at the sultan's request, dictated his reminis-
cences to a writer, Ibn Juzayy (died 1355), who embellished
the simple prose of Ibn Baṭṭūṭah's account with an ornate
style and fragments of poetry. After that he passes from
sight. He is reported to have held the office of *qāḍī* in a
town in Morocco before his death, details of which remain
uncertain. It has been suggested that he died in 1368/69 or
1377 and was buried in his native town of Tangier.

Ibn Baṭṭūṭah was a remarkably intrepid traveler for
any era or time. He covered some 75,000 miles (about
120,000 km), which he described in one of the world's
most famous travel books, the *Riḥlah* (*Travels*). This work
is an important document shedding light on many aspects

of the social, cultural, and political history of a great part of the Muslim world. A curious observer interested in the ways of life in various countries, he describes his experiences with a human approach rarely encountered in official historiography.

TRAVELS OF MARCO POLO

The Venetian merchant and adventurer Marco Polo (1254–1324) traveled from Europe to Asia in 1271–95, remaining in China for 17 of those years. His *Il milione* ("The Million"), known in English as the *Travels of Marco Polo*, also is a classic of travel literature.

Journeys of the Polo Family

Polo's way was paved by the pioneering efforts of his ancestors, especially his father, Niccolò, and his uncle, Maffeo. The family had traded with the Middle East for a long time, acquiring considerable wealth and prestige. Although it is uncertain if the Polos were of the nobility, the matter was of little importance in Venice, a city of republican and mercantile traditions.

The Polo family appears to have been shrewd, alert, and courageous. In about 1260 they foresaw a political change in Constantinople (e.g., the overthrow of the Crusaders who had ruled since 1204 by Michael VIII Palaeologus in 1261), liquidated their property there, invested their capital in jewels, and set off for the Volga River, where Berke Khan, sovereign of the western territories in the Mongol Empire, held court at Sarai or Bulgar. The Polos apparently managed their affairs well at Berke's court, where they doubled their assets. When political events prevented their return to Venice, they traveled eastward to Bukhara (Bokhara) and ended their journey in 1265, probably at the grand khan's summer residence, Shangdu (immortalized as Xanadu by

English poet Samuel Taylor Coleridge). Establishing friendly relations with the great Kublai Khan, they eventually returned to Europe as his ambassadors, carrying letters asking the pope to send Kublai 100 intelligent men "acquainted with the Seven Arts"; they also bore gifts and were asked to bring back oil from the lamp burning at the Holy Sepulchre in Jerusalem.

Polo's Journey to Asia

Little is known about Marco's early years except that he probably grew up in Venice. He was age 15 or 16 when his father and uncle returned to meet him and learned that the pope, Clement IV, had recently died. Niccolò and Maffeo remained in Venice anticipating the election of a new pope, but in 1271, after two years of waiting, they departed with Marco for the Mongol court. In Acre (now 'Akko, Israel) the papal legate, Teobaldo of Piacenza, gave them letters for the Mongol emperor. The Polos had been on the road for only a few days when they heard that their friend Teobaldo had been elected pope as Gregory X. Returning to Acre, they were given proper credentials, and two friars were assigned to accompany them, though they abandoned the Polos shortly after the expedition resumed.

From Acre, the Polo brothers proceeded to Ayas ("Laiazzo" in Marco's writings, now Yumurtalik, on the Gulf of İskenderun, also called the Gulf of Alexandretta, in southeastern Turkey). During the early part of 1272, they probably passed through Erzurum, in what is now eastern Turkey, and Tabriz, in what is now northern Iran, later crossing inhospitable deserts infested with brigands before reaching Hormuz on the Persian Gulf. There the Polos decided not to risk a sea passage to India and beyond but to proceed overland to the Mongol capital.

They next traveled through deserts of "surpassing aridity" toward the Khorasan region in what is now eastern

Iran. Turning gradually to the northeast, they reached more hospitable lands; Badakhshān ("Balascian"), in Afghanistan, in particular, pleased the travelers. Marco suggests that they remained there for a year; detained, perhaps, by illness (possibly malaria) that was cured by the benign climate of the district. It is also believed that Marco visited territories to the south (other parts of Afghanistan, Kafiristan in the Hindu Kush mountain range, Chitral in what is now Pakistan, and perhaps Kashmir) during this period. It is, however, difficult to establish which districts he traversed and which he may have described from information gathered en route.

Leaving Badakhshān, the Polos proceeded toward the Pamirs range, but the route they followed to cross these Central Asian highlands remains uncertain. Descending on the northeastern side of the chain, they reached Kashgar ("Cascar") in what is now the Uygur Autonomous Region of Xinjiang, China. By this point the Polos were on the main Silk Road, and they probably followed along the oases to the south and east of the Takla Makan Desert—Yarkant ("Yarcan"), Hotan ("Cotan"), Che'erchen ("Ciarcian"), and Lop Nur (Lop Lake). These stepping-stones led to Shazhou ("Saciu") on the borders of China, a place now called Dunhuang.

Before reaching Shazhou, the Polos had traveled primarily among Muslim peoples, though they also encountered Nestorian Christians, Buddhists, Manichaeans, and Zoroastrians. In the vast province of Gansu (called "Tangut" by Marco), an entirely different civilization—mainly Buddhist in religion but partly Chinese in culture—prevailed. The travelers probably stopped in Suzhou ("Sukchu," now Jiuquan) and Ganzhou ("Campiciu," now Zhangye) before entering the Ningxia area. It is not clear whether they reached the Mongol summer capital of Shangdu ("Ciandu") directly or after a detour; in any event, sometime in 1275 (1274, according to the research of Japanese scholar Matsuo Otagi) the Polos were again at the Mongol court, presenting the sacred oil from Jerusalem and the papal letters to their patron, Kublai Khan.

SILK ROAD

Linking China with the West, the Silk Road (also called the Silk Route) was an ancient trade route that carried goods and ideas between the two great civilizations of Rome and China. Silk came westward, while wools, gold, and silver went east. China also received Nestorian Christianity and Buddhism (from India) via the route.

Originating at Xi'an (Sian), the 4,000-mile (6,400-km) road, actually a caravan tract, followed the Great Wall of China to the northwest, bypassed the Takla Makan Desert, climbed the Pamirs, crossed Afghanistan, and went on to the Levant; from there, the merchandise was shipped across the Mediterranean Sea. Few persons traveled the entire route, and goods were handled in a staggered progression by middlemen.

With the gradual loss of Roman territory in Asia and the rise of Arabian power in the Levant, the Silk Road fell into disrepair and became increasingly unsafe. In the 13th and 14th centuries the route was revived under the Mongols, and used by Marco Polo to travel to China.

The Silk Road now partially exists in the form of a paved highway connecting Pakistan and the Uygur Autonomous Region of Xinjiang, China. The old route has been the impetus behind a United Nations plan for a trans-Asian highway, and a railway counterpart of the road has been proposed by the UN Economic and Social Commission for Asia and the Pacific (UNESCAP). The road inspired cellist Yo Yo Ma to found the Silk Road Project in 1999, which has explored cultural traditions along its route.

Sojourn in China

For the next 16 or 17 years the Polos lived in the emperor's dominions, which included, among other places, Cathay (now North China) and Mangi, or Manzi (now South China). They may have moved with the court from Shangdu, to the winter residence, Dadu, or Taidu (now Beijing).

Unfortunately, because Marco's book *Il milione* is only incidentally a biography and autobiography, it is exceedingly difficult to ascertain where the Polos went and what they did during these years. Nevertheless, it is well known that many foreigners were in the employ of the state, since the Mongol rulers did not trust their Chinese subjects; so it would have been natural for the Polos to fit in most honourably and successfully with this motley society.

The extent of their success and the specific roles they filled, however, remains an open question. The elder Polos were probably employed in some technical capacity. Once and very abruptly, a glimpse in *Il milione* is obtained of them acting as military advisers during the siege of "Saianfu" (formerly Xiangyang, now Xiangfan), a city that was finally taken, according to Marco, thanks to some "great mangonels" (missile-throwing engines) built according to the Polos' specifications. The whole episode is dubious, however.

Marco was about age 20 when he reached Cathay. Although he knew little or no Chinese, he did speak some of the many languages then used in East Asia—most probably Turkish (in its Coman dialect) as spoken among the Mongols, Arabized Persian, Uighur (Uygur), and perhaps Mongol. He was favoured by Kublai, who took great delight in hearing of strange countries and repeatedly sent him on fact-finding missions to distant parts of the empire. One such journey took Polo to Yunnan in southwestern China and perhaps as far as Tagaung in Myanmar (Burma). On another occasion Polo visited southeastern China, later enthusiastically describing the city of "Quinsay" (now Hangzhou) and the populous regions recently conquered by the Mongols.

Apart from the missions he undertook for the emperor, Polo may have held other administrative responsibilities, including inspection of the customs duties and revenues collected from the trade in salt and other commodities. According to some versions of *Il milione*, he governed the city of Yangzhou for three years sometime between 1282 and 1287, but this assertion seems questionable. There is, however, ample evidence to show that Polo considered himself an adoptive son of his new country. The most detailed descriptions and the greatest superlatives were reserved for Cambaluc, capital of Cathay, whose splendours were beyond compare. To this city, he said:

> ... *everything that is most rare and valuable in all parts of the world finds its way: ... for not fewer than 1,000 carriages and pack-horses loaded with raw silk make their daily entry; and gold tissues and silks of various kinds are manufactured to an immense extent.*

It is no wonder that Europeans became enthralled when reading Polo's accounts of China.

The Return to Venice

Sometime around 1292 (1290 according to Otagi), a Mongol princess was to be sent to Persia to become the consort of Arghun Khan, and the Polos offered to accompany her. Marco wrote that Kublai had been unwilling to let them go but finally granted permission. They were eager to leave, in part, because Kublai was nearly 80, and his death (and the consequent change in regime) might have been dangerous for a small group of isolated foreigners. Naturally, they also longed to see their native Venice and their families again.

The princess, with some 600 courtiers and sailors, and the Polos boarded 14 ships, which left the port of Zaiton (now Quanzhou) and sailed southward. The fleet stopped briefly at Ciamba (now Champa in Vietnam) as well as a number of islands and the Malay Peninsula before settling for five months on the island of Lesser Giaua (now Sumatra) to avoid monsoon storms. There Polo was much impressed by the fact that the North Star appeared to have dipped below the horizon. The fleet then passed near Necuveran (now the Nicobar Islands), touched land again in Seilan or Ceylon (now Sri Lanka), followed the west coast of India and the southern reaches of Persia, and finally anchored at Hormuz. The expedition then proceeded to Khorasan, handing over the princess not to Arghun, who had died, but to his son Maḥmūd Ghāzān.

The Polos eventually departed for Europe, but their movements at this point are unclear. They possibly stayed for a few months in Tabriz. Unfortunately, as soon as they left the Mongol dominions and set foot in a Christian country, at Trebizond (now Turkey), they were robbed of most of their hard-won earnings. After further delays, they reached Constantinople and finally Venice (1295). The story of their dramatic recognition by relatives and neighbours who had thought them long since dead is a part of Polo lore that is well known.

ZHENG HE

The Chinese admiral and diplomat Zheng He (c. 1371–1433) undertook several long sea voyages and helped to extend China's maritime and commercial influence throughout the regions bordering the Indian Ocean. A Muslim, he was born Ma Sanbao (later Ma He) in a family that claimed descent from a Mongol governor of Yunnan province. When the forces of the new Ming dynasty conquered Yunnan, the young Ma was captured, castrated, and sent into the army as an orderly. However, by 1390 Ma He had distinguished himself as a junior officer, skilled in war and diplomacy; he also made influential friends at court. His commander, the prince of Yan, became the Yongle emperor (reigned 1402–24) of the Ming. The emperor having conferred on Ma He (who had become a court eunuch of great influence) the surname Zheng, he was henceforth known as Zheng He.

For 300 years the Chinese had been extending their power out to sea. An extensive seaborne commerce had developed to meet the taste of the Chinese for spices and aromatics and the need for raw industrial materials. Chinese travelers abroad, as well as Indian and Muslim visitors, widened the geographic horizon of the Chinese. Technological developments in shipbuilding and in the arts of seafaring reached new heights by the beginning of the Ming. Zheng was selected by the emperor to be commander in chief of the missions to the "Western Oceans," and he first set sail in 1405, commanding 62 ships and 27,800 men. The fleet visited Champa (now in southern Vietnam), Siam (Thailand), Malacca (Melaka), and Java; then over the Indian Ocean to Calicut (Kozhikode), Cochin (Kochi), and Ceylon (Sri Lanka). Zheng He returned to China in 1407.

On his second voyage, in 1409, Zheng He encountered treachery from King Alagonakkara of Ceylon. Zheng He defeated his forces and took the king back to Nanjing as a captive. In 1411 he set out on his third voyage. This time, going beyond the seaports of India, he sailed to Hormuz on the Persian Gulf. On his return he touched at Samudra, on the northern tip of what is now Sumatra.

On his fourth voyage in 1413 Zheng He left China. After stopping at the principal ports of Asia, he proceeded westward from India to Hormuz. A detachment of the fleet cruised southward down the Arabian coast, visiting Djofar and Aden. A Chinese mission visited Mecca and continued to Egypt. The fleet visited Brava and Malindi and almost reached the Mozambique Channel. On his return to China in 1415, Zheng He brought the envoys of more than 30 states of South and Southeast Asia to pay homage to the Chinese emperor.

During Zheng He's fifth voyage (1417–19), the Ming fleet revisited the Persian Gulf and the east coast of Africa. A sixth voyage was launched in 1421 to take home the foreign emissaries from China. Again he visited Southeast Asia, India, Arabia, and Africa. In 1424 the Yongle emperor died. In the shift of policy his successor, the Hongxi emperor, suspended naval expeditions abroad. Zheng He was appointed garrison commander in Nanjing, with the task of disbanding his troops.

Zheng He's seventh and final voyage left China in the winter of 1431, visiting the states of Southeast Asia, the coast of India, the Persian Gulf, the Red Sea, and the east coast of Africa. He died in Calicut in 1433, and the fleet returned to China.

Zheng He was the best known of the Yongle emperor's diplomatic agents. Although some historians see no achievement in the naval expeditions other than flattering the emperor's vanity, these missions did have the effect of extending China's political sway over maritime Asia for half a century. Admittedly, they did not, like similar voyages of European merchant-adventurers, lead to the establishment of trading empires. Yet, in their wake, Chinese emigration increased, resulting in Chinese colonization in Southeast Asia and the accompanying tributary trade, which thrived into the 19th century.

Chapter 2: The Age of Discovery

lthough Ibn Baṭṭūṭah had written a vivid and perspicacious account of his travels, his book was not known to Christian Europe for centuries. Rather, it was Marco Polo's book *Il milione* that was the most popular. Some 138 manuscripts of it survive: it was translated before 1500 into Latin, German, and Spanish, and the first English translation was published in 1577. For centuries Europe's maps of the Far East were based on the information provided by Marco Polo.

A few travelers followed the Polos. Giovanni da Montecorvino, a Franciscan friar from Italy, became archbishop of Beijing and lived in China from 1294 to 1328. Friar Oderic of Pordenone, an Italian monk, became a missionary, journeying throughout the greater part of Asia between 1316 and 1330. He reached Beijing by way of India and Malaya, then traveled by sea to Guangzhou (Canton). He returned to Europe by way of Central Asia, visiting Tibet in 1325—the first European to do so. Friar Oderic's account of his journeys had considerable influence in his day: it was from it that a spurious traveler, the English writer Sir John Mandeville, quarried most of his stories.

Christopher Columbus possessed and annotated a copy of the Latin edition (1483–85) of Marco Polo's book, and in his journal he identified many of his own discoveries with places that Marco Polo describes. Thus, with Ptolemy in one hand and Marco Polo in the other, the European explorers of the Age of Discovery set forth to try to reach Cathay and Cipango (Japan) by new ways.

World map by J.M. Contarini, 1506, depicting the expanding horizons becoming known to European geographers in the Age of Discovery. Courtesy of the trustees of the British Museum; photograph, J.R. Freeman & Co., Ltd.

Ptolemy promised that the way to Asia was short; Marco Polo promised that the reward was great.

In the 100 years from the mid-15th to the mid-16th century, a combination of circumstances stimulated men to seek new sea routes to the East. It was new routes—rather than new lands—that filled the minds of kings and commoners, scholars and seamen. First, toward the end of the 14th century, the vast empire of the Mongols was breaking up; thus, Western merchants could no longer be ensured of safe-conduct along land routes. Second, the growing power of the Ottoman Turks, who were hostile to Christians, blocked yet more firmly the outlets to the Mediterranean of the ancient sea routes from the East. Third, new nations on the Atlantic shores of Europe were increasingly interested in overseas trade and adventure.

THE SEA ROUTE
EAST BY SOUTH TO CATHAY

Henry the Navigator, prince of Portugal, initiated the first great enterprise of the Age of Discovery—the search for a sea route east by south to Cathay. His motives were mixed. He was curious about the world; he was interested in new navigational aids and better ship design and was eager to test them; he was also a crusader and hoped that, by sailing south and then east along the coast of Africa, Arab power in North Africa could be attacked from the rear. The promotion of profitable trade was yet another motive; he aimed to divert the Guinea trade in gold and ivory away from its routes across the Sahara to the Moors of Barbary (now North Africa) and instead channel it via the sea route to Portugal.

Expedition after expedition was sent forth throughout the 15th century to explore the coast of Africa. In 1445 the Portuguese navigator Dinís Dias reached the mouth of the Sénégal, which "men say comes from the Nile, being one of the most glorious rivers of Earth, flowing from the Garden of Eden and the earthly paradise." Once the desert coast had been passed, the sailors pushed on. In 1455 and 1456 Alvise Ca' da Mosto made voyages to Gambia and the Cape Verde Islands. Prince Henry died in 1460 after a career that had brought the colonization of the Madeira Islands and the Azores and the traversal of the African coast to Sierra Leone.

BARTOLOMEU DIAS
AND THE CAPE OF GOOD HOPE

The Portuguese navigator and explorer Bartolomeu Dias, or Diaz (*c.* 1450–1500), led the first European expedition to round the Cape of Good Hope (1488), opening the sea route to Asia via the Atlantic and Indian oceans. He is usually considered to be the greatest of the Portuguese pioneers who explored the Atlantic during the 15th century.

In 1474, King Afonso V had entrusted his son, Prince John (later John II), with the supervision of Portugal's trade with Guinea and the exploration of the western coast of Africa. John sought to close the area to foreign shipping and, after his accession in 1481, he sought to establish two routes to India: the first, a land and sea route through Egypt and Ethiopia to the Red Sea and the Indian Ocean and, the second, a sea route around the southern shores of Africa. The latter was an act of faith, since Ptolemy's map showed a landlocked Indian Ocean. In 1487, a Portuguese emissary, Pêro da Covilhã, successfully followed the first route; but, on returning to Cairo, he reported that, in order to travel to India, the Portuguese "could navigate by their coasts and the seas of Guinea."

John II ordered new voyages of discovery to ascertain the southern limit of the African continent. The navigators were given stone pillars (*padrões*) to stake the claims of the Portuguese crown. Diogo Cão, one of these captains, reached the Congo River and sailed down the coast of Angola to Cape Santa Maria at latitude 13°26′ S, where he planted one of John's markers. Cão was ennobled and rewarded and sailed again. This time he left a marker at 15°40′ and another at Cape Cross, continuing to 22°10′ S. Royal hopes that he would reach the Indian Ocean were disappointed, and nothing more is heard of Cão. John II entrusted command of a new expedition to Dias. In 1486 rumour arose of a great ruler, the Ogané, far to the east, who was identified with the legendary Christian ruler Prester John. John II then sent Pêro da Covilhã and one Afonso Paiva overland to locate India and Abyssinia and ordered Dias to find the southernmost tip of Africa.

Dias' fleet consisted of three ships, his own *São Cristóvão*, the *São Pantaleão* under his associate João Infante, and a supply ship under Dias's brother, whose name is variously given as Pêro or Diogo. The company included some of the leading pilots of the day, among them Pêro de Alenquer and João de Santiago, who earlier had sailed with Cão. A 16th-century historian, João de Barros, places Dias's departure in August 1486 and says that he was away 16 months and 17 days, but since two other contemporaries, Duarte Pacheco and Christopher Columbus, put his return in December 1488, it is now usually supposed that he left in August 1487.

Dias passed Cão's marker, reaching the "Land of St. Barbara" on December 4, Walvis Bay on December 8, and the Gulf of St. Stephen (now Elizabeth Bay) on December 26. After Jan. 6, 1488, he was prevented by storms from proceeding along the coast and sailed south out of sight of land for several days. When he again turned to port, no land appeared, and it was only on sailing north that he sighted land on February 3. He had thus rounded the Cape without having seen it. He called the spot Angra de São Brás (Bay of St. Blaise, whose feast day it was) or the Bay of Cowherds, from the people he found there. Dias's companions were unable to understand these people, who fled but later returned to attack the Portuguese. The expedition went on to Angra da Roca (now Algoa Bay). The crew was unwilling to continue, and Dias recorded the opinions of all his officers, who were unanimously in favour of returning. They agreed to go on for a few more days, reaching

Rio do Infante, named after the pilot of *São Pantaleão*. This is almost certainly the Great Fish (Groot-Vis) River.

Faced with strong currents, Dias turned back. He sighted the Cape itself in May. Barros says that he named it Cape of Storms and that John II renamed it Cape of Good Hope. Duarte Pacheco, however, attributes the present name to Dias himself, and this is likely since Pacheco joined Dias at the island of Príncipe. Little is known of the return journey, except that Dias touched at Príncipe, the Rio do Resgate (now in Liberia), and the fortified trading post of Mina. In 1938, one of Dias's markers, at Padrão de São Gregório, was retrieved from False Island, about 30 miles (48 km) short of the Great Fish River. Another marker was retrieved at the western end of the Gulf of St. Christopher, which has since been renamed Dias Point.

Nothing is known of Dias's reception by John II. Although plans are said to have been made for a voyage to India, none is known to have been attempted for nine years, perhaps pending news of Pêro da Covilhã. Dias died in 1500 after his ship was lost at sea near the Cape of Good Hope.

VASCO DA GAMA AND THE ROUTE TO INDIA

The seaway was now open, but eight years elapsed before it was exploited. In 1492 Columbus had apparently reached the East by a much easier route. By the end of the decade, however, doubts of the validity of Columbus's claim were common. Interest was therefore renewed in establishing the sea route south by east to the known riches of India. Another Portuguese captain, Vasco da Gama (c. 1460–1524), finally established the sea route to India in a series of three voyages (1497–99, 1502–03, 1524).

THE FIRST VOYAGE

Da Gama sailed from Lisbon on July 8, 1497, commanding a fleet of four vessels—two medium-sized three-masted sailing ships, each of about 120 tons, named the *São Gabriel* and the *São Rafael*; a 50-ton caravel, named the *Berrio*; and a 200-ton storeship. With da Gama's fleet went three interpreters—two Arabic speakers and one who spoke several Bantu dialects. The fleet also carried the *padrões* da Gama's predecessors had bourne to mark their discoveries.

Passing the Canary Islands on July 15, the fleet reached São Tiago in the Cape Verde Islands on the 26th, remaining there until August 3. Then, to avoid the currents of the Gulf of Guinea, da Gama undertook a long detour through the South Atlantic before attempting to round the Cape of Good Hope. The fleet reached Santa Helena Bay (in modern South Africa) on November 7. Unfavourable winds and an adverse current delayed the rounding of the cape until November 22. Three days later da Gama anchored in Mossel Bay, erected a *padrão* on an island, and ordered the storeship to be destroyed. Sailing again on December 8, the fleet reached the coast of Natal on Christmas Day. On Jan. 11, 1498, it anchored for five days near the mouth of a small river between Natal and Mozambique, which they called the Rio do Cobre (now Copper River). On January 25, in what is now Mozambique, they reached the Quelimane River, which they called the Rio dos Bons Sinais (the River of Good Omens), and erected another *padrão*. By this time many of the crews were sick with scurvy (a dietary disease caused by a lack of ascorbic acid and that habitually decimated the crews of ships on lengthy voyages). The expedition rested a month while the ships were repaired.

On March 2 the fleet reached the Island of Mozambique, the inhabitants of which believed the Portuguese to be Muslims like themselves. Da Gama learned that they traded with Arab merchants and that four Arab vessels laden with gold, jewels, silver, and spices were then in port. He was also told that Prester John, the long-sought Christian ruler, lived in the interior but held many coastal cities. The Sultan of Mozambique supplied da Gama with two pilots, one of whom deserted when he discovered that the Portuguese were Christians.

The expedition reached Mombasa on April 7 and dropped anchor at Malindi (both now in Kenya) on April 14, where a Gujarati pilot who knew the route to Calicut (now Kozhikode), on the southwest coast of India, was taken aboard. After a 23-day run across the Indian Ocean, the Ghats Mountains of India were sighted, and Calicut was reached on May 20. There da Gama erected a *padrão* to prove he had reached India. The welcome of the Zamorin, the Hindu ruler, of Calicut (then the most important trading centre of southern India), was dispelled by da Gama's insignificant gifts and rude behaviour. Da Gama failed to conclude a treaty—partly because of the hostility of Muslim merchants and partly because of the trumpery presents and cheap goods that he had brought to trade. While the items were suitable for trading with Christians in West Africa, they were hardly in demand in India.

After tension increased, da Gama left at the end of August, taking with him five or six Hindus so that King Manuel might learn about their customs. Ignorance and indifference to local knowledge had led da Gama to choose the worst possible time of year for his departure, and he had to sail against a monsoon. He visited Anjidiv Island (near Goa) before sailing for Malindi, which he reached on Jan. 8, 1499, after nearly three months crossing the Arabian

Sea. Many of the crew died of scurvy. At Malindi, because so many crewmembers had died, da Gama ordered the *São Rafael* to be burned; there he also erected a *padrão*. He set up his last *padrão* in Mozambique, which he reached on February 1. On March 20 the *São Gabriel* and *Berrio* rounded the Cape together but a month later were parted by a storm; the *Berrio* reached the Tagus River in Portugal on July 10. Da Gama, in the *São Gabriel*, continued to Terceira Island in the Azores, whence he is said to have dispatched his flagship to Lisbon. He himself reached Lisbon on September 9 and made his triumphal entry nine days later, spending the interval mourning his brother Paulo, who had died on Terceira. (Out of da Gama's original crew of 170, only 55 men had survived.) Manuel I granted da Gama the title of *dom*, an annual pension of 1,000 cruzados, and estates.

THE SECOND VOYAGE

To exploit da Gama's achievement, Manuel I dispatched the Portuguese navigator Pedro Álvares Cabral to Calicut with a fleet of 13 ships. The profits of this expedition were such that a third fleet was soon fitted out in Lisbon. The command of this fleet was given to da Gama, who in January 1502 received the title of admiral. Da Gama commanded 10 ships, which were in turn supported by two flotillas of five ships each, each flotilla being under the command of one of his relations. Sailing in February 1502, the fleet called at the Cape Verdes, reaching the port of Sofala in East Africa on June 14. After calling briefly at Mozambique, the Portuguese expedition sailed to Kilwa, (now Tanzania). The ruler of Kilwa, the amīr Ibrāhīm, had been unfriendly to Cabral; da Gama threatened to burn Kilwa if the Amīr did not submit to the Portuguese and swear loyalty to King Manuel, which he then did.

Coasting southern Arabia, da Gama then called at Goa (later the focus of Portuguese power in India) before proceeding to Cannanore, a port in southwestern India to the north of Calicut, where he lay in wait for Arab shipping. After several days an Arab ship arrived with merchandise and between 200 and 400 passengers, including women and children. After seizing the cargo, da Gama is said to have shut up the passengers aboard the captured ship and set it afire, killing all on board. As a consequence, da Gama has been vilified, and Portuguese trading methods have been associated with terror. However, the episode is related only by late and unreliable sources and may be legendary or at least exaggerated.

After da Gama formed an alliance with the ruler of Cannanore, an enemy of the Zamorin, the fleet sailed to Calicut, with the aim of wrecking its trade and punishing the Zamorin for the favour he had shown to Muslim traders. Da Gama bombarded the port and seized and massacred 38 hostages. The Portuguese then sailed south to the port of Cochin, with whose ruler (an enemy of the Zamorin) they formed an alliance. After an invitation to da Gama from the Zamorin had proved to be an attempt to entrap him, the Portuguese had a brief fight with Arab ships off Calicut but put them to full flight. On Feb. 20, 1503, the fleet left Cannanore for Mozambique on the first stage of their return voyage, reaching the Tagus on October 11.

THE THIRD VOYAGE

Obscurity surrounds the reception of da Gama on his return by King Manuel. Da Gama seemingly felt himself inadequately recompensed for his efforts. Controversy broke out between the admiral and the Order of São Tiago over the ownership of the town of Sines, which the admiral had been promised but which the order refused to

yield. Da Gama had married a lady of good family, Caterina
de Ataíde—perhaps in 1500 after his return from his first
voyage—and he then appears to have retired to the town
of Évora. He was later granted additional privileges and
revenues, and his wife bore him six sons. Until 1505 he
continued to advise the King on Indian matters, and he
was created count of Vidigueira in 1519. Not until after
King Manuel died was he again sent overseas. At that time,
in 1524, King John III nominated da Gama as Portuguese
viceroy in India.

Arriving in Goa in September 1524, da Gama immediately set himself to correct the many administrative abuses
that had crept in under his predecessors. Whether from
overwork or other causes, he soon fell ill and died in
Cochin in December. In 1538 his body was taken back to
Portugal.

COLUMBUS'S VOYAGES TO THE NEW WORLD

It is not known when the idea originated of sailing westward in order to reach China. Many 15th-century sailors
set forth searching for islands in the west; and it was widely
held that the east could be reached by sailing west, but to
do so remained impractical. Christopher Columbus
(known in Italian as Cristoforo Colombo and in Spanish as
Cristóbal Colón; 1451–1506) was a Genoese navigator who
had settled in Lisbon in about 1476. Columbus argued that
Cipango, or Cipangu (i.e., Japan), lay a mere 2,500 nautical
miles (4,630 km) west of the Canary Islands in the eastern
Atlantic. He accepted Ptolemy's exaggerated west-east
extent of Asia and then added to it the lands described by
Marco Polo, thus incorrectly reducing the true distance
between the Canaries and Cipango by about one-third.

PREPARATION FOR THE FIRST VOYAGE

In 1484, Columbus began seeking support for an Atlantic crossing from King John II of Portugal but was denied aid. (Some conspiracy theorists have alleged that Columbus made a secret pact with the monarch, but there is no evidence of this.) By 1486 Columbus was firmly in Spain, asking for patronage from King Ferdinand and Queen Isabella. After at least two rejections, he at last obtained royal support in January 1492. This was achieved chiefly through the interventions of the Spanish treasurer, Luis de Santángel, and of the Franciscan friars of La Rábida, near Huelva, with whom Columbus had stayed in the summer of 1491. Juan Pérez of La Rábida had been one of the queen's confessors and perhaps procured him the crucial audience.

An explosion of energy to launch the first voyage was fueled by a desire to spread Christianity, the power of Castile and Aragon, the fear of Portugal, the lust for gold, the desire for conquest and adventure, and Europe's genuine need for a reliable supply of medicinal herbs and spices for cooking and preserving food. Columbus had been present at the siege of Granada, which was the last Moorish stronghold to fall to Spain (Jan. 2, 1492), and he was in fact riding back from Grenada to La Rábida when he was recalled to the Spanish court and the vital royal audience. Granada's fall had produced euphoria among Spanish Christians and encouraged designs of ultimate triumph over the Islamic world. A direct assault eastward could prove difficult, because the Ottoman Empire and other Islamic states in the region had been gaining strength at a pace that was threatening Christian monarchies. The Islamic powers had effectively closed the land routes to the East and made the sea route south from the Red Sea extremely hard to access.

In the letter that prefaces his journal of the first voyage, the admiral vividly evokes his own hopes and binds them together with the conquest of the infidel, the victory of Christianity, and the westward route to discovery and Christian alliance:

> [A]nd I saw the Moorish king come out of the gates of the city and kiss the royal hands of Your Highnesses . . . and Your Highnesses, as Catholic Christians . . . took thought to send me, Christopher Columbus, to the said parts of India, to see those princes and peoples and lands . . . and the manner which should be used to bring about their conversion to our holy faith, and ordained that I should not go by land to the eastward, by which way it was the custom to go, but by way of the west, by which down to this day we do not know certainly that anyone has passed; therefore, having driven out all the Jews from your realms and lordships in the same month of January, Your Highnesses commanded me that, with a sufficient fleet, I should go to the said parts of India, and for this accorded me great rewards and ennobled me so that from that time henceforth I might style myself "Don" and be high admiral of the Ocean Sea and viceroy and perpetual Governor of the islands and continent which I should discover . . . and that my eldest son should succeed to the same position, and so on from generation to generation forever.

Thus a great number of interests were involved in this adventure, which was, in essence, the attempt to find a route to the rich land of Cathay, to India, and to the fabled gold and spice islands of the East by sailing westward over what was presumed to be open sea. Columbus himself clearly hoped to rise from his humble beginnings in this way, to accumulate riches for his family, and to join the ranks of the nobility of Spain. In a similar manner, but at a more exalted level, the Catholic Monarchs hoped that such an enterprise would gain them greater status among the monarchies of Europe, especially against their main rival, Portugal. Then, in alliance with the papacy (in this case, with the Borgia pope Alexander VI [1492–1503]), they might hope to take the lead in the Christian war against the infidel.

At a more elevated level still, Franciscan brethren were preparing for the eventual end of the world, as they believed was prophesied in the Revelation to John. According to that eschatological vision, Christendom would recapture Jerusalem and install a Christian emperor in the Holy Land as a precondition for the coming and defeat of the Antichrist, the Christian conversion of the whole human race, and the Last Judgment. Franciscans and others hoped that Columbus's westward voyage would help to finance a Crusade to the Holy Land that might even be reinforced by, or coordinated with, offensives from the legendary ruler Prester John, who was thought to survive with his descendants in the lands to the east of the infidel. The emperor of Cathay—whom Europeans referred to as the Great Khan of the Golden Horde—was himself held to be interested in Christianity, and Columbus carefully carried a letter of friendship addressed to him by the Spanish monarchs. Finally, Bartolomeu Dias had already pressed southward along the coast of West Africa, beyond São Jorge da Mina, in an effort to find an easterly route to Cathay and India by sea. It would never do to allow the Portuguese to find the sea route first.

THE FIRST VOYAGE

The ships for the first voyage—the *Niña*, *Pinta*, and *Santa María*—were fitted out at Palos, on the Tinto River in Spain. Consortia put together by a royal treasury official and composed mainly of Genoese and Florentine bankers in Sevilla (Seville) provided most of the funds for the expedition, and Columbus supplied more than a third of the sum contributed by the king and queen. Queen Isabella did not, then, have to pawn her jewels (a myth first put about by Bartolomé de Las Casas in the 16th century).

The little fleet left on Aug. 3, 1492. The admiral's navigational genius showed itself immediately, for they sailed southward to the Canary Islands, off the northwest African mainland, rather than sailing due west to the islands of the Azores. The westerlies prevailing in the Azores had defeated previous attempts to sail to the west, but in the Canaries the three ships could pick up the northeast trade winds; supposedly, they could rely on the westerlies for their return. After nearly a month in the Canaries the ships set out from San Sebastián de la Gomera on September 6. On several occasions in September and early October, sailors spotted floating vegetation and various types of birds—all taken as signs that land was nearby. But by October 10 the crew had begun to lose patience, complaining that with their failure to make landfall, contrary winds and a shortage of provisions would keep them from returning home. Columbus allayed their fears, at least temporarily, and on October 12 land was sighted from the *Pinta* (though Columbus, on the *Niña*, later claimed the privilege for himself). The place of the first Caribbean landfall is hotly disputed, but San Salvador, or Watling, Island is currently preferred to Samana Cay, Rum Cay, the Plana Cays, or the Turks and Caicos Islands. Beyond planting the royal banner, however, Columbus spent little time there, being anxious to press on to Cipango. He thought that he had found it in Cuba, where he landed on October 28, but he convinced himself by November 1 that Cuba was the Cathay mainland itself, though he had yet to see evidence of great cities. Thus, on December 5, he turned back southeastward to search for the fabled city of Zaiton, thereby missing his sole chance of setting foot on Florida soil.

Adverse winds carried the fleet to an island called Ayti (now Haiti) by its Taino inhabitants. On December 6 Columbus renamed it La Isla Española, or Hispaniola. He seems to have thought that Hispaniola might be Cipango or, if not Cipango, then perhaps one of the legendarily rich isles from which King Solomon's triennial fleet brought back gold, gems, and spices to Jerusalem (1 Kings 10:11, 22); alternatively, he reasoned that the island could be related to the biblical kingdom of Sheba (Saba'). There Columbus found at least enough gold and prosperity to save him from ridicule on his return to Spain. With the help of a Taino cacique, or Indian chief, named Guacanagarí, he set up a stockade on the northern coast of the island, named it La Navidad, and posted 39 men to guard it until his return. The accidental running aground of the *Santa María* provided additional planks and provisions for the garrison.

On Jan. 16, 1493, Columbus left with his remaining two ships for Spain. The return journey was a nightmare. The westerlies did indeed direct them homeward, but in mid-February a terrible storm engulfed the fleet. The *Niña* was driven to seek harbour at Santa Maria in the Azores, where Columbus led a pilgrimage of thanksgiving to the shrine of the Virgin; however, hostile Portuguese authorities temporarily imprisoned the group. After securing their freedom Columbus sailed on, stormbound, and the damaged ship limped to port in Lisbon. There he was obliged to interview with King John II. These events left Columbus under the suspicion of collaborating with Spain's enemies and cast a shadow on his return to Palos on March 15.

On this first voyage many tensions built up that were to remain through all of Columbus's succeeding efforts. First and perhaps most damaging of all, the admiral's apparently high religious and even mystical aspirations were incompatible with the realities of trading, competition, and colonization. Columbus never openly acknowledged this gulf and so was quite incapable of bridging it. The admiral also adopted a mode of sanctification and autocratic leadership that made him many enemies. Moreover, Columbus was determined to take back both material and human cargo to his sovereigns and for himself, and this could be accomplished only if his sailors carried on looting, kidnapping, and other violent acts, especially on Hispaniola. Although he did control some of his men's excesses, these developments blunted his ability to retain the high moral ground and the claim in particular that his "discoveries" were divinely ordained. Further, the Spanish court revived its latent doubts about the foreigner Columbus's loyalty to Spain, and some of Columbus's companions set themselves against him. Captain Pinzón had disputed the route as the fleet reached the Bahamas. He had later sailed the *Pinta* away from Cuba, and Columbus, on November 21, failing to rejoin him until January 6. The *Pinta* made port at Bayona on its homeward journey, separately from Columbus and the *Niña*. Had Pinzón not died so soon after his return, Columbus's command of the second voyage might have been less than assured. As it was, the Pinzón family became his rivals for reward.

THE SECOND AND THIRD VOYAGES

The gold, parrots, spices, and human captives Columbus displayed for his sovereigns at Barcelona convinced all of the need for a rapid second voyage. Columbus was now at the height of his popularity, and he led at least 17 ships out from Cádiz on Sept. 25, 1493. Colonization and Christian evangelization were openly included this time in the plans, and a group of friars shipped with him. The presence of

some 1,300 salaried men with perhaps 200 private inves-
tors and a small troop of cavalry are testimony to the
anticipations for the expedition.

Sailing again via Gomera in the Canary Islands, the
fleet took a more southerly course than on the first voyage
and reached Dominica in the Lesser Antilles on November
3. After sighting the Virgin Islands, it entered Samaná Bay
in Hispaniola on November 23. Michele de Cuneo, deeply
impressed by this unerring return, remarked that "since
Genoa was Genoa there was never born a man so well
equipped and expert in navigation as the said lord Admiral."

An expedition to Navidad four days later was shocked
to find the stockade destroyed and the men dead. Here
was a clear sign that Taino resistance had gathered strength.
More fortified places were rapidly built, including a city,
founded on January 2 and named La Isabela for the queen.
On February 2 Antonio de Torres left La Isabela with 12
ships, some gold, spices, parrots, and captives (most of
whom died en route), as well as the bad news about Navidad
and some complaints about Columbus's methods of governing. While Torres headed for Spain, two of Columbus's
subordinates, Alonso de Ojeda and Pedro Margarit, took
revenge for the massacre at Navidad and captured slaves.
In March Columbus explored the Cibao Valley (thought
to be the gold-bearing region of the island) and established
the fortress of St. Thomas there. Then, late in April,
Columbus led the *Niña* and two other ships to explore the
Cuban coastline and search for gold in Jamaica, only to
conclude that Hispaniola promised the richest spoils for
the settlers. The admiral decided that Hispaniola was
indeed the biblical land of Sheba and that Cuba was the
mainland of Cathay. On June 12, 1494, Columbus insisted
that his men swear a declaration to that effect—an indica-
tion that he intended to convince his sovereign he had
reached Cathay, though not all of Columbus's company

agreed with him. The following year he began a determined conquest of Hispaniola, spreading devastation
among the Taino. There is evidence, especially in the
objections of a friar, Bernardo Buil, that Columbus's methods remained harsh.

The admiral departed La Isabela for Spain on March
10, 1496, leaving his brothers, Bartholomew and Diego, in
charge of the settlement. He reached Cádiz on June 11 and
immediately pressed his plans for a third voyage upon his
sovereigns, who were at Burgos. Spain was then at war
with France and needed to buy and keep its alliances;
moreover, the yield from the second voyage had fallen well
short of the investment. Portugal was still a threat, though
the two nations had divided the Atlantic conveniently
between themselves in the Treaty of Tordesillas (June 7,
1494). According to the treaty, Spain might take all land
west of a line drawn from pole to pole 370 leagues—i.e.,
about 1,185 miles (1,910 km)—west of the Cape Verde
Islands, whereas Portugal could claim land to the east of
the line. But what about the other side of the world, where
West met East? Also, there might be a previously undis-
covered antipodean continent; who, then, should be
trusted to draw the line there? Ferdinand and Isabella
therefore made a cautious third investment. Six ships left
Sanlúcar de Barrameda on May 30, 1498, three filled with
explorers and three with provisions for the settlement on
Hispaniola. It was clear now that Columbus was expected
both to find great prizes and to establish the flag of Spain
firmly in the East.

Certainly he found prizes, but not quite of the kind his
sponsors required. His aim was to explore to the south of
the existing discoveries, in the hope of finding both a strait
from Cuba (his "Cathay") to India and, perhaps, the
unknown antipodean continent. On June 21 the provision
ships left Gomera for Hispaniola, while the explorers

headed south for the Cape Verde Islands. Columbus began the Atlantic crossing on July 4 from São Tiago Island in Cape Verde. He discovered the principle of compass variation (the variation at any point on Earth's surface between the direction to magnetic and geographic north), for which he made brilliant allowance on the journey from Margarita Island to Hispaniola on the later leg of this voyage. He also observed, though misunderstood, the diurnal rotation of the northern polestar (Polaris). After stopping at Trinidad (named for the Holy Trinity, whose protection he had invoked for the voyage), Columbus entered the Gulf of Paria and planted the Spanish flag on the Paria Peninsula in Venezuela. He sent the caravel *El Corréo* southward to investigate the mouth of the Grande River (a northern branch of the Orinoco River delta), and by August 15 he knew by the great torrents of fresh water flowing into the Gulf of Paria that he had discovered another continent—"another world." But he did not find the strait to India, nor did he find King Solomon's gold mines, which his reading had led him and his sovereigns to expect in these latitudes; and he made only disastrous discoveries when he returned to Hispaniola.

Both the Taino and the European immigrants had resented the rule of Bartholomew and Diego Columbus. A rebellion by the mayor of La Isabela, Francisco Roldán, had led to appeals to the Spanish court, and, even as Columbus attempted to restore order (partly by hangings), the Spanish chief justice, Francisco de Bobadilla, was on his way to the colony with a royal commission to investigate the complaints. It is hard to explain exactly what the trouble was. Columbus's report to his sovereigns from the second voyage, taken back by Torres and so known as the Torres Memorandum, speaks of sickness, poor provisioning, recalcitrant natives, and undisciplined hidalgos (gentry). It may be that these problems had intensified.

But the Columbus family must be held at least partly responsible, intent as it was on enslaving the Taino and shipping them to Europe or forcing them to mine gold on Hispaniola. Under Columbus's original system of gold production, local chiefs had been in charge of delivering gold on a loose per capita basis; the adelantado (governor) Bartholomew Columbus had replaced that policy with a system of direct exploitation led by favoured Spaniards, causing widespread dissent among unfavoured Spaniards and indigenous chiefs. Bobadilla ruled against the Columbus family when he arrived in Hispaniola. He clapped Columbus and his two brothers in irons and sent them promptly back on the ship *La Gorda*, and they arrived at Cádiz in late October 1500.

During that return journey Columbus composed a long letter to his sovereigns that is one of the most extraordinary he wrote and one of the most informative. One part of its exalted, almost mystical, quality may be attributed to the humiliations the admiral had endured (humiliations he compounded by refusing to allow the captain of the *La Gorda* to remove his chains during the voyage) and another to the fact that he was now suffering severely from sleeplessness, eyestrain, and a form of rheumatoid arthritis, which may have hastened his death. Much of what he said in the letter, however, seems genuine. It shows that Columbus had absolute faith in his navigational abilities, his seaman's sense of the weather, his eyes, and his reading. He asserted that he had reached the outer region of the Earthly Paradise, in that, during his earlier approach to Trinidad and the Paria Peninsula, the polestar's rotation had given him the impression that the fleet was climbing. The weather had become extremely mild, and the flow of fresh water into the Gulf of Paria was, as he saw, enormous. All this could have one explanation only—they had mounted toward the temperate heights of the

Earthly Paradise, heights from which the rivers of Paradise ran into the sea. Columbus had found all such signs of the outer regions of the Earthly Paradise in his reading and indeed they were widely known. On this estimate, he was therefore close to the realms of gold that lay near Paradise. He had not found the gold yet, to be sure, but he knew where it was. Columbus's expectations thus enabled him to interpret his discoveries in terms of biblical and classical sources and to do so in a manner that would be comprehensible to his sponsors and favourable to himself.

This letter, desperate though it was, convinced the sovereigns that, even if he had not yet found the prize, he had been close to it after all. They ordered his release and gave him audience at Granada in late December 1500. They accepted that Columbus's capacities as navigator and explorer were unexcelled, although he was an unsatisfactory governor, and on Sept. 3, 1501, they appointed Nicolás de Ovando to succeed Bobadilla to the governorship. Columbus, though ill and importunate, was a better investment than the many adventurers and profiteers who had meantime been licensed to compete with him, and there was always the danger (revealed in some of the letters of this period) that he would offer his services to his native Genoa. In October 1501 Columbus went to Sevilla to make ready his fourth and final expedition.

THE FOURTH VOYAGE AND FINAL YEARS

The winter and spring of 1501–02 were exceedingly busy. The four chosen ships were bought, outfitted, and crewed, and some 20 of Columbus's extant letters and memoranda were written then, many in exculpation of Bobadilla's charges, others pressing even harder the nearness of the Earthly Paradise and the need to reconquer Jerusalem. Columbus took to calling himself "Christbearer" in his letters and to using a strange and mystical signature, never satisfactorily explained. He began also, with these thoughts and pressures in mind, to compile his Book of Privileges, which defends the titles and financial claims of the Columbus family, and his apocalyptic Book of Prophecies, which includes several biblical passages. The first compilation seems an odd companion to the second, yet both were closely linked in the admiral's own mind. He seems to have been certain that his mission was divinely guided. Thus, the loftiness of his spiritual aspirations increased as the threats to his personal ones mounted. In the midst of all these efforts and hazards, Columbus sailed from Cádiz on his fourth voyage on May 9, 1502.

Columbus's sovereigns had lost much of their confidence in him, and there is much to suggest that pity mingled with hope in their support. His four ships contrasted sharply with the 30 granted to the governor Ovando. His illnesses were worsening, and the hostility to his rule in Hispaniola was unabated. Thus, Ferdinand and Isabella forbade him to return there. He was to resume, instead, his interrupted exploration of the "other world" to the south that he had found on his third voyage and to look particularly for gold and the strait to India. Columbus expected to meet the Portuguese navigator Vasco da Gama in the East, and the sovereigns instructed him on the appropriate courteous behaviour for such a meeting—another sign, perhaps, that they did not wholly trust him. They were right. He departed from Gran Canaria on the night of May 25, made landfall at Martinique on June 15 (after the fastest crossing to date), and was, by June 29, demanding entrance to Santo Domingo on Hispaniola. Only on being refused entry by Ovando did he sail away to the west and south. From July to September 1502 he explored the coast of Jamaica, the southern shore of Cuba, Honduras, and the Mosquito Coast of Nicaragua. His feat of Caribbean transnavigation, which took him to Bonacca Island off Cape Honduras on July 30, deserves to be reckoned on a par, as to difficulty, with that of crossing the Atlantic, and the admiral was justly proud of it. The fleet continued southward along Costa Rica. Constantly probing for the strait, Columbus sailed round the Chiriquí Lagoon (in Panama) in October; then, searching for gold, he explored the Panamanian region of Veragua (Veraguas) in the foulest of weather. In order to exploit the promising gold yield he was beginning to find there, the admiral in February 1503 attempted to establish a trading post at Santa María de Belén on the bank of the Belén (Bethlehem) River under the command of Bartholomew Columbus. However, Indian resistance and the poor condition of his ships (of which only two remained, fearfully holed by shipworm) caused him to turn back to Hispaniola. On this voyage disaster again struck. Against Columbus's better judgment, his pilots turned the fleet north too soon. The ships could not make the distance and had to be beached on the coast of Jamaica. By June 1503 Columbus and his crews were castaways.

Columbus had hoped, as he said to his sovereigns, that "my hard and troublesome voyage may yet turn out to be my noblest"; it was in fact the most disappointing of all and the most unlucky. In its explorations the fleet had missed discovering the Pacific (across the isthmus of Panama) and failed to make contact with the Maya of Yucatán by the narrowest of margins. Two of the men— Diego Méndez and Bartolomeo Fieschi, captains of the wrecked ships *La Capitana* and *Vizcaíno*, respectively—left about July 17 by canoe to get help for the castaways. Although they managed to traverse the 450 miles (720 km) of open sea to Hispaniola, Ovando made no great haste to deliver that help. In the meantime, the admiral displayed his acumen once again by correctly predicting an eclipse

of the Moon from his astronomical tables, thus frighten-
ing the local peoples into providing food; but rescuers did
not arrive until June 1504, and Columbus and his men
did not reach Hispaniola until August 13. On November 7
he sailed back to Sanlúcar and found that Queen Isabella,
his main supporter, had made her will and was dying.

Columbus always maintained that he had found the
true Indies and Cathay in the face of mounting evidence
that he had not. Perhaps he genuinely believed that he had
been there; in any event, his disallowances of the "New
World" hindered his goals of nobility and wealth and
dented his later reputation. Columbus had been remote
from his companions and colonists, and he had been a poor
judge of the ambitions, and perhaps the failings, of those
who sailed with him. This combination proved damaging
to almost all of his hopes. Nonetheless, it would be wrong
to suppose that Columbus spent his final two years wholly
in illness, poverty, and oblivion. His son Diego was well
established at court, and the admiral himself lived in Sevilla
in some style. His "tenth" of the gold diggings in Hispaniola,
guaranteed in 1493, provided a substantial revenue (against
which his Genoese bankers allowed him to draw), and one
of the few ships to escape a hurricane off Hispaniola in
1502 (in which Bobadilla himself went down) was that carrying Columbus's gold. He felt himself ill-used and
shortchanged nonetheless, and these years were marred,
for both him and King Ferdinand, by his constant pressing
for redress. Columbus followed the court from Segovia to
Salamanca and Valladolid, attempting to gain an audience.
He knew that his life was nearing its end, and in August
1505 he began to amend his will. He died on May 20, 1506.
First he was laid in the Franciscan friary in Valladolid, and
then taken to the family mausoleum established at the
Carthusian monastery of Las Cuevas in Sevilla. In 1542, by
the will of his son Diego, Columbus's bones were laid with

COLUMBUS'S JOURNALS

The chronicles of the discovery and conquest of the New World are commonly considered to be the most important 16th-century writing in the Americas. This group of documents includes narrative accounts, legal documents (depositions, reports, arguments, etc.), and full-fledged histories. Because of their foundational aura, the most celebrated of the texts are Christopher Columbus's letters and reports to the Catholic monarchs and their functionaries. There is an added charm in Columbus's awkwardness of style (Spanish was not his native tongue), his difficulties in describing objects unknown to Europeans, and his huge mistakes. In spite of these often attractive flaws, his accounts constitute a substantial legacy in the discourse of the West. The most egregious of Columbus's errors was, of course, his belief that he had arrived somewhere in Asia, which led to his adopting the name "Indies" for the lands he "discovered," hence the misnomer "Indians" for all the natives of the American continent.

Columbus's letters and reports were quickly disseminated in the original and in Latin translations. Using these and other early accounts, the Italian humanist Peter Martyr d'Anghiera wrote, during the last years of the 15th and early years of the 16th century, the first history of the New World: *De Orbe Novo decades* (1516; *De Orbe Novo: The Eight Decades of Peter Martyr d'Anghiera*). Whereas Columbus was a navigator who could write a little, Peter Martyr' elegant Latin tract enjoyed a wide readership all over Europe.

his own in the Cathedral of Santo Domingo, Hispaniola (now in the Dominican Republic). After Spain ceded Hispaniola to France, the remains were moved to Havana, Cuba, in 1795 and returned to Sevilla in 1898. In 1877,

however, workers at the cathedral in Santo Domingo
claimed to have found another set of bones that were
marked as those of Columbus. Since 1992 these bones have
been interred in the Columbus Lighthouse (Faro a Colón).

VESPUCCI'S TRAVELS
TO SOUTH AMERICA

The Italian-born Spanish merchant and explorer-navigator
Amerigo Vespucci (1454?–1512) also took part in early voyages to the New World (1499–1500 and 1501–02). Two series
of documents on his voyages are extant. The first series consists of a letter in the name of Vespucci dated from Lisbon,
Port., Sept. 4, 1504, written in Italian, perhaps to the *gonfalo-
nier* (magistrate of a medieval Italian republic) Piero Soderini,
and printed in Florence in 1505 and of two Latin versions of
that letter, printed under the titles of "Quattuor Americi
navigationes" and "Mundus Novus," or "Epistola Alberici de
Novo Mundo." The second series consists of three private
letters addressed to the Medici. In the first series of documents, four voyages by Vespucci are mentioned; in the
second, only two. Until the 1930s, the documents of the first
series were considered from the point of view of the order
of the four voyages. According to a theory of Alberto
Magnaghi, on the contrary, these documents are to be
regarded as the result of skillful manipulations, and the
sole authentic papers would be the private letters, so that
the verified voyages would be reduced to two. The question is fundamental for the evaluation of Vespucci's work
and has given rise to fierce controversy; attempts to recon-
cile the two series of documents were not successful.

The voyage completed by Vespucci between May 1499
and June 1500 as navigator of an expedition of four ships
sent from Spain under the command of Alonso de Ojeda is
certainly authentic. (This is the second expedition of the

traditional series.) Since Vespucci took part as navigator, he certainly cannot have been inexperienced; but it does not seem possible that he had made a previous voyage (1497–98) in this area (i.e., around the Gulf of Mexico and the Atlantic coast from Florida to Chesapeake Bay), though this matter remains unresolved.

In the voyage of 1499–1500, Vespucci would seem to have left Ojeda after reaching the coast of what is now Guyana. Turning south, he is believed to have discovered the mouth of the Amazon River and to have gone as far as Cape St. Augustine (latitude about 6° S). On the way back he reached Trinidad, sighted the mouth of the Orinoco River, and then made for Haiti. Vespucci thought he had sailed along the coast of the extreme easterly peninsula of Asia, where Ptolemy, the geographer, believed the market of Cattigara to be; so he looked for the tip of this peninsula, calling it Cape Cattigara. He supposed that the ships, once past this point, emerged into the seas of southern Asia. As soon as he was back in Spain, he equipped a fresh expedition with the aim of reaching the Indian Ocean, the Gulf of the Ganges (now the Bay of Bengal), and the island of Taprobane or Ceylon (now Sri Lanka). But the Spanish government did not welcome his proposals, and at the end of 1500, Vespucci went into the service of Portugal.

Under Portuguese auspices Vespucci completed a second expedition, which set off from Lisbon on May 13, 1501. After a halt at the Cape Verde Islands, the expedition traveled southwestward and reached the coast of Brazil toward Cape St. Augustine. The remainder of the voyage is disputed, but Vespucci claimed to have continued southward, and he may have sighted (January 1502) Guanabara Bay (now the bay of Rio de Janeiro) and sailed as far as the Río de la Plata, making Vespucci the first European to discover that estuary (Juan Díaz de Solís arrived there in 1516). The ships may have journeyed still farther south, along the coast of Patagonia (now southern Argentina). The return route is unknown. Vespucci's ships anchored at Lisbon on July 22, 1502.

It is uncertain whether Vespucci took part in yet another expedition (1503–04) for the Portuguese government (it is said that he may have been with one under Gonzalo Coelho). In any case, this expedition contributed no fresh knowledge. Although Vespucci subsequently helped to prepare other expeditions, he never again joined one in person. He later returned to Spain and occupied the influential post of *piloto mayor* ("master navigator") in Sevilla from 1508 until his death.

VESPUCCI'S NAMESAKE

The voyage of 1501–02 is of fundamental importance in the history of geographic discovery in that Vespucci himself, and scholars as well, became convinced that the newly discovered lands were not part of Asia but a "New World." In 1507 a humanist, Martin Waldseemüller, reprinted at Saint-Dié in Lorraine the "Quattuor Americi navigationes" ("Four Voyages of Amerigo"), preceded by a pamphlet of his own entitled "Cosmographiae introductio," and he suggested that the newly discovered world be named "ab Americo Inventore... quasi Americi terram sive Americam" ("from Amerigo the discoverer... as if it were the land of Americus or America"). The proposal is perpetuated in a large planisphere of Waldseemüller's, in which the name America appears for the first time, although applied only to South America. The suggestion caught on; the extension of the name to North America, however, came later. On the upper part of the map, with the hemisphere comprising the Old World, appears the picture of Ptolemy; on the part of the map with the New World hemisphere is the picture of Vespucci.

MAGELLAN AND THE
CIRCUMNAVIGATION OF THE EARTH

The Portuguese navigator and explorer Ferdinand Magellan (Fernão de Magalhães in Portuguese and Fernando, or Hernando, de Magallanes in Spanish; *c.* 1480–1521) sailed under the flags of both Portugal (1505–12) and Spain (1519–21). From Spain he sailed around South America, discovering the Strait of Magellan, and across the Pacific. Though he was killed in the Philippines, his ships continued westward to Spain, accomplishing the first circumnavigation of Earth. The Basque navigator Juan Sebastián del Cano successfully terminated that voyage.

In early 1505 Magellan enlisted in the fleet of Francisco de Almeida, first Portuguese viceroy in the East, whose expedition, sent by King Manuel to check Muslim sea power in Africa and India, left Lisbon on March 25. During a naval engagement at Cannanore on the Malabar Coast of India, Magellan is said by the chronicler Gaspar Correia to have been wounded. Though Correia states that during this early period of his Indian service he acquired considerable knowledge of navigation, little is known of Magellan's first years in the East until he appears among those sailing in November 1506 with Nuno Vaz Pereira to Sofala on the Mozambique coast, where the Portuguese established a fort.

In 1508 Magellan was back in India, taking part, on Feb. 2–3, 1509, in the great Battle of Diu, which gave the Portuguese supremacy over most of the Indian Ocean. Reaching Cochin in the fleet of Diogo Lopes de Sequeira, he left as one of the men-at-arms for Malacca. Magellan is mentioned as being sent to warn the commander of impending attack by Malays and during the subsequent fighting courageously saved the life of a Portuguese explorer, Francisco Serrão, who later from the Moluccas (now Maluku) sent him helpful information about those islands. At a council held at Cochin on October 10, to decide on plans for recapturing Goa, Magellan advised against taking large ships at that season, but the new viceroy, Afonso de Albuquerque, did so, the city falling on November 24; Magellan's name does not appear among those who fought. There is no conclusive evidence for the theory that during his Indian service he attained the rank of captain.

The Portuguese victories off the eastern coast of Africa and the western coast of India had broken Muslim power in the Indian Ocean, and the purpose of Almeida's expedition—to wrest from the Arabs the key points of sea trade—was almost accomplished, but without control of Malacca their achievement was incomplete. At the end of June 1511, therefore, a fleet under Albuquerque left for Malacca, which fell after six weeks. This event, in which Magellan took part, was the crowning Portuguese victory in the Far East. Through Malacca passed the wealth of the East to the harbours of the West, and in the command of the Malacca Strait the Portuguese held the key to the seas and ports of Malaysia. It remained to explore the wealth-giving Moluccas, the islands of spice. Accordingly, early in December 1511 they sailed on a voyage of reconnaissance and after reaching Banda, returned with spice in 1512. The claim made by some that Magellan went on this voyage rests on unproved statements by Giovanni Battista Ramusio and Leonardo de Argensola, and the want of evidence argues against its acceptance. Even if he did, in truth, reach the Moluccas, a further voyage—which he later commanded from Spain to the Philippines—was required to complete the circle of navigation.

In 1512 Magellan was back in Lisbon. The following year he joined the forces sent against the Moroccan stronghold of Azamor and in a skirmish after its fall sustained a wound that caused him to limp for the rest of his life.

Returning to Lisbon in November 1514 he asked King Manuel for a token increase in his pension, signifying a rise in rank. But unfounded reports of irregular conduct on his part after the siege of Azamor had reached the king, who, refusing his request, ordered him back to Morocco. Early in 1516 Magellan renewed his petition; the king, refusing once more, told him he might offer his services elsewhere.

ALLEGIANCE TO SPAIN

Magellan therefore went to Spain, reaching Sevilla on Oct. 20, 1517. The Portuguese cosmographer Rui Faleiro joined him, and together they traveled to the court at Valladolid. There, having renounced their nationality, the two men offered their services to King Charles I (later, Emperor Charles V). Magalhães henceforward became known by the Spanish version of his name—Fernando de Magallanes.

By decree of a papal bull in 1493, all new territories dis-covered or that should be discovered east of a line of demarcation (redrawn 1494) were assigned to Portugal, all that lay west to Spain. Magellan and Faleiro now proposed by sailing west to give practical proof of their claim that the Spice Islands lay west of the line of demarcation—that is, within the Spanish, not the Portuguese, hemisphere. On March 22, 1518, their proposal received royal assent; they were appointed joint captains general of an expedi-tion directed to seek an all-Spanish route to the Moluccas. The government of any lands discovered was to be vested in them and their heirs, and they were to receive a one-twentieth share of the net profits from the venture; both were invested with the Order of Santiago. Magellan was convinced that he would lead his ships from the Atlantic to the "Sea of the South" by discovering a strait through Tierra Firme (the South American mainland). This idea did not originate with him; others had sought a passage by

which vessels sailing continuously westward would reach
the East and thus avoid the Cape of Good Hope, which
was controlled by the Portuguese; in the royal agreement
Magellan and Faleiro were directed to find "the" strait.
The officials entrusted with East Indian affairs were
instructed to furnish five ships for the expedition, prepared in Sevilla, where an unsuccessful attempt to wreck
the project was made by Portuguese agents. Magellan's
flagship, the *Trinidad*, had as consorts the *San Antonio*,
Concepción, *Victoria*, and *Santiago*. An attack of insanity
prevented Faleiro from sailing.

Magellan and his ships left Sanlúcar de Barrameda on
Sept. 20, 1519, carrying about 270 men of various ethnic and
national origins. The fleet reached Tenerife on September
26, sailing on October 3 for Brazil; becalmed off the Guinea
coast, it met storms before reaching the line. On November
29 it was 27 leagues southwest of Cape St. Augustine.
Rounding Cabo Frio, Magellan entered the Bay of Rio de
Janeiro on December 13, then sailed south to the Río de la
Plata and vainly probed the estuary, seeking the strait. On
March 31 he reached Port St. Julian in latitude 49°20′ S,
where on Easter day at midnight Spanish captains led a serious mutiny against the Portuguese commander. Magellan
with resolution, ruthlessness, and daring quelled it, execut-
ing one of the captains and leaving another to his fate ashore
when, on Aug. 24, 1520, the fleet left St. Julian.

DISCOVERY OF THE STRAIT OF MAGELLAN

After reaching the mouth of the Santa Cruz, near which the
Santiago had been wrecked earlier while scouting, Magellan
started south again, on October 21 rounding the Cape of
the Virgins (Cabo Vírgenes) and at approximately 52°50′ S
entered the passage that proved to be the strait of his seeking, later to bear his name. The *San Antonio* having deserted,

only three of his ships reached the western end of the passage. At the news that the ocean had been sighted the iron-willed admiral broke down and cried with joy.

On November 28 the *Trinidad, Concepción*, and *Victoria* entered the "Sea of the South," from their calm crossing later called the Pacific Ocean. Tortured by thirst, stricken by scurvy, feeding on fouled biscuits, finally reduced to eating the leather off the yardarms, the crews, driven first by the Peru Current and throughout the voyage by the relentless determination of Magellan, made the great crossing of the Pacific. Until December 18 they had sailed near the Chilean coast; then Magellan took a course northwestward. Land was not sighted until Jan. 24, 1521, probably Pukapuka in the Tuamotu Archipelago. Crossing the equinoctial line at approximately 158° W on February 13, the voyagers on March 6 made first landfall at Guam in the Marianas, where they obtained fresh food for the first time in 99 days. A *Memorial*, sent by Magellan to King Charles before leaving Spain, suggests that he knew (probably partly from Serrão's letters) the approximate position of the Moluccas; in sailing now to the Philippines instead of direct to the Spice Islands, he was doubtless dominated by thoughts of obtaining more food and supplies as well as the advantage of securing a base before visiting the Moluccas.

Leaving on March 9, Magellan steered west-southwest to islands later called the Philippines, where at Massava he secured the first alliance in the Pacific for Spain, and at Cebú the conversion to Christianity of the ruler and his chief men. Less than two months later, however, Magellan was killed in a fight with natives on Mactan Island.

CIRCUMNAVIGATION OF THE GLOBE

After Magellan's death only two of the ships, the *Trinidad* and *Victoria*, reached the Moluccas; only one, the *Victoria*

STRAIT OF MAGELLAN

The Strait of Magellan (Estrecho de Magallanes) is a channel linking the Atlantic and Pacific oceans, between the mainland tip of South America and Tierra del Fuego Island. Lying entirely within Chilean territorial waters, except for its easternmost extremity touched by Argentina, it is 350 miles (560 km) long and 2–20 miles (3–32 km) wide. It extends westward from the Atlantic between Cape Vírgenes and Cape Espíritu Santo, proceeds southwestward, and curves to the northwest at Froward Cape on the southern tip of Brunswick Peninsula to reach the Pacific Ocean after passing Cape Pillar on Desolación Island. The strait's major port is Punta Arenas, on the Brunswick Peninsula.

Ferdinand Magellan and his company were the first Europeans to navigate the strait (Oct. 21–Nov. 28, 1520) while his expedition was en route to the first circumnavigation of the world. Although the strait follows a somewhat tortuous course among numerous islands and channels and has a cold, foggy climate, it was an important sailing-ship route before the building of the Panama Canal (completed in 1914) shortened the Atlantic-Pacific passage by several thousand miles.

(85 tons), returned to Spain, under command of Cano, originally master on the *Concepción* and participator in the mutiny at Port St. Julian. The leaking but spice-laden ship returned home on Sept. 8, 1522, with only 17 other European survivors and 4 Indians, "weaker than men have ever been before." Upon his arrival Cano received from the emperor an augmentation to his coat of arms, a globe with the inscription "Primus circumdedisti me" ("You were the first to encircle me").

C hapter 3: Colonial Exploration of the New World

T he age of modern colonialism began about 1500, following the European discoveries of a sea route around Africa's southern coast (1488) and of America (1492). With these events sea power shifted from the Mediterranean to the Atlantic and to the countries that developed their maritime power. By discovery, conquest, and settlement, these nations expanded and colonized throughout the world, spreading European institutions and culture.

SPAIN: THE CONQUESTS

Only gradually did the Spaniards realize the possibilities of America. They had completed the occupation of the larger West Indian islands by 1512, though they largely ignored the smaller ones, to their ultimate regret. Thus far they had found lands nearly empty of treasure, populated by inhabitants who died off rapidly on contact with Europeans. In 1508 an expedition did leave Hispaniola to colonize the mainland, and, after hardship and decimation, the remnant settled at Darién on the Isthmus of Panama, from which in 1513 Vasco Núñez de Balboa made his famous march to the Pacific. On the Isthmus the Spaniards heard garbled reports of the wealth and splendour of Inca Peru. Balboa was succeeded (and judicially murdered) by Pedrarias Dávila, who turned his attention to Central America and founded Nicaragua.

Expeditions sent by Diego Velázquez, governor of Cuba, made contact with the decayed Mayan civilization of Yucatán and brought news of the cities and precious metals of Aztec Mexico. Hernán Cortés entered Mexico from Cuba in 1519 and spent two years overthrowing the Aztec confederation, which dominated Mexico's civilized heartland. The Spaniards used firearms effectively but did most of their fighting with pikes and blades, aided by numerous Indian allies who hated the dominant Aztecs. The conquest of Aztec Mexico led directly to that of Guatemala and about half of Yucatán, whose geography and warlike inhabitants slowed Spanish progress.

Mexico yielded much gold and silver, and the conquerors imagined still greater wealth and wonders to the north. None of this existed, but it seemed real when a northern wanderer, Alvar Núñez Cabeza de Vaca, in 1536 brought to Mexico an exciting but fanciful report of the fabulous lands. Expeditions explored northern Mexico and the southern part of what is now the United States—notably the expedition of Juan Rodríguez Cabrillo by sea along what are now the California and Oregon coasts and the expeditions of Hernando de Soto and Francisco Vázquez Coronado through the southeastern and southwestern United States. These brought geographical knowledge but nothing of value to the Spaniards, who for years thereafter ignored the northern regions.

Meanwhile, the Pizarro brothers—Francisco Pizarro and his half-brothers Gonzalo and Hernando—entered the Inca empire from Panama in 1531 and proceeded with its conquest. Finding the huge realm divided by a recent civil war over the throne, they captured and executed the incumbent usurper, Atahuallpa. But the conquest took years to complete; the Pizarros had to crush a formidable native rising and defeat their erstwhile associate, Diego de Almagro, who felt cheated of his share of the spoils. The Pizarros and their followers took and divided a great amount of gold and silver, with prospects of more from the mines of Peru and Bolivia. By-products of the Inca conquest were the seizure of northern Chile by Pedro de Valdivia and the descent of the entire Amazon by Francisco de Orellana. Other conquistadors entered the regions of what became Ecuador, Colombia, and Argentina.

BALBOA REACHES THE PACIFIC

The Spanish conquistador and explorer Vasco Núñez de Balboa (1475–1519) was head of the first stable settlement on the South American continent (1511) and led the first Europeans to sight the Pacific Ocean (Sept. 25 [or 27], 1513).

In 1500 Balboa sailed with Rodrigo de Bastidas on a voyage of exploration along the coast of what is now Colombia. Later, he settled in Hispaniola (now Haiti), but he did not prosper as a pioneer farmer and had to escape his creditors by embarking as a stowaway on an expedition organized by Martín Fernández de Enciso (1510) to bring aid and reinforcements to a colony founded by Alonso de Ojeda on the coast of Urabá, in Colombia. The expedition found the survivors of the colony, led by Francisco Pizarro, but Ojeda had departed. On the advice of Balboa the settlers moved across the Gulf of Urabá to Darién, on the less hostile coast of the Isthmus of Panama, where they founded Santa María de la Antigua, the first stable settlement on the continent, and began to acquire gold by barter or war with the local Indians. The colonists soon deposed Enciso, Ojeda's second in command, and elected a town council; one of its two alcaldes, or magistrates, was Balboa. With the subsequent departure of Enciso for Hispaniola, Balboa became the undisputed head of the colony. In December 1511, King Ferdinand II sent orders that named Balboa interim governor and captain general of Darién.

The Spaniards were told by Indians that to the south lay a sea and a province infinitely rich in gold—a reference to the Pacific and perhaps to the Inca empire. The

conquest of that land, their informants declared, would
require 1,000 men. Balboa hastened to send emissaries to
Spain to request reinforcements; the news they brought
created much excitement, and a large expedition was
promptly organized. But Balboa was not given command.
Charges brought against him by his enemies had turned
King Ferdinand against him, and, as commander of the
armada and governor of Darién, the king sent out the elderly, powerful nobleman Pedro Arias Dávila (Pedrarias).
The expedition, numbering 2,000 persons, left Spain in
April 1514.

Discovery of the Pacific

Meanwhile, Balboa, without waiting for reinforcements,
had sailed on Sept. 1, 1513, from Santa María for Acla, at
the narrowest part of the isthmus. Accompanied by 190
Spaniards and hundreds of Indian carriers, he marched
south across the isthmus through dense jungles, rivers,
and swamps and ascended the cordillera; on Sept. 25 (or
27), 1513, standing "silent, upon a peak in Darién," he
sighted the Pacific. Some days later he reached the shore
of the Gulf of San Miguel and took possession of the Mar
del Sur (South Sea) and the adjacent lands for the king of
Castile. He then recrossed the isthmus, arriving at Santa
María in January 1514. His letters and those of a royal agent
who had been sent to Darién to prepare the ground for the
coming of Pedrarias, announcing the discovery of the
"South Sea," restored Balboa to royal favour. He was
named *adelantado* (governor) of the Mar del Sur and of the
provinces of Panamá and Coiba but remained subject to
the authority of Pedrarias, who arrived in Darién, now a
royal colony renamed Castilla del Oro, in June 1514.

Relations between the two men were, from the first,
troubled by distrust and jealousy. The ailing and suspicious Pedrarias pursued a tortuous policy designed to

frustrate Balboa at every turn; but he at last gave Balboa grudging permission to explore the South Sea. By dint of enormous efforts Balboa had a fleet of ships built and transported in pieces across the mountains to the Pacific shore, where he explored the Gulf of San Miguel (1517–18). At the same time, the stream of charges of misconduct and incapacity levelled against Pedrarias by Balboa and others had finally convinced the crown of Pedrarias' inability to govern; news arrived in Darién of his imminent replacement by a new governor who subjected Pedrarias to a *residencia* (judicial review). Pedrarias doubtless feared that Balboa's presence and testimony would contribute to his ruin and decided to get rid of his rival. Summoned home on the pretext that Pedrarias wished to discuss matters of common concern, Balboa was seized and charged with rebellion, high treason, and mistreatment of Indians, among other misdeeds. After a farcical trial presided over by Gaspar de Espinosa, Pedrarias' chief justice, Balboa was found guilty, condemned to death, and beheaded with four alleged accomplices in 1519.

CORTÉS AND THE CONQUEST OF THE AZTECS

Hernán Cortés, or Cortéz (1485–1547), was the Spanish conquistador who overthrew the Aztec empire (1519–21) and won Mexico for the crown of Spain.

Cortés, excited by Christopher Columbus's stories of the Indies, sailed for the island of Hispaniola in 1506 when he was 19 years old. In Hispaniola he became a farmer and notary to a town council. He contracted syphilis and, as a result, missed the ill-fated expeditions of Diego de Nicuesa and Alonso de Ojeda, which sailed for the South American mainland in 1509. By 1511 he had recovered, and he sailed with Diego Velázquez to conquer Cuba. There Velázquez was appointed governor, and Cortés clerk to the treasurer. Cortés received a *repartimiento* (gift of land and Indian slaves) and the first house in the new capital of Santiago. He was now in a position of power and the man to whom dissident elements in the colony began to turn for leadership.

Cortés was twice elected alcalde (mayor) of Santiago and was a man who "in all he did, in his presence, bearing, conversation, manner of eating and of dressing, gave signs of being a great lord." It was therefore to Cortés that Velázquez turned when, after news had come of the progress of Juan de Grijalba's efforts to establish a colony on the mainland, it was decided to send him help. An agreement appointing Cortés captain general of a new expedition was signed in October 1518. Experience of the rough-and-tumble of New World politics advised Cortés to move fast, before Velázquez changed his mind. His sense of the dramatic, his experience as an administrator, the knowledge gained from so many failed expeditions, and his ability as a speaker enabled him to quickly gather six ships and 300 men in less than a month. The reaction of Velázquez was predictable; his jealousy aroused, he resolved to place leadership of the expedition in other hands. Cortés, however, put hastily to sea to raise more men and ships in other Cuban ports.

The Expedition to Mexico

When Cortés finally sailed for the coast of Yucatán on Feb. 18, 1519, he had 11 ships, 508 soldiers, about 100 sailors, and—most important—16 horses. In March 1519 he landed at Tabasco, where he stayed for a time in order to gain intelligence from the local Indians. He won them over and received presents from them, including 20 women, one of whom, Marina ("Malinche"), became his mistress and interpreter and bore him a son, Martín.

Cortés sailed to another spot on the southeastern Mexican coast and founded Veracruz, mainly to have himself elected captain general and chief justice by his soldiers as citizens, thus shaking off the authority of Velázquez. On the mainland Cortés did what no other expedition leader had done: he exercised and disciplined his army, welding it into a cohesive force. But the ultimate expression of his determination occurred when he purposely sank his ships. By that single action he committed himself and his entire force to survival by conquest.

Cortés then set out for the Mexican interior, relying sometimes on force, sometimes on amity toward the local Indian peoples, but always careful to keep conflict with them to a strict minimum. The key to Cortés's subsequent conquests lay in the political crisis within the Aztec empire. The Aztecs were bitterly resented by many of the subject peoples who had to pay tribute to them. The ability of Cortés as a leader is nowhere more apparent than in his quick grasp of the situation—a grasp that ultimately gave him more than 200,000 Indian allies. The nation of Tlaxcala, for instance, which was in a state of chronic war with Montezuma II, ruler of the Aztec empire of Mexico, resisted Cortés at first but became his most faithful ally. Rejecting all of Montezuma's threats and blandishments to keep him away from Tenochtitlán or Mexico, the capital (now Mexico City), Cortés entered the city on Nov. 8, 1519, with his small Spanish force and only 1,000 Tlaxcaltecs. In accordance with the diplomatic customs of Mexico, Montezuma received him with great honour. Cortés soon decided to seize Montezuma in order to hold the country through its monarch and achieve not only its political conquest but its religious conversion.

Spanish politics and envy were to bedevil Cortés throughout his meteoric career. Cortés soon heard of the

arrival of a Spanish force from Cuba, led by Pánfilo
Narváez, to deprive Cortés of his command at a time
(mid-1520) when he was holding the Aztec capital of
Tenochtitlán by little more than the force of his personal-
ity. Leaving a garrison in Tenochtitlán of 80 Spaniards and
a few hundred Tlaxcaltecs commanded by his most reckless captain, Pedro de Alvarado, Cortés marched against
Narváez, defeated him, and enlisted his army in his own
forces. On his return, he found the Spanish garrison in
Tenochtitlán besieged by the Aztecs after Alvarado had
massacred many leading Aztec chiefs during a festival.
Hard pressed and lacking food, Cortés decided to leave
the city by night. The Spaniards' retreat from the capital
was performed but with a heavy loss in lives and most of
the treasure they had accumulated. After six days of
retreat, Cortés won the battle of Otumba over the Aztecs
sent in pursuit (July 7, 1520).

Cortés eventually rejoined his Tlaxcalan allies and
reorganized his forces before again marching on
Tenochtitlán in December 1520. After subduing the neighbouring territories he laid siege to the city itself, conquering
it street by street until its capture was completed on Aug.
13, 1521. This victory marked the fall of the Aztec empire.
Cortés had become the absolute ruler of a huge territory
extending from the Caribbean Sea to the Pacific Ocean.

In the meantime, Velázquez was mounting an insidi-
ous political attack on Cortés in Spain through Bishop
Juan Rodríguez de Fonseca and the Council of the Indies.
Fully conscious of the vulnerability of a successful conqueror whose field of operations was 5,000 miles (8,000
km) from the centre of political power, Cortés countered
with lengthy and detailed dispatches—five remarkable
letters to the Spanish king Charles V. His acceptance by
the Indians and even his popularity as a relatively benign

ruler was such that he could have established Mexico as an independent kingdom. Indeed, this is what the Council of the Indies feared. But his upbringing in a feudal world in which the king commanded absolute allegiance was against it.

Later Years

In 1524 Cortés's restless urge to explore and conquer took him south to the jungles of Honduras. The two arduous years he spent on this disastrous expedition damaged his health and his position. His property was seized by the officials he had left in charge, and reports of the cruelty of their administration and the chaos it created aroused concern in Spain. Cortés's fifth letter to the Spanish king attempts to justify his reckless behaviour and concludes with a bitter attack on "various and powerful rivals and enemies" who have "obscured the eyes of your Majesty." But it was his misfortune that he was not dealing simply with a king of Spain but with an emperor who ruled most of Europe and who had little time for distant colonies, except insofar as they contributed to his treasury. The Spanish bureaucrats sent out a commission of inquiry under Luis Ponce de León, and, when he died almost immediately, Cortés was accused of poisoning him and was forced to retire to his estate.

In 1528, Cortés sailed for Spain to plead his cause in person with the king. He brought with him a great wealth of treasure and a magnificent entourage. King Charles received him at his royal court at Toledo, confirmed Cortés as captain general (but not as governor), and named him marqués del Valle. He also remarried, into a ducal family. He returned to New Spain in 1530 to find the country in a state of anarchy. Many accusations were made against him—even that he had murdered his first wife, Catalina, who had died that year. After reasserting his position and reestablishing some sort of order, Cortés retired to his estates at Cuernavaca, about 30 miles (48 km) south of Mexico City. There he concentrated on the building of his palace and on Pacific exploration.

Finally a viceroy was appointed, after which, in 1540, Cortés returned to Spain. By then he had become thoroughly disillusioned, his life made miserable by litigation. All the rest is anticlimax. "I am old, poor and in debt . . . again and again I have begged your Majesty . . ." In the end he was permitted to return to Mexico, but he died before he had even reached Sevilla.

CHOCOLATE

At the court of Montezuma, the Aztec ruler of Mexico, in 1519, Hernán Cortés was served xocoatl, a bitter cocoa-bean drink, which he then introduced to Spain. Sweetened, flavoured with cinnamon and vanilla, and served hot, the beverage remained a Spanish secret for almost 100 years before its introduction to France. In 1657 a Frenchman opened a shop in London, at which solid chocolate for making the beverage could be purchased at 10 to 15 shillings a pound. At this price only the wealthy could afford to drink it, and there appeared in London, Amsterdam, and other European capitals fashionable chocolate houses, some of which later developed into famous clubs. In about 1700 the English improved chocolate by the addition of milk. The reduction of the cost of the beverage was hampered in Great Britain by the imposition of high import duties on the raw cocoa bean, and it was not until the mid-19th century, when the duty was lowered to a uniform rate of 1 penny a pound, that chocolate became popular.

FRANCISCO PIZARRO AND THE CONQUEST OF THE INCAS

Francisco Pizarro (1475–1541) was the Spanish conqueror of the Inca empire and founder of the city of Lima, Peru.

In 1502, Pizarro went to Hispaniola with the new governor of the Spanish colony. He had little inclination toward the settled life of a colonizer, and in 1510 he enrolled in an expedition of the explorer Alonso de Ojeda to Urabá in Colombia. He was considered a hard, silent, and apparently unambitious man who could be trusted in difficult situations. Three years later, acting as captain, he participated in an expedition led by Vasco Núñez de Balboa that discovered the Pacific Ocean. From 1519 to 1523 he was mayor and magistrate of the newly founded town of Panamá, accumulating a small fortune.

Discovery and Conquest of Peru

It was not until 1523, when Pizzaro was 48 years old, that he embarked upon the adventure that was to lead to his lasting fame. In partnership with a soldier, Diego de Almagro, and a priest, Hernando de Luque, he made preparations for a voyage of discovery and conquest down the west coast of South America. Many hardships were endured along the Colombian coast during the first (1524–25) and second (1526–28) expeditions. Bartolomé Ruiz, who joined Pizarro and Almagro for the latter expedition, sailed ahead and crossed the Equator, encountering a trading raft carrying embroidered fabrics and precious metals from Peru. He returned and led the expedition as far south as Ecuador. Pizarro and others remained on coastal islands while Almagro was sent back to Panama for reinforcements. The new governor of Panama, however, sent back orders that the expedition be abandoned to save lives. At this point Pizarro is reputed to have drawn a line on the ground with his sword, inviting those who desired wealth and glory to cross it. The "famous thirteen" who did cross the line continued their exploration of the coast as far as latitude 9° S, obtaining distinct accounts of a great Indian empire as well as many Inca artifacts. They christened the new land Peru, probably a corruption of Virú, the name of a local river.

Finding the governor of Panama still opposed to their now promising enterprise, the explorers decided that Pizarro should go to Spain to ask the emperor Charles V (Charles I of Spain) for permission to undertake conquest. Sailing in the spring of 1528, Pizarro was in Sevilla at the same time as Hernán Cortés and was able to win Charles over to his scheme. He was decorated, granted a coat of arms, and, in July 1529, made governor and captain general of the province of New Castile for a distance of some 600 miles (965 km) south of Panama along the newly discovered coast. Pizarro was invested with all the authority and prerogatives of a viceroy, and Almagro and Luque were left in subordinate positions. All the "famous thirteen" received substantial rights and privileges in the new territories.

Joined by four of his brothers, Pizarro sailed for Panama in January 1530 and by January of the following year was ready to set off for Peru. He set sail with one ship, 180 men, and 37 horses, being joined later by two more ships. By April they had made contact with emissaries of Atahuallpa, emperor of the Incas, who was residing near the city of Cajamarca with an army of about 30,000 men. Somewhat scornful of Pizarro's small force, the Inca accepted a proposal that the two leaders meet in that city.

Arriving on November 15, Pizarro immediately set up his artillery and sent his brother Hernando and another Spaniard to request an interview. After a day of tense waiting, Atahuallpa, borne on a litter, entered the great square of Cajamarca with an escort of between 3,000 and 4,000 men, who were either unarmed or carrying short clubs and slings beneath their tunics. Pizarro sent out a priest, Vicente de Valverde, to exhort the Inca to accept Christianity and Charles V as his master. Atahuallpa disputed both the religion and the sovereignty of the Spaniards and, after examining a Bible offered by the priest, flung the book to the ground. Valverde reported these events to Pizarro, who immediately ordered an attack. The astonished Incas were cut down from all sides, Pizarro himself seizing Atahuallpa.

Atahuallpa was held as hostage and failed to win his release, though he fulfilled a promise to fill the chamber in which he was held with gold and silver. Accused of ordering the execution of his brother Huascar, a rival for the title of Inca, and of plotting to overthrow the Spaniards, Atahuallpa was put to death by strangulation on Aug. 29, 1533. With news of Atahuallpa's death, the Inca armies surrounding Cajamarca retreated, and Pizarro progressed toward Cuzco, the royal capital, which was occupied without a struggle in November 1533. The Spaniards declared Manco Capac, Huascar's brother, as Inca.

For the remainder of his life, Pizarro was engaged in consolidating the Spanish hold on Peru and in defending his and his brothers' share of the spoils. A certain enmity and rivalry developed between him and Almagro as a result of Pizarro's overriding powers from the king of Spain. Almagro at one stage seized Cuzco but was persuaded by Pizarro to depart for Chile. Disappointed by the poverty of that country, however, he returned to Peru, where he was made prisoner and later executed by Hernando Pizarro.

Francisco Pizarro, meanwhile, was in Lima, a city that he had founded in 1535 and to which he devoted the last two years of his life. Almagro's former adherents had grouped around Almagro's son in Lima, where they were confined and watched. Suspecting that they were in danger, they decided to move first, attacking Pizarro's palace on June 26, 1541. Pizarro died that day a protracted death, drawing a cross of his own blood on the ground, kissing it, and crying "Jesus" as he fell.

FRANCISCO DE ORELLANA

The Spanish soldier Francisco de Orellana (*c.* 1490–*c.* 1546) was the first European explorer of the Amazon River. After participating with Francisco Pizarro in the conquest of Peru in 1535, Orellana moved to Guayaquil and was named governor of that area in 1538. When Pizarro's half brother, Gonzalo, prepared an expedition to explore the regions east of Quito, Orellana was appointed his lieutenant. In April 1541 he was sent ahead of the main party to seek provisions, taking a brigantine with 50 soldiers. He reached the junction of the Napo and Marañón Rivers, where his group persuaded him of the impossibility of returning to Pizarro. Instead, he entered upon an exploration of the Amazon system. Drifting with the current, he reached the mouth of the river in August 1542. Proceeding to Trinidad, he finally returned to Spain, where he told of hoards of gold and cinnamon and of encounters with tribes led by women resembling the Amazons of Greek mythology—a comparison that is presumed to have led him to name the river the Amazon.

Orellana sought the right to explore and exploit the lands that he had discovered. Because the Spanish crown was involved in controversy with Portugal over the ownership of the area, it could provide him with only some assistance but no official support. His return to the Amazon proved a disaster. Ships and men were lost on the passage to America, and Orellana's vessel capsized near the mouth of the Amazon and he drowned.

DE SOTO AND THE DISCOVERY
OF THE MISSISSIPPI RIVER

The Spanish explorer and conquistador Hernando (or Fernando) de Soto (c. 1496/97–1542) participated in the conquests of Central America and Peru and, in the course of exploring what was to become the southeastern United States, discovered the Mississippi River.

De Soto's parents intended him to be a lawyer, but in 1514, while still in his teens, he left for Sevilla. Despite his youth, de Soto's zeal and his prowess as a horseman helped gain him a place on the 1514 expedition of Pedro Arias Dávila to the West Indies. In Panama, de Soto quickly made his mark as a trader and expeditioner, reaping high profits by his skill and daring. By 1520 he had accumulated considerable capital through his slave trading in Nicaragua and on the Isthmus of Panama, after successful partnerships with Hernán Ponce de León and Francisco Campañón. In 1524–27 de Soto defeated his archrival, Gil González de Ávila, in a struggle for control of Nicaragua, and he subsequently expanded his trade in Indian slaves.

In 1530, de Soto lent Francisco Pizarro two ships to investigate reports of gold located south of Darién on the Pacific coast (now in northwestern Colombia). After de Soto's patron, Dávila, died in 1531 and Pizarro's expedition confirmed the reports of gold, de Soto joined the enterprise. In return for the use of his ships, Pizarro named de Soto his chief lieutenant, and the conquest of Peru began the following year in 1532. De Soto, as the expedition's captain, was the driving force in the Spaniards' defeat of the Incas at Cajamarca, and he was the first European to make contact with the Inca emperor Atahuallpa.

Following the Spaniards' capture of Atahuallpa, de Soto seized Cuzco, the Inca capital. For political reasons, he became the emperor's friend and protector, but Pizarro, fearing Atahuallpa's influence over his Inca subjects, had the emperor executed even though the latter's subjects had raised an enormous ransom in gold and silver in order to ensure his release. Dissatisfied with Pizarro's leadership and coveting a governorship of his own, de Soto returned to Spain in 1536. The shares that he had accumulated in the sack of Peru, though less than half of Pizarro's, made him one of the wealthiest of the returning conquistadors.

Exploration of Southern North America

In 1537 de Soto sought special permission to conquer Ecuador, but he was commissioned by the Spanish crown to conquer what is now Florida. In addition, he was made governor of Cuba. In April 1538 de Soto embarked from the port of Sanlúcar de Barrameda in command of 10 ships and 700 men. After a brief stop in Cuba, the expedition landed in May 1539 on the coast of Florida, at a point somewhere between present-day Tampa Bay and Charlotte Harbor. After spending the winter at a small village of the Apalache Indians (near present-day Tallahassee, now the Florida panhandle), de Soto moved northward and through Georgia and then westward through the Carolinas and Tennessee, led by native guides whom he abducted along the way. Though he did not find the gold he was looking for, he did collect a valuable assortment of pearls at a place called Cofitachequi, in eastern Georgia. Near Lookout Mountain, in southeastern Tennessee, de Soto and his men turned southward into Alabama and headed toward Mobile Bay where they expected to rendezvous with their ships. But at the fortified Indian town of Mauvila (now Mobile), a confederation of Indians attacked the Spaniards in October 1540. The natives were decimated, but the Spanish were also severely crippled, losing most of their equipment and all their pearls.

After a month's rest, de Soto decided to turn north once again and head inland in search of treasure. This was a fateful decision that had disastrous results. Moving northwest through Alabama and then west through Mississippi, de Soto's party was attacked relentlessly by Indians. On May 21, 1541, the Spaniards saw for the first time the Mississippi River, the "Father of the Water" south of Memphis, Tenn. They crossed the river and made their way through Arkansas and Louisiana. Then, early in 1542, de Soto turned back to the Mississippi River. Overcome by fever, he died in Louisiana, and his comrades buried his body in the Mississippi. Luis de Moscoso, whom de Soto had named his successor, led the expedition's remnants (half the original party) down the Mississippi on rafts, and they reached Mexico in 1543.

Coronado's Expeditions in Southwestern North America

Francisco Vázquez de Coronado (c. 1510–54) is the best-known Spanish explorer of the North American Southwest. His expeditions resulted in the discovery of many physical landmarks, including the Grand Canyon, but he failed to find the treasure-laden cities he sought.

Coronado went to New Spain (Mexico) with Antonio de Mendoza, the Spanish viceroy, in 1535 and earned early distinction in pacifying Indians. He was appointed governor of Nueva Galicia in 1538. Fray Marcos de Niza, sent north in 1539 by Mendoza to explore, had come back with reports of vast riches in the legendary Seven Golden Cities of Cíbola, which perhaps corresponded in reality to the

Zuni Pueblos (now New Mexico). Mendoza organized an ambitious expedition to make a more thorough exploration. It consisted of 300 Spaniards, hundreds of Indians and native slaves, horses, and herds of sheep, pigs, and cattle, in addition to two ships under the command of Hernando de Alarcón, who sailed up the Gulf of California to discover the mouth of the Colorado River on Aug. 26, 1540. In February 1540, the main force under Coronado left Compostela and proceeded up the west coast of Mexico to Culiacán. A smaller unit rode north from there and encountered the Pueblos of Zuni in July 1540 but found no great wealth or treasure. Another side exploration made García López de Cárdenas the first European to view the Grand Canyon of the Colorado River (in Arizona). The groups united to spend the winter on the Rio Grande at Kuana (now Santa Fe, N.M.). Several Indian groups attempted to attack them there but were beaten back with severe reprisals.

In the spring of 1541, the force moved into Palo Duro Canyon (now Texas). Once there, Coronado left most of his men and proceeded north with 30 horsemen to another supposedly fabulously wealthy country, Quivira (now Kansas), only to find a seminomadic Indian village and disillusionment again. In 1542 Coronado returned to Mexico, reported his disappointing findings to Mendoza, and resumed his governorship of Nueva Galicia.

An official inquiry, or *residencia*, normally called after an expedition, brought Coronado an indictment for his conduct; but the Mexican audiencia (a governing body in the Spanish colonies) found him innocent in February 1546. In his residencia following his governorship he was also indicted, and in this instance he was fined and lost a number of Indians from his landed estate. He retained his seat, however, on the Council of Mexico City until his death.

JUAN PONCE DE LEÓN: FLORIDA AND THE FOUNTAIN OF YOUTH

The Spanish explorer Juan Ponce de León (1460–1521) founded the oldest settlement in Puerto Rico and later discovered Florida (1513) while searching for the mythical Fountain of Youth.

Born into a noble family, it is possible that Ponce de León began his career of exploration in 1493 as part of Christopher Columbus's second expedition to the New World. In 1502 he was in the West Indies as a captain serving under Nicolás de Ovando, governor of Hispaniola. As a reward for suppressing an Indian mutiny, Ponce de León was named by Ovando to be the provincial governor of the eastern part of Hispaniola. Hearing persistent reports of gold to be found on Puerto Rico, Ponce de León in 1508–09 explored and settled that island, founding the colony's oldest settlement, Caparra, near what is now San Juan. He then returned to Hispaniola and was named governor of Puerto Rico but was soon displaced from the governorship through the political maneuvering of rivals.

The Spanish crown encouraged Ponce de León to continue searching for new lands. He learned from Indians of an island called Bimini (now in the Bahamas) on which there was a miraculous spring or fountain that could rejuvenate those who drank from it (the Fountain of Youth). In search of this fountain, he led a privately outfitted expedition from Puerto Rico in March 1513 and in April of that year landed on the coast of Florida near the site of modern St. Augustine. At the time he did not realize that he was on the mainland of North America and instead supposed he had landed on an island. He named the region Florida because it was discovered at

Easter (Spanish: Pascua Florida) and because it abounded in lush, florid vegetation. He coasted southward, sailing through the Florida Keys and ending his search near Charlotte Harbor on Florida's west coast. He then returned to Puerto Rico and thence to Spain, where he secured the title in 1514 of military governor of Bimini and Florida with permission to colonize those regions.

In 1521 Ponce de León sailed again for Florida with two ships and 200 men, landing near Charlotte Harbor. On this occasion he was wounded by an arrow during an Indian attack, and he died after being returned to Cuba. Puerto Rico's third largest city, Ponce, is named in his honour.

ST. AUGUSTINE

St. Augustine, in northeastern Florida, is the oldest continuously settled city in the United States. It is situated on a peninsula between two saltwater rivers, the San Sebastian (west) and Matanzas (east), and on the mainland west of the San Sebastian, just inland from the Atlantic coast, and is about 40 miles (65 km) southeast of Jacksonville.

Juan Ponce de León, in search of the legendary Fountain of Youth, landed there in 1513 and took possession of the territory for Spain. In 1564 France established Fort Caroline near the mouth of the St. Johns River, about 35 miles (55 km) north. A year later, in order to maintain Spanish sovereignty over Florida, Pedro Menéndez de Avilés destroyed the French colony and founded the city, which he named for St. Augustine, bishop of Hippo, upon whose feast day he had sighted the coast. Except for the 20 years (1763–83) that Florida belonged to England, throughout the following 256 years it was the main northern outpost of the Spanish colonial empire.

Since 1821 the city has been a part of the United States. A remaining symbol of former Spanish power is the massive Castillo de San Marcos, built in 1672–95 near the southern tip of the peninsula; the oldest masonry fort standing in the United States, it is now a national monument. The city was plundered (1586) by the English sea raider Sir Francis Drake, burned (1702) by Governor James Moore of Carolina, and besieged (1740) by the British general and leader of the Georgia Colony, James Edward Oglethorpe. St. Augustine became a refuge for loyalists during the American Revolution and during the Seminole Wars provided a prison for captured Seminole Indians, including Osceola. Union troops occupied it the last three years of the American Civil War.

Bridge of Lions spanning Matanzas Bay, St. Augustine, Fla. © Corbis

FRANCE IN NORTH AMERICA

France probably could have become the leading European colonial power in the 17th and 18th centuries. It had the largest population and wealth of any European country, the best army while Louis XIV ruled, and, for a time during his reign, the strongest navy. But France pursued a spasmodic overseas policy, largely because of an intense preoccupation with domestic and wider European affairs.

The Italian navigator Giovanni da Verrazzano (or Verrazano) reconnoitered the North American coast for France in 1524, and in the next decade Jacques Cartier explored the St. Lawrence River; however, his plans to establish a colony amounted to nothing. During most of the rest of the 16th century, French colonization efforts were confined to short-lived settlements at Guanabara Bay (now Rio de Janeiro, Braz.) and Florida. Both met sad ends. France, meanwhile, was troubled by internal religious strife and, for a time, was influenced by Philip II of Spain. But at the beginning of the 17th century, with Spanish power declining and domestic religious peace restored by King Henry IV's Edict of Nantes (1598), granting religious liberty to the Huguenots (French Protestants), the king chartered a Compagnie d'Occident ("Western Company"). This led to further exploration and to a small Acadian (Nova Scotian) settlement, and in 1603, Samuel de Champlain went to Canada, where he claimed lands as New France. Champlain became Canada's outstanding leader, founding Quebec in 1608, defeating the Iroquois of New York, stimulating fur trade, and exploring westward to Lake Huron in 1615. He introduced Recollet (Franciscan) friars for conversion of the American Indians, but the Jesuit order (the Society of Jesus) soon became the principal missionary body in Canada.

VERRAZZANO'S EXPLORATION
OF THE EASTERN COAST

Giovanni da Verrazzano (1485–1528) was the first European to sight New York and Narragansett Bays. After his education in Florence, he moved to Dieppe, Fr., and entered that nation's maritime service. He made several voyages to the Levant, and in 1523, he secured two ships for a voyage backed by the French king to discover a westward passage to Asia.

In January 1524 he sailed one of those vessels, *La Dauphine*, to the New World and reached Cape Fear (North Carolina) in March. Verrazzano then sailed northward, exploring the eastern coast of North America. He made several discoveries on the voyage—including the sites of present-day New York Bay, Block Island, and Narragansett Bay—and was the first European explorer to name newly discovered North American sites for persons and places in the Old World. Verrazzano wrote interesting, though sometimes inaccurate, accounts of the lands and inhabitants that he encountered. His explorations on this first journey concluded at the eastern part of Newfoundland. His return to France on July 8, 1524, gave King Francis I his nation's claim to the New World.

Verrazzano undertook two more voyages to the Americas. In 1527, he commanded a fleet of ships on an expedition to Brazil that returned profitable dyewood to France. His final voyage began in 1528, when he sailed with his brother, Girolamo, from Dieppe with two or three ships. The fleet sailed to Florida, the Bahamas, and finally the Lesser Antilles. He anchored there off one of the islands (apparently Guadeloupe), went ashore, and was captured, killed, and eaten by cannibals.

CARTIER'S EXPLORATION
OF THE ST. LAWRENCE RIVER

The French mariner Jacques Cartier (1491–1557) led the explorations of the North American coast and the St. Lawrence River (1534, 1535, and 1541–42) that laid the basis for later French claims to Canada. He appears also to have voyaged to Brazil. King Francis I of France decided in 1534 to commission Cartier to explore the northern lands in the hope of discovering gold, spices, and a passage to Asia.

Cartier's party sailed from Saint-Malo on April 20, 1534, with two ships and 61 men; he explored the Gulf of St. Lawrence as far as Anticosti Island then seized two Indians at Gaspé and sailed back to France. His report piqued the curiosity of Francis I sufficiently for him to send Cartier back the following year, with three ships and 110 men, to explore further. Guided by the two Indians he had brought back, he sailed up the St. Lawrence as far as what is now Quebec and established a base near an Iroquois village. In September he proceeded with a small party as far as the island of Montreal, where navigation was barred by rapids. He was warmly welcomed by the resident Iroquois, but he spent only a few hours among them before returning to winter at his base. He had, however, learned from the Indians that two rivers led farther west to lands where gold, silver, copper, and spices abounded.

The severity of the winter came as a terrible shock; no Europeans since the Vikings had wintered that far north on the American continent, and a mild winter was expected because Quebec lay at a lower latitude than Paris. Scurvy claimed 25 of Cartier's men. To make matters worse, the explorers earned the enmity of the Iroquois. Thus, in May, as soon as the river was free of ice, they treacherously seized some of the Iroquois chiefs and sailed for France. Cartier was able to report only that great riches lay farther in the interior and that a great river, said to be 800 leagues (about 2,000 miles [3,200 km]) long, possibly led to Asia.

War in Europe prevented Francis I from sending another expedition until 1541. This time, to secure French title against the counterclaims of Spain, he commissioned a nobleman, Jean-François de La Rocque de Roberval, to establish a colony in the lands discovered by Cartier, who was appointed Roberval's subaltern. Cartier sailed first, arriving at Quebec on August 23; Roberval was delayed until the following year. Cartier again visited Montreal, but as before, he remained only a few hours and failed to go even the few miles necessary to get beyond the rapids. The subsequent maps based on the knowledge he provided fail to indicate that he had reached a large island at the confluence of the Ottawa and St. Lawrence rivers.

The winter at his new base above Quebec proved as severe as the earlier one. Cartier appears to have been unable to maintain discipline among his men, and their actions again aroused the hostility of the local Indians. But what were thought to be gold and diamonds were found in abundance. In the spring, not waiting for Roberval to arrive with the main body of colonists, Cartier abandoned the base and sailed for France. En route he stopped at Newfoundland, where he encountered Roberval, who ordered him back to Quebec. Cartier, however, stole away during the night and continued back to France. There, his mineral specimens were found to be valueless. Roberval enjoyed no better success. After one winter he abandoned the plan to found a colony and returned to France. The disappointment at these meagre results was very great. Not for more than half a century did France again show interest in these new lands.

THE ST. LAWRENCE RIVER AND SEAWAY

Efforts to sail into the heart of the North American continent date to Jacques Cartier's journey up the St. Lawrence River in 1535 while seeking a northwest passage to the Far East. However, he found his path blocked by the Lachine Rapids, southwest of what is now Montreal. The digging of shallow St. Lawrence canals for bateaux and Durham boats (long, tapering boats with flat bottoms and auxiliary sails) in the early 1780s; the construction of the Erie Canal from Buffalo, N.Y., to the Hudson River from 1817 to 1825; the opening of the first canal around Niagara Falls in 1829; and the completion of the first lock, at Sault Ste. Marie, Mich., in 1855, all fostered the dream of a navigable waterway into the continental interior. The United States, however, proved a reluctant partner in a venture, pursued by Canada from the beginning of the 20th century, to open the Great Lakes to sea traffic. The U.S. Senate rejected the Seaway Treaty of 1932 and allowed a second treaty, signed in 1941, to remain unratified for eight years. Faced with the likelihood that Canada would proceed independently, the U.S. Congress finally approved participation in the project in May 1954.

The U.S.-Canadian St. Lawrence Seaway waterway and lock system, along the upper St. Lawrence River, links the Atlantic Ocean with the Great Lakes. Its construction, carried out in 1954–59, involved clearing a 186-mile (299-km) stretch of the St. Lawrence River between Montreal and Lake Ontario. Its course includes lakes, rivers, locks, and canals that extend for 2,340 miles (3,766 km) to connect Duluth, Minn., with the head of the Gulf of St. Lawrence. With the Great Lakes, it provides some

9,500 miles (15,285 km) of navigable waterways and allows deep-draft ocean vessels access to the Great Lakes' rich industrial and agricultural regions. It is navigable from April to mid-December.

SAMUEL DE CHAMPLAIN

The French explorer Samuel de Champlain (1567–1635) is the acknowledged founder of the city of Quebec (1608) and consolidator of the French colonies in the New World. He discovered the lake that bears his name (1609) and made other explorations of what are now northern New York state, the Ottawa River, and the eastern Great Lakes.

Champlain was probably born a commoner, but, after acquiring a reputation as a navigator (having taken part in an expedition to the West Indies and Central America), he received an honorary if unofficial title at the court of Henry IV. In 1603 he accepted an invitation to visit what he called the River of Canada (St. Lawrence River). He sailed, as an observer in a longboat, upstream from the mother ship's anchorage at Tadoussac, a summer trading post, to the site of Montreal and its rapids. His report on the expedition was published in France, and in 1604 he accompanied a group of ill-fated settlers to Acadia, a region surrounding the Bay of Fundy.

Champlain spent three winters in Acadia—the first on an island in the St. Croix River, where scurvy killed nearly half the party, and the second and third, which claimed the lives of fewer men, at Annapolis Basin. During the summers he searched for an ideal site for colonization. His explorations led him down the Atlantic coast southward to Massachusetts Bay and beyond, mapping in detail the

Samuel de Champlain. Encyclopædia Britannica, Inc.

harbours that his English rivals had only touched. In 1607 the English came to Kennebec (now in Maine) in southern Acadia. They spent only one winter there, but the threat of conflict increased French interest in colonization.

Heading an expedition that left France in 1608, Champlain undertook his most ambitious project—the founding of Quebec. On earlier expeditions he had been a subordinate, but this time he was the leader of 32 colonists.

Champlain and eight others survived the first winter at Quebec and greeted more colonists in June. Allied by an earlier French treaty with the northern Indian tribes, he joined them in defeating Iroquois marauders in a skirmish on Lake Champlain. That and a similar victory in 1610 enhanced French prestige among the allied tribes, and fur trade between France and the Indians increased.

The fur trade had heavy financial losses in 1611, which prompted Quebec's sponsors to abandon the colony, but Champlain (who had returned to France in 1610) persuaded Louis XIII to intervene. Eventually the king appointed a viceroy, who made Champlain commandant of New France. In 1613, he reestablished his authority at Quebec and immediately embarked for the Ottawa River on a mission to restore the ruined fur trade. The following year he organized a company of French merchants to finance trade, religious missions, and his own exploration.

Champlain next went to Lake Huron, where native chiefs persuaded him to lead a war party against a fortified village south of Lake Ontario. The Iroquois defenders wounded him and repulsed his Huron-Algonquin warriors, a somewhat disorganized but loyal force that carried him to safety. After spending a winter in their territory, he again returned to France, where political maneuvers were endangering the colony's future. In 1620 the king reaffirmed Champlain's authority over Quebec but forbade his personal exploration, directing him instead to employ his talents in administrative tasks.

The colony, still dependent on the fur trade and only experimenting in agriculture, hardly prospered under his care or under the patronage of a new and strong company. English privateers, however, considered Quebec worth besieging in 1628, when England and France were at war.

Champlain manned the walls until the following summer, when his distressed garrison exhausted its food and gunpowder. Although he surrendered the fort, he did not abandon his colony. Taken to England as a prisoner, he argued that the surrender had occurred after the end of French and English hostilities. In 1632 the colony was restored to France, and in 1633, a year after publishing his seventh book, he made his last voyage across the Atlantic Ocean to Quebec.

Only a few more settlers were aboard when his ships dropped anchor at Quebec, but others continued to arrive each year. Before he died of a stroke in 1635, his colony extended along both shores of the St. Lawrence River.

QUEBEC

The Canadian city and port of Quebec (French: Québec) lies at the confluence of the St. Lawrence and Saint-Charles rivers, about 150 miles (240 km) northeast of Montreal. Jacques Cartier, the first European to visit the area (1535), founded the Huron Indian village of Stadacona on the site. In 1608 Samuel de Champlain installed the first permanent base in Canada at Quebec, which grew as a fur-trading settlement. In 1629 Quebec was captured by the British, who held it until 1632, when the Treaty of Saint-Germain-en-Laye restored Quebec to France. The colony was then developed rapidly.

In 1690 the fleet of Sir William Phipps, governor of Massachusetts, attempted to take Quebec but was beaten back with troops led by its governor, the comte (count) de Frontenac. In 1711, a second attempt to take the city also failed when a British armada crashed on the reefs of the St. Lawrence before reaching Quebec.

Quebec city at dusk, Quebec, Can. © Creatas/JupiterImages

The city fell to the British in 1759 and was ceded to Great Britain by the Treaty of Paris in 1763. During the American Revolution, the Americans, under Richard Montgomery and Benedict Arnold, failed in an attempt to capture the city.

In 1791 Quebec was designated as the provincial capital of Lower Canada, which later became the province of Quebec. It was incorporated in 1832 and was given its actual charter in 1840. In 1864 Quebec was the seat of the conference of British North American colonies to plan the confederation of Canada. During World War II U.S. Pres. Franklin D. Roosevelt and British Prime Minister

Winston Churchill twice met in Quebec to plan the invasion of Europe. The city observed its 400th anniversary in 2008 with a number of commemorations and special events.

Quebec is home to a number of historical buildings. Many are religious in nature, some dating from the 17th century. On the Place Royale stands the modest Church of Notre-Dame des Victoires (1688). Other significant buildings include the Ursuline monastery, the seminary, the Anglican cathedral (the first such in Canada), the Catholic basilica (where many of the bishops of Quebec are buried), and the provincial Parliament Building.

The Parliament Building, home to Quebec's National Assembly, in Quebec city. © Creatas/JupiterImages

LA SALLE'S EXPLORATION OF THE INTERIOR

The French explorer of North America René-Robert Cavelier, sieur (lord) de La Salle (1643–87), led an expedition down the Illinois and Mississippi rivers and claimed the region watered by the Mississippi and its tributaries for Louis XIV of France; he named the region "Louisiana." A few years later, in a luckless expedition seeking the mouth of the Mississippi, he was murdered by his men.

Early Years in North America

In 1666 La Salle, seeking adventure and exploration, set out for Canada to find his fortune. With a grant of land at the western end of Île de Montréal, La Salle acquired at one stroke the status of a seigneur (landholder) and the opportunities of a frontiersman.

The young landlord farmed his land near the Lachine Rapids and, at the same time, set up a fur-trading outpost. Through contact with the Indians who came to sell their pelts, he learned various Indian dialects and heard stories of the lands beyond the settlements. He soon became obsessed with the idea of finding a way to the Far East through the rivers and lakes of the Western frontier. Having sold his land, La Salle set out in 1669 to explore the Ohio region. His discovery of the Ohio River, however, is not accepted by modern historians.

La Salle found a kindred spirit in the Count de Frontenac, the "Fighting Governor" of New France from 1672 to 1682. Together, they pursued a policy of extending French military power by establishing a fort on Lake Ontario (Fort-Frontenac), holding the Iroquois in check, and intercepting the fur trade between the Upper Lakes and the Dutch and English coastal settlements.

Their plans were strongly opposed by the Montreal merchants, who feared the loss of their trade, and by the missionaries (especially the Jesuits), who were afraid of losing their influence over the Indians of the interior. Nevertheless, Fort-Frontenac was built where Kingston, Ont., now stands, and La Salle was installed there as seigneur in 1675 after a visit to the French court as Frontenac's representative. Louis XIV was sufficiently impressed by him to grant him a title of nobility.

Attempts to Expand New France

At Fort-Frontenac, La Salle had control of a large share of the fur trade, and his affairs prospered. But his restless ambition drove him to seek greater ends. On another visit to France in 1677 he obtained from the king authority to explore "the western parts of New France" and permission to build as many forts as he wished, as well as to hold a valuable monopoly of the trade in buffalo hides.

When he returned to Canada in 1678, La Salle was accompanied by an Italian soldier of fortune, Henri de Tonty, who became his most loyal friend and ally. Early in the following year, he built the *Griffon*, the first commercial sailing vessel on Lake Erie, which he hoped would pay for an expedition into the interior as far as the Mississippi. From the Seneca Indians above the Niagara Falls he learned how to make long journeys overland, on foot in any season, subsisting on game and a small bag of corn. His trek from Niagara to Fort-Frontenac in the dead of winter won the admiration of a normally critical member of his expeditions, the friar Louis Hennepin.

La Salle's great scheme of carrying cargo in sailing vessels like the *Griffon* on the lakes and down the Mississippi was frustrated by the wreck of that ship and by the destruction and desertion of Fort-Crèvecoeur on the Illinois

River, where a second ship was being built in 1680. Proud and unyielding by nature, La Salle tried to bend others to his will and often demanded too much of them, though he was no less hard on himself. After several disappointments, he at last reached the junction of the Illinois with the Mississippi and saw for the first time the river he had dreamed of for so long. But he had to deny himself the chance to explore it. Hearing that Tonty and his party were in danger, he turned back to aid them.

After many vicissitudes, La Salle and Tonty succeeded in canoeing down the Mississippi and reached the Gulf of Mexico. There, on April 9, 1682, the explorer proclaimed the whole Mississippi Basin for France as Louisiana. In name, at least, he acquired for France the most fertile half of the North American continent.

The following year La Salle built Fort-Saint-Louis at Starved Rock on the Illinois River (now a state park), and there he organized a colony of several thousand Indians. To maintain the new colony he sought help from Quebec; but Frontenac had been replaced by a governor hostile to La Salle's interests, and La Salle received orders to surrender Fort-Saint-Louis. He refused and left North America to appeal directly to the king. Welcomed in Paris, La Salle was given an audience with Louis XIV, who favoured him by commanding the governor to make full restitution of La Salle's property.

Last Expedition

The last phase of La Salle's extraordinary career centred on his proposal to fortify the mouth of the Mississippi and to invade and conquer part of the Spanish province of Mexico. He planned to accomplish this with some 200 Frenchmen, aided by buccaneers and an army of 15,000 Indians—a venture that caused his detractors to question

JOLLIET AND MARQUETTE

The French-Canadian explorer and cartographer Louis Jolliet (1645–1700) and French Jesuit missionary and explorer Jacques Marquette were the first Europeans to traverse the Mississippi River from its confluence with the Wisconsin River to the mouth of the Arkansas River in Arkansas.

Marquette—popularly called Père (Father) Marquette—arrived in Quebec in 1666. After a study of Indian languages, he assisted in founding a mission at Sault Ste. Marie (now in Michigan) in 1668 and another at Michilimackinac (St. Ignace, also in Michigan) in 1671. In 1672 Jolliet (or Joliet) was commissioned by Louis, comte (count) de Frontenac, governor of New France, to find the direction and the mouth of the Mississippi, and he was joined by Marquette.

On May 17, 1673, the party set out in two birchbark canoes from St. Ignace for Green Bay, on Lake Michigan. Continuing up the Fox River in central Wisconsin and, after a portage, down the Wisconsin, they entered the Mississippi near present-day Prairie du Chien about a month later. Pausing along the way to make notes, to hunt, and to glean scraps of information from Indians, they arrived in July at the Quapaw Indian village about (40 miles [65 km] north of present-day Arkansas City, Ark.) at the mouth of the Arkansas River. From personal observations and from the friendly Quapaw Indians, they concluded that the Mississippi flowed south into the Gulf of Mexico—and, hence, through hostile Spanish domains—not, as they had hoped, into the Pacific Ocean.

In mid-July the party returned homeward via the Illinois River and Green Bay. Marquette was exhausted when he reached Green Bay, and he remained there while Jolliet continued on to Canada. Their journey is described in Marquette's journal, which has survived.

In 1674 Marquette set out to found a mission among the Illinois Indians, but, caught by the winter, he and two companions camped near the site of the city of Chicago and thus became the first Europeans to live there. Marquette reached the Indians near what is now Utica, Ill., in the spring, but illness forced his return. While en route to St. Ignace he died in western Michigan at the mouth of a river now known as Père Marquette. Jolliet later traveled to Hudson Bay, the Labrador coast, and a number of Canadian rivers. In 1697 he was made royal hydrographer of New France.

his sanity. But the king saw a chance to harass the Spaniards, with whom he was at war, and approved the project, giving La Salle men, ships, and money.

The expedition was doomed from the start. It had hardly left France when quarrels arose between La Salle and the naval commander. Vessels were lost by piracy and shipwreck, while sickness took a heavy toll of the colonists. Finally, a gross miscalculation brought the ships to Matagorda Bay in Texas, 500 miles west of their intended landfall. After several fruitless journeys in search of his lost Mississippi, La Salle met his death at the hands of mutineers near the Brazos River. His vision of a French empire died with him.

Chapter 4: Journeys of Inquiry

The earlier European explorers in the Pacific were primarily in search of trade or booty; the later ones were primarily in search of information. By the end of the 16th century, Portugal held only the ports of Goa and Diu, in India, and Macau, in China, in the East. The English dominated the trade of India, and the Dutch that of the East Indies (Indonesia). It was the Dutch, trading on the fringes of the known world, who were the explorers. Outfitting their ships at the Cape of Good Hope, they soon learned that, by sailing east for some 3,000 miles (5,000 km) before turning north, they would encounter favourable winds in setting a course toward the Spice Islands (now the Moluccas). Before long, reports were received of landfalls made on an unknown coast; as early as 1618 a Dutch skipper suggested using this coast in order to get a fixed course for Java. Thereafter, the west coast of Australia was gradually charted. It was identified by some as the coast of the great southern continent shown on Gerardus Mercator's world map and, by others, as the continent of Loach or Beach mentioned by Marco Polo, interpreted as lying to the south of Malacca (Melaka); Polo, however, was probably describing the Malay Peninsula. In 1642, Anthony van Diemen, a farsighted governor-general of the profitable Dutch East India Company, sent out the Dutch navigator Abel Tasman for the immediate purpose of making an exploratory voyage but with the ultimate aim of developing trade.

Other traders in the Pacific, for the most part Spaniards, established land portages from harbours on the Caribbean to harbours on the west coast of Central and South America; from the Pacific coast ports of the Americas, they then set a course westward to the Philippines. Many of their ships crossed and recrossed the Pacific without making a landfall; many islands were found, named, and lost, only to be found again without recognition, renamed, and perhaps lost yet again. In the days before longitude could be accurately fixed, such uncertainty was not surprising.

Some voyages—for example, those of Álvaro de Mendaña de Neira, the Spanish explorer, in 1567 and 1568; Mendaña and the Portuguese navigator Pedro Fernández de Quirós in 1595; Quirós and another Portuguese explorer, Luis de Torres, in 1606—had, among other motives, the purpose of finding the great southern continent. Quirós was sure that in Espíritu Santo in the New Hebrides he had found his goal; he "took possession of the site on which is to be founded the New Jerusalem." Torres sailed from there to New Guinea and thence to Manila, in the Philippines. In doing so, he coasted the south shore of New Guinea, sailing through Torres Strait, unaware that another continent lay on his left.

The English were rivals of the Spaniards in the search for wealth in unknown lands in the Pacific. Two English seamen, Sir Francis Drake and Thomas Cavendish, circumnavigated the world from west to east in 1577 to 1580 and 1586 to 1588, respectively. One of Drake's avowed objects was the search for Terra Australis. Despite the fact that he participated in several buccaneering voyages, the English seaman William Dampier, who was active in the late 17th and early 18th centuries, may be regarded as the first to travel mainly to satisfy scientific curiosity. He wrote: "I was well satisfied enough knowing that, the further [sic] we went, the more knowledge and experience I should get, which was the main thing I regarded." His book *A New Voyage Round the World* (1697) further popularized the idea of a great southern continent.

In the late 18th century, the final phase of Pacific exploration occurred. The French sent the explorer Louis-Antoine de Bougainville to the Pacific in 1768. He appears to have been more of a skeptic than many of his contemporaries, for, while he agreed "that it is difficult to conceive such a number of low islands and almost drowned lands without a continent near them," at the same time he maintained that "if any considerable land existed hereabouts we could not fail meeting with it."

The British, for their part, commissioned John Byron in 1764 and Samuel Wallis and Phillip Carteret in 1766 "to discover unknown lands and to explore the coast of New Albion." For all the navigational skill and personal endurance shown by captains and crews, the rewards of these voyages in increasing geographical knowledge were not great. The courses sailed were in the familiar waters of the southern tropics; none was through the dangerous waters of higher latitudes. Capt. James Cook, the English navigator, in three magnificent voyages at long last succeeded in demolishing the fables about Pacific geography.

TASMAN'S DISCOVERIES IN THE SOUTH PACIFIC

Abel Janszoon Tasman (1603?–1659/61),the greatest of the Dutch navigators and explorers, discovered Tasmania, New Zealand, Tonga, and the Fiji Islands. He entered the service of the Dutch East India Company in 1632 or 1633 and made his first voyage of exploration to the island of Ceram (now Seram, Indon.) as captain in 1634. He sailed in 1639 on an expedition in search of the "islands of gold and silver" in the seas east of Japan. After a series of trading voyages to Japan, Formosa (Taiwan), Cambodia, and Sumatra, he was chosen by the governor-general van Diemen to command an ambitious exploration of the Southern Hemisphere.

By 1642, Dutch navigators had discovered discontinuous stretches of the western coast of Australia, but whether these coasts were continental and connected with the hypothetical southern continent of the Pacific Ocean remained unknown. Tasman was assigned to solve this problem, following instructions based on a memoir by Frans Jacobszoon Visscher, his chief pilot. He was instructed to explore the Indian Ocean from west to east, south of the ordinary trade route, and, proceeding eastward into the Pacific (if this proved possible), to investigate the practicability of a sea passage eastward to Chile, to rediscover the Solomon Islands of the Spaniards, and to explore New Guinea.

Leaving Batavia (now Jakarta) on Aug. 14, 1642, with two ships, the *Heemskerk* and *Zeehaen*, Tasman sailed to Mauritius (September 5–October 8), then southward and eastward, reaching his southernmost latitude of 49° S at about longitude 94° E. Turning north he discovered land on November 24 at 42°20' S and skirted its shores, naming it Van Diemen's Land (now Tasmania). A council of officers on December 5 decided against further investigation, so he missed the opportunity of discovering Bass Strait. Continuing eastward, he sighted on December 13, at 42°10' S, the coast of South Island, New Zealand, and explored it northward, entering the strait between North Island and South Island, supposing it to be a bay. He left New Zealand on Jan. 4, 1643, at North Cape, under the impression that he had probably discovered the west coast of the southern continent, which might be connected with the "Staten Landt" (Staten Island) discovered by W.C. Schouten and Jacques Le Maire south of South America—hence the name of Staten Landt, which Tasman gave to his discovery in honour of the States General (the Dutch legislature).

Convinced by the swell that the passage to Chile existed, Tasman now turned northeast, and on January 21 he discovered Tonga and on February 6 the Fiji Islands. Turning northwest, the ships reached New Guinea waters on April 1 and Batavia on June 14, 1643, completing a

10-month voyage on which only 10 men had died from illness. Tasman had circumnavigated Australia without seeing it, thus establishing that it was separated from the hypothetical southern continent.

The council of the company decided, however, that Tasman had been negligent in his investigation of the lands that he discovered and of the passage to Chile. They sent him on a new expedition to the "South Land" in 1644 with instructions to establish the relationships of New Guinea, the "great known South Land" (western Australia), Van Diemen's Land, and the "unknown South Land." Tasman sailed from Batavia on February 29, steering southeast along the south coast of New Guinea, sailing southeast into Torres Strait (which he mistook for a shallow bay), coasting Australia's Gulf of Carpentaria, and then following the north coast and then the west coast of Australia to 22° S.

Although he was rewarded with the rank of commander and was made a member of the Council of Justice of Batavia, his second voyage was also a disappointment to the company because it had failed to reveal lands of potential wealth. In 1647, Tasman commanded a trading fleet to Siam (now Thailand), and in the following year he commanded a war fleet against the Spaniards in the Philippines. He left the service of the Dutch East India Company several years later.

DUTCH EAST INDIA COMPANY

The Dutch East India Company was founded in 1602 to protect Dutch trade in the Indian Ocean and to assist the Dutch in their war of independence from Spain. The trading company prospered through most of the 17th century as the instrument of the powerful Dutch commercial empire in the East Indies. It was dissolved in 1799.

The Dutch government granted the company a trade monopoly in the waters between the Cape of Good Hope and the Straits of Magellan with the right to conclude treaties with native princes, to build forts and maintain armed forces, and to carry on administrative functions through officials who were required to take an oath of loyalty to the Dutch government. Under the administration of forceful governors-general, most notably Jan Pieterszoon Coen (1618–23) and Governor-general van Diemen (1636–45), the company was able to defeat the British fleet and largely displace the Portuguese in the East Indies.

In 1619 the company renamed Jacatra Batavia (now Jakarta) and used it as a base to conquer Java and the outer islands. By the late 17th century the company had declined as a trading and sea power and had become more involved in the affairs of Java. By the 18th century the company had changed from a commercial-shipping enterprise to a loose territorial organization interested in the agricultural produce of the Indonesian archipelago. Toward the end of the 18th century the company became corrupt and seriously in debt. The Dutch government eventually revoked the company's charter and took over its debts and possessions in 1799.

DRAKE'S CIRCUMNAVIGATION

The English admiral Sir Francis Drake (c. 1540–96) was the most renowned seaman of the Elizabethan Age. In 1577–80 he led an expedition that circumnavigated the world. Drake went to sea at about age 18 and gained a reputation as an outstanding navigator. He became wealthy by raiding and plundering Spanish colonies in the New World.

In 1577, Drake was chosen as the leader of an expedition intended to pass around South America through the Strait of Magellan and to explore the coast that lay beyond. The expedition was backed by Queen Elizabeth I herself. Nothing could have suited Drake better. He had official approval to benefit himself and the queen, as well as to cause the maximum damage to the Spaniards. The explicit object was to "find out places meet to have traffic." Drake, however, devoted the voyage to piracy, without official reproof in England. He set sail in December with five small ships, manned by fewer than 200 men, and reached the Brazilian coast in the spring of 1578. His flagship, the *Pelican*, which Drake later renamed the *Golden Hind* (or *Hinde*), weighed only about 100 tons. It seemed little enough with which to undertake a venture into the domain of the most powerful monarch and empire in the world.

Upon arrival in South America, Drake alleged a plot by unreliable officers, and its supposed leader, Thomas Doughty, was tried and executed. Drake was always a stern disciplinarian, and he clearly did not intend to continue the venture without making sure that everyone in his small company was loyal to him. Two of his smaller vessels, having served their purpose as store ships, were then abandoned after their provisions had been taken aboard the others, and on Aug. 21, 1578, he entered the Strait of Magellan. It took 16 days to sail through and reach the Pacific Ocean. Then, as he wrote, "God by a contrary wind and intolerable tempest seemed to set himself against us." During the gale, Drake's vessel and that of his second in command had been separated; the latter, having missed a rendezvous with Drake, ultimately returned to England, presuming that the *Golden Hind* had sunk. It was, therefore, only Drake's flagship that made its way into the Pacific and up the coast of South America. He passed along the coast like a whirlwind, for the Spaniards were quite unguarded, having never known a hostile ship in their waters. He seized provisions at Valparaíso, attacked passing Spanish merchantmen, and captured two very rich prizes that were carrying bars of gold and silver, minted Spanish coinage, precious stones, and pearls. He claimed then to have sailed to the north as far as 48° N, on a parallel with Vancouver [Canada], to seek the Northwest Passage back into the Atlantic. Bitterly cold weather defeated him, and he coasted southward to anchor near what is now San Francisco, Ca. He named the surrounding country New Albion and took possession of it in the name of Queen Elizabeth.

In July 1579 Drake sailed west across the Pacific and after 68 days sighted a line of islands (probably the remote Palau group). From there he went on to the Philippines, where he replenished provisions before sailing to the Moluccas. There he was well received by a local sultan and succeeded in buying spices. Drake's navigation skills were excellent, but in those totally uncharted waters his ship struck a reef. He was able to get her off without any great damage and, after calling at Java, set his course across the Indian Ocean for the Cape of Good Hope. Two years after it had nosed its way into the Strait of Magellan, the *Golden Hind* came back into the Atlantic with only 56 of the original crew of 100 left aboard.

On Sept. 26, 1580, Drake took his ship into Plymouth Harbour. It was laden with treasure and spices, and Drake's fortune was permanently made. Despite Spanish protests about his piratical conduct while in their imperial waters, Queen Elizabeth herself went aboard the *Golden Hind*, which was lying at Deptford in the Thames estuary, and personally bestowed knighthood on him.

DRAKE PASSAGE

The Drake Passage is a deep waterway, 600 miles (1,000 km) wide, connecting the Atlantic and Pacific oceans between Cape Horn (the southernmost point of South America) and the South Shetland Islands; it is situated about 100 miles (160 km) north of the Antarctic Peninsula. The passage defines the zone of climatic transition separating the cool, humid, subpolar conditions of Tierra del Fuego and the frigid, polar regions of Antarctica. Though bearing the name of the famous English seaman and global circumnavigator Sir Francis Drake, the passage was first traversed in 1616 by a Flemish expedition led by Willem Schouten. The Drake Passage played an important part in the trade of the 19th and early 20th centuries before the opening of the Panama Canal in 1914. The stormy seas and icy conditions made the rounding of Cape Horn through the passage a rigorous test for ships and crews alike, especially for the sailing vessels of the day.

The passage has an average depth of about 11,000 feet (3,400 metres) with deeper regions of up to 15,600 feet (4,800 metres) near the northern and southern boundaries. The winds over the passage are predominantly from the west and are most intense to the north around Cape Horn. Cyclones (atmospheric low pressure systems) formed in the Pacific sweep west to east across the southern edge of the passage. The mean annual air temperature ranges from 41 °F (5 °C) in the north to 27 °F (-3 °C) in the south. Surface water temperatures vary from 43 °F (6 °C) in the north to 30 °F (-1 °C) in the south.

The sea ice cover extending northward from Antarctica varies seasonally. In the late summer (February) the passage is ice-free. In September the maximum ice cover occurs; 25 percent to full cover extends to latitude 60° S, with occasional ice floes reaching Cape Horn.

Water within the Drake Passage flows predominantly from west to east and forms part of the Antarctic Circumpolar Current, the most voluminous current in the world. Accelerated by the physical constriction of the passage, the Antarctic Circumpolar Current increases rapidly in velocity, especially at 60° S.

LA PÉROUSE AND DUMONT D'URVILLE'S EXPLORATIONS OF THE PACIFIC

Two French navigators—Jean-François de Galaup, count de La Pérouse (1741–c. 1788), and his successor, Jules-Sébastien-César Dumont d'Urville (1790–1842)—conducted wide-ranging explorations in the Pacific Ocean in the late 18th and early 19th centuries, respectively. La Pérouse disappeared in 1788 while on a voyage in the South Pacific, and it was not until d'Urville's journey there three decades later that information on the earlier party's fate came to light. Both expeditions led to increased understanding of the region but that of d'Urville in 1826–29 resulted in extensive revisions of existing charts and discovery or redesignation of island groups.

Commanding the ship *La Boussole*, which was accompanied by the *Astrolabe*, La Pérouse sailed from France on Aug. 1, 1785. After rounding Cape Horn, he made a stop in the South Pacific at Easter Island (April 9, 1786). Investigating tropical Pacific waters, he visited the Sandwich Islands (now Hawaii) and, with the object of locating the Northwest Passage from the Pacific, he made his way to North America. He reached the southern shore

of Alaska, near Mount St. Elias, in June 1786 and explored
the coast southward beyond what is now San Francisco to
Monterey. He then crossed the Pacific and reached the
South China coast at Macau on Jan. 3, 1787. Leaving Manila
on April 9, he began to explore the Asian coast. He sailed
through the Sea of Japan up to the Tatar Strait, which separates the mainland from the island of Sakhalin, and also
visited the strait, named for him, that separates Sakhalin
from Hokkaido, Japan. At Petropavlovsk, on the Siberian
peninsula of Kamchatka, he dispatched his expedition
journal and maps overland to France. The ships then made
for the Navigators' (now Samoa) Islands, where the commander of the *Astrolabe* and 11 of his men were murdered.
La Pérouse then went to the Friendly (now Tonga) and
Norfolk islands on his way to Botany Bay in eastern
Australia, from which he departed on March 10, 1788, and
was never heard from again. However, his records survived
and were published in 1797.

D'Urville had previously served on a circumnavigation of the world (1822–25) before embarking on his great
voyage to the South Pacific. A main objective of this next
mission was to search for traces of La Pérouse. During the
journey he charted parts of New Zealand and visited
the Fiji and Loyalty islands, New Caledonia, New Guinea,
Amboyna, Van Diemen's Land (now Tasmania), the
Caroline Islands, and the Celebes.

In 1826–27 the English captain-adventurer Peter
Dillon found evidence that La Pérouse's ships had been
near Vanikoro, one of the Santa Cruz Islands (now in
Solomon Islands). In February 1828 d'Urville also sighted
wreckage at Vanikoro, and he learned from islanders
that about 30 men from the ships had been massacred
on shore, though others who were well armed managed
to escape.

LA PEROUSE STRAIT

La Perouse Strait (Russian: Proliv Laperuza; Japanese: Sōya-kaikyō) is an international waterway between the islands of Sakhalin (Russia) and Hokkaido (Japan). The strait, named for the French explorer Jean-François de Galaup, count de La Pérouse, separates the Sea of Okhotsk from the Sea of Japan. It is 27 miles (43 km) wide at its narrowest part, between Cape Krilon (Sakhalin) and Cape Sōya (Hokkaido) and varies in depth from 167 to 387 feet (51 to 118 metres). The strait is characterized by extremely strong marine currents. It is closed by ice in the winter.

The expedition returned to France on March 25, 1829. The voyage resulted in extensive revision in charts of South Sea waters and redesignation of island groups into Melanesia, Micronesia, Polynesia, and Malaysia. D'Urville also returned with about 1,600 plant specimens, 900 rock samples, and information on the languages of the islands he had visited.

VOYAGES OF JAMES COOK

The renowned British naval captain, navigator, and explorer James Cook (1728–79) was one of the most intrepid of the great discoverers. Over the course of two decades he led expeditions that explored the seaways and coasts of Canada (1759 and 1763–67) and conducted three expeditions to the Pacific Ocean (1768–71, 1772–75, and 1776–79), ranging from the Antarctic ice fields to the Bering Strait and from the coasts of North America to Australia and New Zealand.

Early Career

Cook went to sea at the age of 18 as a merchant seaman, learning to sail stout, seaworthy collier-barks made at the town of Whitby and receiving splendid practical navigational training in the treacherous waters of the North Sea. In 1855 he joined the Royal Navy. During the Seven Years' War between Great Britain and France (1756–63), he spent much of the war in North America, during which time he charted and marked the more difficult reaches of the St. Lawrence River. Between 1763 and 1768, after the war had ended, he commanded a schooner while surveying the coasts of Newfoundland.

Voyages and Discoveries

In 1768 the Royal Society, in conjunction with the Admiralty, was organizing the first scientific expedition to the Pacific, and the rather obscure 40-year-old Cook was appointed commander of the expedition. He was given a homely looking but extremely sturdy Whitby coal-hauling bark that was renamed HMS *Endeavour*. Cook's orders were to convey gentlemen of the Royal Society and their assistants to Tahiti to observe the transit of the planet Venus across the Sun. That done, on June 3, 1769, he was to find the southern continent, the so-called Terra Australis, which philosophers argued must exist to balance the landmasses of the Northern Hemisphere. The leader of the scientists was the rich and able Joseph Banks, age 26, who was assisted by Daniel Solander, a Swedish botanist, as well as astronomers and artists. Cook carried an early nautical almanac and brass sextants but no chronometer on the first voyage.

Striking south and southwest from Tahiti, where his predecessors had sailed west and west-northwest with the favouring trade winds, Cook found and charted all of New Zealand, a difficult job that took six months. After that, instead of turning before the west winds for the homeward run around Cape Horn, he crossed the Tasman Sea westward and, on April 19, 1770, came on the southeast coast of Australia. Running north along its 2,000-mile (3,200-km) eastern coast, surveying as he went, Cook successfully navigated Queensland's Great Barrier Reef—since reckoned as one of the greatest navigational hazards in the world—taking the Coral Sea and the Torres Strait in his stride. Once the bark touched on a coral spur by night, but it withstood the impact and was refloated. After the *Endeavour* was grounded on the nearby Queensland coast and repaired, Cook sailed it back to England. He stopped briefly at Batavia (now Jakarta) for supplies, and, although the crew had been remarkably healthy until then, 30 died of fever and dysentery contracted while on land. None of the crew, however, died of scurvy. This was because, in addition to ensuring cleanliness and ventilation in the crew's quarters, Cook insisted on an appropriate diet that included watercress, sauerkraut, and a kind of orange extract. The health in which he maintained his sailors in consequence made his name a naval byword.

Back in England, Cook soon began to organize another ambitious voyage. The success of the expedition of Joseph Banks and his scientists (which established the useful principle of sending scientists on naval voyages— e.g., Charles Darwin in the *Beagle*, T.H. Huxley in the *Rattlesnake*, and J.D. Hooker with Sir James Ross to the Ross Sea in the Antarctic) stimulated interest not only in the discovery of new lands, but in the knowledge of many other scientific subjects. The wealth of scientifically collected material from the *Endeavour* voyage was unique. Cook was now sent out with two ships to make the first circumnavigation of and penetration into the Antarctic.

Between July 1772 and July 1775 Cook made what ranks as one of the greatest sailing ship voyages, again with a small former Whitby ship, the *Resolution*, and a consort ship, the *Adventure*. He found no trace of Terra Australis, though he sailed beyond latitude 70° S in the Antarctic, but he successfully completed the first west–east circumnavigation in high latitudes, charted Tonga and Easter Island during the winters, and discovered New Caledonia in the Pacific and the South Sandwich Islands and South Georgia Island in the Atlantic. He showed that a real Terra Australis existed only in the landmasses of Australia, New Zealand, and whatever land might remain frozen beyond the ice rim of Antarctica.

There was yet one secret of the Pacific to be discovered: whether there existed a northwest passage around Canada and Alaska or a northeast one around Siberia, between the Atlantic and Pacific. Although the passages had long been sought in vain from Europe, it was thought that the search from the North Pacific might be successful. The man to undertake the search obviously was Cook, and in July 1776 he went off again on the *Resolution,* with another Whitby ship, the *Discovery*. This search was unsuccessful, for neither a northwest nor a northeast passage usable by sailing ships existed, and the voyage led to Cook's death. In a brief fracas with Hawaiians over the stealing of a cutter, Cook was slain on the beach at Kealakekua by the Polynesian natives.

Cook had set new standards of thoroughness in discovery and seamanship, in navigation, cartography, and the sea care of men, in relations with natives both friendly and hostile, and in the application of science at sea; and he had peacefully changed the map of the world more than any other single man in history.

GEORG FORSTER

The explorer and scientist Georg Forster (1754–94) helped to establish the literary travel book as a favoured genre in German literature. With his father, Johann Reinhold Forster, he emigrated to England in 1766. Both were invited to accompany Capt. James Cook on his second voyage around the world (1772–75). Georg Forster's account of the journey, *A Voyage Towards the South Pole and Round the World* (1777), was based on his father's journals; it later appeared in a German version, *Reise um die Welt* (1778–80). A work of travel, science, and literature, the book not only established Forster as one of the most accomplished stylists of the time but also influenced German scientific and literary writing, including that of Johann Wolfgang von Goethe, Johann Gottfried von Herder, and Alexander von Humboldt. A superb essayist, Forster contributed to the scientific, especially botanical, knowledge of the South Seas.

HUMBOLDT'S EXPLORATION OF SOUTH AMERICA

The German naturalist and explorer Alexander von Humboldt (1769–1859) was a major figure in the classical period of physical geography and biogeography—areas of science now included in the earth sciences and ecology. With his book *Kosmos* he made a valuable contribution to the popularization of science. The Peru, or Humboldt, Current off the west coast of South America originally was named for him.

As an adolescent, Humboldt obtained some training in engineering and in his late teens became passionately interested in botany. He then took up an interest in mineralogy and geology, trained intensively for two years, and began working for the mining department of the Prussian government. However, Humboldt had a growing conviction that his real aim in life was scientific exploration. He resigned his post in 1797 to thoroughly prepare himself for the task. In 1799 he obtained permission from the Spanish government to visit the Spanish colonies in the New World. That summer he set sail from Marseille accompanied by the French botanist Aimé Bonpland, whom he had met in Paris. The estate he had inherited at the death of his mother enabled Humboldt to finance the expedition entirely out of his own pocket. Humboldt and Bonpland spent five years (1799–1804) in Central and South America, covering more than 6,000 miles (9,650 km) on foot, on horseback, and in canoes. It was a life of great physical exertion and serious deprivation.

Starting from Caracas, they traveled south through grasslands and scrublands until they reached the banks of the Apure River, a tributary of the Orinoco River. They continued their journey on the river by canoe as far as the Orinoco. Following its course and that of the Casiquiare River, they proved that the Casiquiare River formed a connection between the vast river systems of the Amazon and the Orinoco. For three months Humboldt and Bonpland moved through dense tropical rain forests, tormented by clouds of mosquitoes and stifled by the humid heat. Their provisions were soon destroyed by insects and rain; the lack of food finally drove them to subsist on ground wild cacao beans and river water. Yet both travelers, buoyed by the excitement provided by the new and overwhelming impressions, remained healthy and in the best of spirits until their return to civilization, when they succumbed to a severe bout of fever.

After a short stay in Cuba, Humboldt and Bonpland returned to South America for an extensive exploration of the Andes. From Bogotá to Trujillo, Peru, they wandered over the Andean highlands—following a route now traversed by the Pan-American Highway, in their time a series of steep, rocky, and often very narrow paths. They climbed a number of peaks, including all the volcanoes in the surroundings of Quito, Ecu.; Humboldt's ascent of Chimborazo (20,702 feet [6,310 metres]) to a height of 19,286 feet (5,878 metres), but short of the summit, remained a world mountain-climbing record for nearly 30 years. All these achievements were carried out without the help of modern mountaineering equipment, without ropes, crampons, or oxygen supplies; hence, Humboldt and Bonpland suffered badly from altitude (mountain) sickness. But Humboldt turned his discomfort to advantage: he became the first person to ascribe altitude sickness to lack of oxygen in the rarefied air of great heights. He also studied the oceanic current off the west coast of South America that was originally named for him but is now known as the Peru Current. When the pair arrived, worn and footsore, in Quito, Humboldt, the experienced mountaineer and indefatigable collector of scientific data, had no difficulty in assuming the role of courtier and man of the world when he was received by the Viceroy and the leaders of Spanish society.

In the spring of 1803, the two travelers sailed from Guayaquil to Acapulco, Mex., where they spent the last year of their expedition in a close study of this most developed and highly civilized part of the Spanish colonies. After a short stay in the United States, where Humboldt was received by Pres. Thomas Jefferson, they sailed for France.

Humboldt and Bonpland returned with an immense amount of information. In addition to a vast collection of new plants, there were determinations of longitudes and latitudes, measurements of the components of Earth's geomagnetic field, and daily observations of temperatures and barometric pressure, as well as statistical data on the social and economic conditions of Mexico.

PERU CURRENT

With a width of about 550 miles (900 km), the Peru Current (also called Humboldt Current) is a cold-water current of the southeast Pacific Ocean. Relatively slow and shallow, it is an eastern boundary current similar to the California Current of the North Pacific. The West Wind Drift flows east toward South America south of latitude 40° S, and while most of it continues through the Drake Passage around the southern tip of South America to the Atlantic, a shallow stream turns north to parallel the continent as far as latitude 4° S, where it turns west to join the Pacific South Equatorial Current.

As it is a cold current, except at times of the phenomenon known as El Niño, the Peru Current brings fog to the nearby coast but also helps to keep the coast one of the most intensely arid areas in the world. The cold flow is intensified by upwelling of deep water caused by the combined effects of the drag of surface winds of the Southeast Trades and Earth's rotation. Upwelling brings abundant nutrients close to the surface, and the beneficial effects of sunlight, which enable rich plankton growth, make the waters off Peru, Chile, and Ecuador one of the world's greatest fishing grounds for anchovies and the larger fish, such as tuna, that feed on them. Another economic benefit is the guano, used for fertilizer, deposited by the flocks of birds that feed on the anchovies.

INTO THE HEART OF AFRICA

The river systems were the key to African geography. The existence of a great river in the interior of West Africa was known to the Greeks, but the questions of which direction it flowed and whether it found an outlet in the Sénégal, the Gambia, the Congo, or even the Nile, were in dispute. A young Scottish surgeon, Mungo Park, was asked to explore it by the African Association of London. In 1796, Park, who had traveled inland from the Gambia, saw "the long sought for majestic Niger flowing slowly *eastwards*." On a second expedition, attempting to follow its course to the mouth, he was drowned near Bussa, in what is now Nigeria. In 1830 an English explorer, Richard Lander, traveled from the Bight of Benin, on the West African coast, to Bussa, and he then navigated the river down to its mouth, which was revealed as being one of the delta tributaries that, because of the trade in palm oil, were known to traders as "the oil rivers" on the Gulf of Guinea.

The Zambezi, in south central Africa, was not known at all until the Scottish missionary-explorer David Livingstone traveled its length in the mid-19th century. Livingstone later investigated the complex drainage system between Lakes Nyasa and Tanganyika and explored the headwaters of the Congo River. He refused to return to England with the British American explorer Henry Morton Stanley, who was sent to his rescue in 1871, because he was still uncertain of the position of the watershed between the Nile and the Congo; however, he died at Lake Bangweulu in 1873.

The whereabouts of the source of the Nile had intrigued men since the days of the Egyptian pharaohs. A Scottish explorer, James Bruce, traveling in Ethiopia in 1770, visited the two fountains in Lake Tana, the source of the Blue Nile, first discovered by the Spanish priest Paez in 1618. The English explorers Richard Burton and John Hanning Speke discovered Lake Tanganyika in 1857. Speke then traveled north alone and reached the southern creek of a lake, which he named Victoria Nyanza. Without exploring farther, he returned to England, sure that he had found the source of the Nile. He was right—but he had not seen the outlet, and Burton did not believe him. In 1862 Speke, traveling with the Scottish explorer James Grant, found the Ripon Falls, in Uganda (which was submerged following the construction of the Owen Falls Dam [now the Nalubaale Dam] in 1954), and "saw without any doubt that Old Father Nile rises in Victoria Nyanza." Stanley completed the puzzle in 1875, when he circumnavigated the lake and then followed the Congo to its mouth. The pattern made by the river systems of Africa was elucidated at last.

LIVINGSTONE'S JOURNEYS INTO THE CONTINENTAL CENTRE

Scottish missionary and explorer David Livingstone (1813–73) studied theology and medicine in Glasgow before being ordained in 1840. He then decided to explore Africa to open up the interior for colonization, extend the Gospel, and abolish the slave trade. He set sail for South Africa in 1840 and arrived in Capetown on March 14, 1841.

Initial Explorations

For the next 15 years, Livingstone was constantly on the move into the African interior. He strengthened his missionary determination, responded wholeheartedly to the delights of geographic discovery, clashed with the Boers and the Portuguese, whose treatment of the Africans he came to detest, and built a remarkable reputation as a dedicated Christian, a courageous explorer, and a fervent antislavery advocate. So impassioned was his commitment to Africa, in fact, that he neglected his duties as husband and father.

From a mission at Kuruman on the Cape frontier, which Livingstone reached on July 31, 1841, he soon pushed his search for converts northward into untried country where the population was reputed to be more numerous. This suited his purpose of spreading the Gospel through "native agents." By the summer of 1842, he had already gone farther north than any other European into the difficult Kalahari country and had familiarized himself with the local languages and cultures. His mettle was dramatically tested in 1844 when, during a journey to Mabotsa to establish a mission station, he was mauled by a lion. The resulting injury to his left arm was complicated by another accident, and he could never again support the barrel of a gun steadily with his left hand and thus was obliged to fire from his left shoulder and to take aim with his left eye.

By the early 1850s Livingstone had already achieved a small measure of fame as surveyor and scientist of a small expedition responsible for the first European sighting of Lake Ngami (Aug. 1, 1849), for which he was awarded a gold medal and monetary prize by the British Royal Geographical Society. This was the beginning of his life-long association with the society, which continued to encourage his ambitions as an explorer and to champion his interests in Britain.

Opening the Interior

Livingstone was now ready to push Christianity, commerce, and civilization—the trinity that he believed was

destined to open up Africa—northward beyond the frontiers of South Africa and into the heart of the continent.
In a famous statement in 1853 he made his purpose clear:
"I shall open up a path into the interior, or perish." On
Nov. 11, 1853, from Linyanti at the approaches to the
Zambezi River and in the midst of the Makololo peoples
whom he considered eminently suitable for missionary
work, Livingstone set out northwestward with little equipment and only a small party of Africans. His intention was
to find a route to the Atlantic coast that would permit
legitimate commerce to undercut the slave trade. He also
sought a route that would be more suitable for reaching
the Makololo than the one through Boer territory. (In 1852
the Boers had destroyed his home at Kolobeng and
attacked his African friends.) After an arduous journey
that might have wrecked the constitution of a lesser man,
Livingstone reached Luanda on the west coast on May 31,
1854. In order to take his Makololo followers back home
and to carry out further explorations of the Zambezi, as
soon as his health permitted—on Sept. 20, 1854—he began
the return journey. He reached Linyanti nearly a year later
on Sept. 11, 1855. Continuing eastward on November 3,
Livingstone explored the Zambezi regions and reached
Quelimane in Mozambique on May 20, 1856. His most
spectacular visit on this last leg of his great journey was to
the thundering, smokelike waters on the Zambezi at which
he arrived on Nov. 17, 1855. With typical patriotism, he
named those waters Victoria Falls for his queen.

Livingstone returned to England on Dec. 9, 1856, a
national hero. News from and about him during the
previous three years had stirred the imagination of
English-speaking peoples everywhere to an unprecedented
degree. He recorded his accomplishments modestly but
effectively in his *Missionary Travels and Researches in South*

Victoria Falls on the Zambezi River as seen from Zambia. G. Holton—
Photo Researchers

Africa (1857), which quickly sold more than 70,000 copies and took its place in publishing history. Honours flowed in upon him, and he became financially independent.

After the completion of his book, Livingstone spent six months speaking all over the British Isles. In his Senate House address at Cambridge on Dec. 4, 1857, he foresaw that he would be unable to complete his work in Africa, and he called on young university men to take up the task that he had begun. The publication of *Dr. Livingstone's Cambridge Lectures* (1858) roused almost as much interest as his first book, and out of his Cambridge visit came the Universities' Mission to Central Africa in 1860, on which Livingstone set high hopes during his second expedition to Africa.

The Zambezi Expedition

This time Livingstone was away from Britain from March 12, 1858, to July 23, 1864. This expedition was infinitely better organized than Livingstone's previous solitary journeys. It had a paddle steamer, impressive stores, 10 Africans, and 6 Europeans (including his brother Charles and an Edinburgh doctor, John Kirk). But it was soon revealed that Livingstone's legendary leadership skills had limitations. Quarrels broke out among the Europeans, and some were dismissed. Disillusionment with Livingstone set in among members both in his own expedition and of the abortive Universities' Mission that followed it to central Africa. It proved impossible to navigate the Zambezi by ship, and Livingstone's two attempts to find a route along the Ruvuma River bypassing Portuguese territory to districts around Lake Nyasa (Lake Malawi) also proved impractical. On Sept. 17, 1859, Livingstone and his party became the first Britons to reach the districts that held out promise of colonization.

The British government recalled the expedition in 1863, when it was clear that Livingstone's optimism about economic and political developments in the Zambezi regions was premature. Livingstone, however, showed something of his old fire when he took his little vessel, the *Lady Nyassa*, with a small untrained crew and little fuel, on a hazardous voyage of 2,500 miles (4,000 km) across the Indian Ocean to India and left it for sale in Bombay (now Mumbai). Furthermore, within the next three decades the Zambezi expedition proved to be anything but a disaster. It had amassed a valuable body of scientific knowledge. The association of the Lake Nyasa regions with Livingstone's name and the prospects for colonization that he envisaged there were important factors for the creation in 1893 of the British Central Africa Protectorate, which in 1907 became Nyasaland and in 1966 the republic of Malawi.

Back in Britain in the summer of 1864, Livingstone, with his brother Charles, wrote his second book, *Narrative of an Expedition to the Zambesi and Its Tributaries* (1865). Livingstone was advised at this time to have a surgical operation for the hemorrhoids that had troubled him since his first great African journey. He refused, and it is probable that severe bleeding hemorrhoids were the cause of his death at the end of his third and greatest African journey.

Quest for the Nile

Livingstone returned to Africa, after another short visit to Bombay, on Jan. 28, 1866, with support from private and public bodies and the status of a British consul at large. His aim, as usual, was the extension of the Gospel and the abolition of the slave trade on the East African coast, but a new objective was the exploration of the central African watershed and the possibility of finding the ultimate sources of the Nile. This time Livingstone went without European subordinates and took only African and Asian followers. Trouble, however, once more broke out among his staff, and Livingstone, prematurely aged from the hardships of his previous expeditions, found it difficult to cope. Striking out from Mikindani on the east coast, he was compelled by Ngoni raids to give up his original intention of avoiding Portuguese territory and reaching the country around Lake Tanganyika by passing north of Lake Nyasa. The expedition was instead forced south, and in September, some of Livingstone's followers deserted him. To avoid punishment when they returned to Zanzibar, they concocted a story that the Ngoni had killed Livingstone. Although it was proved the following year that he was alive, a touch of drama was added to the reports circulating abroad about his expedition.

Drama mounted as Livingstone moved north again from the south end of Lake Nyasa. Early in 1867 a deserter carried off his medical chest, but Livingstone pressed on into central Africa. He was the first European to reach Lake Mweru (Nov. 8, 1867) and Lake Bangweulu (July 18, 1868). Assisted by Arab traders, Livingstone reached Lake Tanganyika in February 1869. Despite illness, he went on and arrived on March 29, 1871, at his ultimate northwesterly point, Nyangwe, on the Lualaba leading into the Congo River. This was farther west than any European had penetrated.

When he returned to Ujiji on the eastern shore of Lake Tanganyika on Oct. 23, 1871, Livingstone was a sick and failing man. Search parties had been sent to look for him because he had not been heard from in several years, and Henry M. Stanley, a correspondent of the *New York Herald* newspaper, found the explorer, greeting him with the now famous quote, "Dr. Livingstone, I presume?" (The exact date of the encounter is unclear, as the two men wrote different dates in their journals; Livingstone's journal suggests that the meeting took place sometime in Oct. 24–28, 1871, while Stanley reported November 10.) Stanley brought much-needed food and medicine, and Livingstone soon recovered. He joined Stanley in exploring the northern reaches of Lake Tanganyika and then accompanied him to Unyanyembe, 200 miles (320 km) eastward. But he refused all Stanley's pleas to leave Africa with him, and on March 14, 1872, Stanley departed for England to add, with journalistic fervour, to the saga of David Livingstone.

Livingstone moved south again, obsessed by his quest for the Nile sources and his desire for the destruction of the slave trade, but his illness overcame him. In May 1873, at Chitambo in what is now northern Zambia, Livingstone's African servants found him dead, kneeling by his bedside as if in prayer. In order to embalm Livingstone's body, they removed his heart and viscera and buried them in African soil. In a difficult journey of nine months, they carried his body to the coast. It was taken to England and, in a great Victorian funeral, was buried in Westminster Abbey on April 18, 1874. *The Last Journals of David Livingstone* were published in the same year.

STANLEY'S EXPLORATIONS

Unquestionably, Sir Henry Morton Stanley (1841–1904), famous for his rescue of David Livingstone, was equally as renowned for his explorations of central Africa, especially his discoveries in and development of the Congo region.

Stanley was born John Rowlands to unmarried parents and grew up partly in the charge of reluctant relatives and

VICTORIA FALLS

The Victoria Falls is a spectacular waterfall located about midway along the course of the Zambezi River, at the border between Zambia to the north and Zimbabwe to the south. Approximately twice as wide and twice as deep as Niagara Falls, the waterfall spans the entire breadth of the Zambezi River at one of its widest points (more than 5,500 feet [1,700 metres]). At the falls, the river plunges over a sheer precipice to a maximum drop of 355 feet (108 metres). The falls' mean flow is almost 33,000 cubic feet (935 cubic metres) per second.

The Zambezi River does not gather speed as it nears the drop, the approach being signaled only by the mighty roar and characteristic veil of mist for which the Kalolo-Lozi people named the falls Mosi-oa-Tunya ("The Smoke That Thunders"). The lip of the falls' precipice is split into several parts by various small islands, depressions, and promontories along its edge. The eastern portions of the falls are mostly dry during times of low river flow.

The waters of Victoria Falls do not drop into an open basin but rather into a chasm that varies in width from 80 to 240 feet (25 to 75 metres). This chasm is formed by the precipice of the falls and by an opposite rock wall of equal height. The chasm's only outlet is a narrow channel cut in the barrier wall at a point about three-fifths of the way from the western end of the falls, and through this gorge, which is less than 210 feet (65 metres) wide and 390 feet (120 metres) long, flows the entire volume of the Zambezi River. At the gorge's end is the Boiling Pot, a deep pool into which the waters churn and foam at flood time. Just below the Boiling Pot, the gorge is spanned by the Victoria Falls (Zambezi) Bridge, which carries rail, automobile, and pedestrian traffic between Zambia and Zimbabwe. The river's waters then emerge into an enormous zigzag trough that forms the beginning of Batoka Gorge, which has been cut by the river to a depth of 400–800 feet (120–240 metres) through a basalt plateau for a distance of 60 miles (100 km).

In addition to the falls themselves, the surrounding Victoria Falls National Park (Zimbabwe) and Mosi-oa-Tunya National Park (Zambia) abound with large and small game and offer recreational facilities. Victoria Falls and the adjoining parklands were collectively designated a World Heritage site in 1989.

The Victoria Falls Bridge across the Zambezi River, connecting Zambia and Zimbabwe. © Brian A. Vikander/West Light

partly in a workhouse. In 1859 he sailed from Liverpool as
a cabin boy and landed at New Orleans, La., in 1859. There
Rowlands was befriended by a merchant, Henry Hope
Stanley, whose first and last names the boy adopted; the
name "Morton" was added later. For some years Stanley
led a roving life, as a soldier in the American Civil War, a
seaman on merchant ships and in the U.S. Navy, and a journalist in the early days of frontier expansion; he even
managed a trip to Turkey.

In 1867 Stanley offered his services to James Gordon
Bennett of the *New York Herald* as a special correspondent
with the British expeditionary force in Ethiopia, and
Stanley was the first to report the fall of Magdala in 1868.
An assignment to report on the Spanish Civil War followed, and in 1869 he received instructions to undertake a
roving commission in the Middle East, which was to
include the relief of Livingstone, of whom little had been
heard since his departure for Africa in 1866.

Relief of Livingstone

On Jan. 6, 1871, Stanley reached Zanzibar, the starting
point for expeditions to the African interior, and, intent
on a scoop, left on March 21 without disclosing his intentions. Leading a well-equipped caravan and backed by
American money, Stanley forced his way through country
disturbed by fighting and stricken by sickness to Ujiji on
Lake Tanganyika, Livingstone's last known port of call.
There he found the old hero, ill and short of supplies. A
cordial friendship sprang up between the two men, and,
when Stanley returned to the coast, he dispatched fresh
supplies that enabled Livingstone to continue the search
for the Nile that culminated in his death a year later in the
swamps of Lake Bangweulu, a region that in fact gives rise
to the Congo River.

How I Found Livingstone was published soon after Stanley's arrival in England in the late summer of 1872, when the exploits of this hitherto unknown adventurer gave rise to controversy. Members of the Royal Geographical Society (RGS) resented an American journalist having succeeded in relieving the famous traveler when they, his friends, had failed. Stanley did, however, receive the RGS Patron's Gold Medal. In 1873 Stanley went to Asante (Ashanti; now in modern Ghana) as war correspondent for the *New York Herald*.

Discovery and Development of the Congo

When Livingstone died in 1873, Stanley resolved to take up the exploration of Africa where he had left off. The problem of the Nile sources and the nature of the central African lakes had been only partly solved by earlier explorers. Stanley secured financial backing from the *New York Herald* and the *Daily Telegraph* of London for an expedition to pursue the quest, and the caravan left Zanzibar on Nov. 12, 1874, heading for Lake Victoria. His visit to King Mutesa I of Buganda led to the admission of Christian missionaries to the area in 1877 and to the eventual establishment of a British protectorate in Uganda. Circumnavigating Lake Victoria, Stanley confirmed John Hanning Speke's estimate of its size and importance. Skirmishes with suspicious tribespeople on the lakeshore, which resulted in a number of casualties, gave rise in England to criticism of this new kind of traveler with his journalist's outlook and forceful methods. Lake Tanganyika was next explored and found to have no connection with the Nile system. Stanley and his men pressed on west to the Lualaba River (the very river that Livingstone had hoped was the Nile, but that proved to be the headstream of the Congo). There they joined forces with the Arab

trader Tippu Tib, who accompanied them for a few laps
downriver, then left Stanley to fight his way first to Stanley
Pool (now Malebo Pool) and then (partly overland) down
to the great cataracts he named Livingstone Falls. Stanley
and his men reached the sea on Aug. 12, 1877, after an epic
journey described in *Through the Dark Continent* (1878).

Failing to enlist British interests in the development of
the Congo region, Stanley took service with the king
of Belgium, Leopold II, whose secret ambition it was to
annex the region for himself. From August 1879 to June
1884 Stanley was in the Congo basin, where he built a road
from the lower Congo up to Stanley Pool and launched
steamers on the upper river. (It is from this period, when
Stanley persevered in the face of great difficulties, that
he earned, from his men, the nickname of Bula Matari
["Breaker of Rocks"]). Originally under international auspices, Stanley's work was to pave the way for the creation
of the Congo Free State, under the sovereignty of King
Leopold.

Relief of Emin Paşa

Stanley's last expedition in Africa was for the relief of
Mehmed Emin Paşa, governor of the Equatorial Province
of Egypt, who had been cut off by the Mahdist revolt of
1882 in the environs of Lake Albert. Stanley was appointed
to lead a relief expedition and decided to approach Lake
Albert by way of the Congo River, counting on Tippu
Tib to supply porters. Stanley left England in January
1887 and arrived at the mouth of the Congo in March.
The expedition reached the navigable head of the river
in June, and there, at Yambuya, Stanley left a rear column
with orders to await Tippu Tib's porters. The failure of
the rear column to rejoin the main body later gave rise to
controversy harmful to Stanley's reputation. Eventually

ITURI FOREST

The Ituri Forest is a dense region of tropical rainforest lying on the northeastern lip of the Congo River basin in the Democratic Republic of the Congo. Situated in Central Africa between latitudes 0° and 3° N and longitudes 27° and 30° E, the precise geographic limits of the Ituri are poorly defined, especially along its southern and western extensions. The forest owes its name to the Ituri River, which flows east-west across the forest into the Aruwimi River and thence to the Congo.

The Ituri, with its constant high humidity and dark interior, may seem oppressive to some. Certainly the novelist Joseph Conrad thought so when he referred to the forest as the "heart of darkness." But the overwhelming impression for even the most squeamish visitor is not of darkness, nor of oppressive gloom but of life in its most vibrant and exciting form. The magnificence of the tropical rain forest of the Ituri cannot help but inspire the modern-day observer with the same poetic enthusiasm displayed by Henry Morton Stanley when he described his crossing of the area in 1887–88.

The trees of the forest range in size from small saplings just inches in diameter to gigantic hardwoods reaching to heights of 170 feet (52 metres). Like the pillars of a Gothic cathedral, these giant trees are buttressed; roots run down their sides and extend great distances across the forest floor, making the ground a labyrinth of roots that anchor the trees and grab scarce nutrients from the shallow forest soil. In places where the high canopy is nearly continuous, only small, elusive patches of sunlight reach the forest floor. The lack of light at lower levels is accentuated by the darkness of the foliage of the few shrubs and small trees that can grow under such shaded conditions. Where gaps occur in the upper canopy, herbaceous plants with long leaves resembling those of the banana plant take advantage of the available light and grow in dense stands. In many places the forest has been disturbed, either by human activity or by natural treefalls that cut large swathes through the canopy and open up the forest to the strong equatorial sun. There, the vegetation near the ground is a dense tangle of nettles, creepers, and competing species of fast-growing, short-lived trees, which make walking through the forest difficult if not impossible.

Everywhere on the ground there is a profusion of fallen nuts and fruits, some as large as basketballs and many partially eaten by monkeys, antelope (duikers), and rodents. During some seasons the air is filled with the nectar of numerous species of flower, including many epiphytes, which cling to the surface of other plants and draw their sustenance from the air. Always there is the sound of myriad insects. Cicadas perch on tree trunks and emit an irritating buzz that seems designed to drive any intruder to madness. Army ants advance in columns, audibly cracking the bodies of their insect prey. Seemingly endless lines of migrating butterflies flutter through the understory and sometimes congregate in colourful displays along streambeds. The buzzing of bees, busily plying the treetops in search of sweet nourishing nectar, is ever present

Efforts to preserve the fauna and flora are largely confined to the Maiko National Park on the southern edge of the Ituri and the Okapi Wildlife Reserve (designated a UNESCO World Heritage site in 1996) to the northeast. Both offer some protection for such animals as the forest elephant, the okapi, the Congo peacock, the aardvark, and the chimpanzee, but poaching activities and destruction of forest habitat seriously threaten these and other species both outside and inside the park. Conservation efforts have also been disrupted by civil strife that began in the late 1990s.

Lombi tree (Dalbergia glandulosa) *supported by buttress roots in the Ituri Forest, Congo (Kinshasa).* © Alan Watson/Forest Light

the expedition was assembled at Lake Albert, and, despite Emin's initial reluctance to leave his province, some 1,500 persons set out for the east coast on April 10, 1889, and arrived at Bagamoyo on December 4. On the way, the Ruwenzori Range was revealed to explorers for the first time (identified as Ptolemy's Mountains of the Moon), and the Semliki River was shown to link Lakes Edward and Albert; thus were cleared up the few doubtful geographic points regarding the Nile sources. *In Darkest Africa* (1890) is Stanley's own account of his last adventure on the African continent. He received a Special Gold Medal from the RGS.

Stanley was renaturalized a British subject in 1892. (He had become a U.S. citizen in 1885.) He was made a Knight Grand Cross of the Order of the Bath in 1899, becoming Sir Henry Morton Stanley. The remaining years before his death were spent mainly at a small estate that he bought in Surrey in 1898.

RICHARD BURTON AND THE SOURCE OF THE NILE

The English scholar-explorer Sir Richard Burton (1821–90) who is widely known as an Orientalist, also won renown for his role in the discovery of the source of the Nile River. In 1842 he went to India as a subaltern officer. There he disguised himself as a Muslim and wrote detailed reports of merchant bazaars and urban brothels. He then traveled to Arabia, again disguised as a Muslim, and became the first non-Muslim European to penetrate the forbidden holy cities. He recounted his adventures in *Pilgrimage to El-Medinah and Mecca* (1855–56), a classic account of Muslim life.

By this time Burton had become fascinated by the idea of discovering the source of the White Nile and in 1855 planned an expedition with three officers of the British East India Company, including John Hanning Speke, intending to push across Somaliland. Africans attacked the party near Berbera, however, killing one member of the party and seriously wounding Speke. Burton himself had a javelin hurled through his jaw and was forced to return to England. After recovery, in July 1855, he volunteered for service in the Crimean War.

After the war, Burton turned again to the Nile search, leading an expedition inland from Zanzibar with John Speke in 1857–58. They suffered almost every kind of hardship Africa could inflict. When they finally arrived on the shores of Lake Tanganyika, Burton was so ill from malaria he could not walk, and Speke was virtually blind. Ailing, and disappointed by native information that the Rusizi River to the north poured into rather than out of the lake, Burton wished to return and prepare a new expedition. Speke, however, who had recovered more quickly, pushed on alone to the northeast and discovered Lake Victoria, which he was convinced was the true Nile source. Burton's unwillingness to accept this theory without further exploration led to quarrels with Speke and their eventual estrangement.

Speke was the first to return to London, where he was lionized and given funds to return to Africa. Burton, largely ignored and denied financing for a new exploration of his own, felt betrayed. His *Lake Regions of Central Africa* (1860) attacked Speke's claims and exacerbated their by then public feud.

Burton now entered the British Foreign Office as consul in Fernando Po, a Spanish island off the coast of West Africa. During his three years there, he made many short trips of exploration into West Africa, gathering enough material to fill five books. His explicit descriptions of

LAKE VICTORIA

Lake Victoria (or Victoria Nyanza) is the largest lake in Africa and the chief reservoir of the Nile. It lies mainly in Tanzania and Uganda but also borders Kenya. Among the freshwater lakes of the world it is exceeded in size only by Lake Superior in North America, its area being 26,828 square miles (69,484 square km).

An irregular quadrilateral in shape, its shores, except on the west, are deeply indented. Its greatest length from north to south is 210 miles (337 km), and its greatest breadth is 150 miles (240 km). Its coastline exceeds 2,000 miles (3,220 km). Its waters fill a shallow depression in the centre of the great plateau that stretches between the Western and Eastern Rift Valleys. The lake's greatest ascertained depth is 270 feet (82 metres). Its only outlet is the Victoria Nile, which exits from the northern coast.

The lake's southwestern coast is backed by precipices 300 feet (90 metres) high, which give way on the western coast to papyrus and ambatch swamps marking the delta of the Kagera River, the largest and most important of the lake affluents. The lake's deeply indented northern coast is flat and bare; the Ugandan cities of Kampala and Entebbe lie along or near it. At the lake's southeastern corner is Speke Gulf, and at the southwestern corner, Emin Pasha Gulf. Of the numerous islands in the lake, Ukerewe, north of Speke Gulf, is the largest.

The search by Europeans for the source of the Nile led to the sighting of the lake by the British explorer John Hanning Speke in 1858. Formerly known to the Arabs as Ukerewe, the lake was named by Speke in honour of Queen Victoria of England. A detailed survey of the lake was made by Sir William Garstin in 1901. Plans for gradually raising the level of the lake's waters were completed in 1954 with the construction of the Owen Falls Dam (now the Nalubaale Dam) on the Victoria Nile at Jinja, Ugan. The dam, which provides hydroelectric power on a large scale, made the lake a vast reservoir. A second dam, Kiira, was later constructed near Nalubaale. It was completed in 1999 and began producing hydroelectric power the next year.

tribal rituals concerning birth, marriage, and death, as well as fetishism, ritual murder, cannibalism, and bizarre sexual practices, though admired by modern anthropologists, won him no favour with the Foreign Office, which considered him eccentric if not dangerous.

Returning to London on leave in September 1864, Burton was invited to debate with Speke before the British Association for the Advancement of Science. Speke, who with James Augustus Grant had made a memorable journey from Zanzibar to Lake Victoria and then down the whole length of the Nile, was expected to defend his conviction that Lake Victoria was the true Nile source. After the preliminary session on September 15, Speke went hunting, dying mysteriously, and the debate was never concluded.

Chapter 5:
Arctic Exploration

The earliest references to Arctic exploration are shrouded in obscurity as a result both of inaccurate ideas of the shape of Earth and of primitive navigation techniques, which make it difficult to interpret early maps and accounts of voyages. Probably the first to approach the Arctic regions was a Greek, Pytheas, who in the 4th century BCE made a voyage from the Mediterranean, around Britain, to a place he called Thule, variously identified as the Shetland Islands, Iceland, and Norway. Pytheas's accounts were for centuries discredited, but the idea of Thule, shrouded in fog and believed to be the "end" of the Earth, caught the imagination of many.

Iceland is known to have been visited by Irish monks in the 8th and 9th centuries CE, but it was the Vikings from Norway who settled the island, late in the 9th century. In the course of the next four centuries, these hardy sailors established trade routes to the White Sea, visited Greenland (c. 982) and founded two settlements on the southwest coast (which disappeared, for unknown reasons, before the 16th century), reached the coast of North America, and probably also reached Svalbard and Novaya Zemlya. However, they left scant records of their voyages, and many of the places they visited had to be rediscovered by others.

ENGLISH AND DUTCH EXPLORATION OF THE EURASIAN ARCTIC

After a long period of inactivity following the decline of the Vikings, leadership in Arctic exploration was assumed in the early 16th century by the Dutch and the English.

The motive was trade with the Far East. The known sea routes around the southern tips of Africa and South America had been claimed as a monopoly by Portugal and Spain, respectively, and were long and arduous besides; the overland routes were even worse. There remained, however, the northern latitudes, and the attempts by English and Dutch merchants to find a Northeast and a Northwest Passage strongly stimulated Arctic exploration.

In 1553 the English sent three ships to the northeast under the command of Sir Hugh Willoughby, with Richard Chancellor as chief pilot. Willoughby, with two ships, wintered in a harbour on the Kola Peninsula, where he and all his men perished. Chancellor, who in the *Edward Bonaventure* had become separated from the others in a gale, reached what is now Archangel (Arkhangelsk) and made an overland journey to Moscow (some 1,500 miles [2,400 km]) before returning home to England. It is interesting to note that these waters were already well known to Russian sailors, who used the route around North Cape (in Norway) to western Europe as early as 1496, but this was not generally known at the time.

After Chancellor's voyage the Muscovy Company was formed, and a lucrative trade developed with Russia—the success of which rather distracted the minds of the English from the Northeast Passage. Nevertheless, in 1556 Stephen Borough sailed in the *Searchthrift* to try to reach the Ob River, but he was stopped by ice and fog at the entrance to the Kara Sea. Not until 1580 did another English expedition, under Arthur Pet and Charles Jackman, attempt its passage. They too failed to penetrate it, and England lost interest in searching for the Northeast Passage.

In the meantime, however, the Dutch had taken up the search, largely because of the efforts of merchant and explorer Olivier Brunel, who in 1565 established a trading post at Archangel. In the course of an eventful career, Brunel made an overland journey to the Ob and in 1584 tried to reach it by sea, but like Pet and Jackman he got no farther than Yugorsky Shar Strait. He was followed by Willem Barents, an outstanding seaman and navigator, who in 1594 discovered Novaya Zemlya and sailed to its northern tip. As Barents coasted north, he noted the wreckage of ships and grave markers at many points along the shore, indicating that Russians had been there before him. His two companions, Cornelis Nai and Brant Tetgales, penetrated a little way through Yugorsky Shar Strait into the Kara Sea. In 1596, with Jan Cornelisz Rijp and Jacob van Heemskerck, he was more successful. Heading due north from Norway instead of following the coast around, Barents discovered Bear Island and Svalbard, which he mistook for Greenland. Rijp then went home with one ship, but Barents and Heemskerck in the other headed east and rounded the north end of Novaya Zemlya. They were forced to winter in Ice Haven on the northeast coast and thus became the first Europeans known to have wintered successfully in the Arctic. They built a house of driftwood and passed the season with remarkable fortitude and success; only two in their company died of scurvy. In the spring, the ship being hopelessly damaged, they escaped across the open Barents Sea in two small boats. Barents died on the journey.

HUDSON'S EXPEDITIONS

The English navigator and explorer Henry Hudson (c. 1565–1611) sailed three times for the English (1607, 1608, and 1610–11) and once for the Dutch (1609), trying to discover a short route from Europe to Asia through the Arctic Ocean. He was a competent navigator who materially extended the explorations of his predecessors. His contribution to geographical knowledge was great, while his discoveries formed the basis for the Dutch colonization of the Hudson River and for English claims to much of Canada. A river, a strait, and a bay in North America are named for him.

Of Hudson's early life, nothing is known. Several Hudsons were associated with his sponsors, the Muscovy Company of London, a generation before his own time. A 1585 voyage by the English navigator John Davis, who sailed to the Arctic to make the first attempt to find a Northwest Passage from Europe to Asia, was planned in the home of a Thomas Hudson in Limehouse, now in London's East End. Henry Hudson may have been present on that occasion and consequently developed a lifelong interest in Arctic exploration. It is certain that he was well informed about Arctic geography and that his competence as a navigator was such that two wealthy companies chose him to conduct hazardous explorations.

THE SEARCH FOR THE NORTHEAST PASSAGE

In the spring of 1607, sailing for the Muscovy Company, Hudson, his son John, and 10 companions set forth "for to discover a Passage by the North Pole to Japan and China." Believing that he would find an ice-free sea around the North Pole, Hudson struck out northward. On reaching the edge of the polar ice pack, he followed it east until he reached the Svalbard (Spitsbergen) archipelago. From there he extended explorations made earlier by the 16th-century Dutch navigator Willem Barents, who had also sought a Northeast Passage to Asia.

A year later, the Muscovy Company again sent Hudson to seek a Northeast Passage, this time between Svalbard and the islands of Novaya Zemlya, which lie to the east of the Barents Sea. Finding his way again blocked by ice fields, he returned to England.

Shortly after his return, Hudson was lured to Amsterdam to undertake a third northeast voyage under contract to the Dutch East India Company. While there, he heard reports of two possible channels to the Pacific across North America. One of these, said to be in about latitude 62° N, was described in the logbooks of a voyage made in 1602 by an English explorer, Capt. George Weymouth. The other, said to be in the vicinity of about latitude 40° N, was newly reported from Virginia by the English soldier, explorer, and colonist Capt. John Smith. Although his interest in a Northwest Passage had been aroused, Hudson agreed to return directly to Holland if his northeast voyage should prove unsuccessful.

Hudson sailed from Holland in the *Half Moon* on April 6, 1609. When head winds and storms forced him to abandon his northeast voyage, he ignored his agreement and proposed to the crew that they should instead seek the Northwest Passage. Given their choice between returning home or continuing, the crew elected to follow up Smith's suggestion and seek the Northwest Passage around 40° N. While cruising along the Atlantic seaboard, Hudson put into the majestic river that was discovered by Giovanni da Verrazzano in 1524 but that was thenceforth to be known as the Hudson. After ascending it for about 150 miles (240 km) to the vicinity of what is now Albany, N.Y., Hudson concluded that the river did not lead to the Pacific.

On his way to Holland, Hudson docked at Dartmouth, Eng. The English government then ordered him and the English members of his crew to desist from further explorations for other nations. His log and papers were sent to Holland, where his discoveries were soon made known.

Hudson now made ready a voyage to America to follow up Weymouth's suggestion. Weymouth had described an inlet (now Hudson Strait) where a "furious overfall" of water rushed out with every ebb tide. This phenomenon suggested that a great body of water lay beyond the strait. Hudson was confident that it was the Pacific Ocean. The British East India Company contributed £300 ($475) toward his voyage, and the Muscovy Company presumably furnished a like amount. Hudson's private sponsors included 5 noblemen and 13 merchants.

THE VOYAGE TO HUDSON BAY

Sailing from London on April 17, 1610, in the 55-ton vessel *Discovery*, Hudson stopped briefly in Iceland, then proceeded to the "furious overfall." Passing through it and entering Hudson Bay, he then followed the east coast southward, rather than striking boldly westward. Finding himself in James Bay at the southernmost extremity of Hudson Bay and with no outlet to the Pacific to be found, Hudson cruised aimlessly until winter overtook him.

In the close confinement of an Arctic winter, quarrels arose. Hudson angered one of his crew, Henry Green, by first giving him a gray gown and then, when Green displeased him, taking it back and giving it to another. Some of his crew suspected that Hudson was secretly hoarding food for his favourites, and tempers flared when Hudson ordered the crew's own sea chests searched for extra victuals. Robert Juet, the mate, had been demoted, and he conspired with Green and others to mutiny. Once the homeward voyage had begun, the mutineers seized Hudson, his son, and seven others, casting them adrift in Hudson Bay in a small open boat on June 22, 1611. Although the *Discovery* sailed home to England, neither

Henry Hudson being abandoned by the crew of the Discovery *in Hudson Bay, Can., on June 22, 1611; lithograph by Lewis & Browne.* Library of Congress, Washington, D.C.

of the ringleaders returned with her, having been killed, together with several others, in a fight with Inuit. No more was ever heard of Hudson and his small party, although in 1631 to 1632 another explorer found the ruins of a shelter, possibly erected by the castaways.

EARLY RUSSIAN EXPLORATION

By the end of the 16th century, the Russians had established a commercial route via the Arctic to the fur-trading centre of Mangazeya on the Taz River in western Siberia. From the mouth of the Northern (Severnaya) Dvina River, the route ran coastwise, through Yugorsky Shar Strait to the west coast of Yamal. To avoid the difficult ice conditions farther north, the shallow-drafted vessels crossed the peninsula to the Gulf of Ob via two opposing rivers and an intervening portage. Use of this route was officially discontinued relatively soon afterward as a result of prohibitions in 1616 and 1619, aimed in part against foreign interlopers and in part to control trade better.

In 1581–82 the Cossack leader Yermak crossed the Urals and conquered the Tatar khanate of Sibir, defeating its leader, Kuchum. In the summer of 1641, a detachment of Cossacks descended the Okhota River to the Pacific. Furs, extracted as tribute from the indigenous peoples, were the driving force behind this phenomenal east-ward surge, and the routes used were mainly riverine—by boat in summer and by sledge in winter. Nonetheless, during or shortly after this eastern expansion, attempts were made to utilize the central section of the Northeast Passage around the Taymyr Peninsula as a commercial route.

In 1940 and 1945 workers at archaeological sites on Faddeya Island and on the mainland at Simsa Gulf in northeastern Taymyr recovered a remarkable collection of artifacts, including parts of a boat, the ruins of a log hut, human skeletal remains, firearms, bows and arrows, fragments of cloth and leather garments and footwear, abundant remains of furs, and 3,482 Russian coins, the latest of which dated to 1619. Interpretation of the evidence varies, but most likely these are the remains of a Russian expedition shipwrecked on this coast while attempting to sail from east to west (possibly from the Lena River) sometime about 1640. There are only vague references to this expedition in the literature—perhaps because it represented a clandestine attempt to circumvent official prohibitions on use of the riverine and overland routes farther south; i.e., these early Arctic seafarers did not want to advertise their activities.

Farther east there was already substantial regular use of the Lena-Kolyma section of the Northeast Passage by the mid-17th century. The first Cossacks descended the Lena to its delta in 1633, and within a decade, the entire coast from the mouth of the Olenek River to the mouth of the Kolyma River had been explored. By 1645 the first trading vessels were plying between the Kolyma and the Lena along the Arctic coast.

In 1648, seven vessels under the command of the Cossack Semyon Dezhnyov sailed east from the mouth of the Kolyma bound for the Anadyr River basin east of the Kolyma Mountains, which was rumoured to be rich in furs. Three of the vessels reached Cape Dezhnyov (the entrance to the Bering Strait), where one was wrecked. Running south, Dezhnyov's own vessel made a final landfall at Cape Olyutorsky, whence he and his men made their way north overland to the Anadyr. Thus, Dezhnyov was the first European to sail through the Bering Strait.

In the 1720s Peter the Great mounted an ambitious operation to determine the geography of the Bering Strait area, because the documentation from Dezhnyov's voyage was still filed in the obscurity of the archives. He commissioned Vitus Bering, a Danish officer in the Russian navy, for the task, and, after three years of preparation, Bering put to sea from the east coast of Kamchatka in the summer of 1728. He discovered St. Lawrence Island and the Diomedes and pushed well north through the Bering Strait into the Chukchi Sea but without sighting the Alaskan coast either outward or homeward bound. Hence, he could not know for sure that he had been in the Arctic Ocean. Four years later, during an expedition aimed at subduing the Chukchi people, Ivan Fyodorov and Mikhail Gvozdev sailed east from Cape Dezhnyov, discovered Cape Prince of Wales, and explored the coast to the vicinity of Nome, thereby becoming the first Europeans to see Alaska.

At that point the Russian Admiralty mounted an operation that to the present day has had no equal in the history of polar exploration: the Great Northern Expedition of 1733–43. The undertaking was again under the command of Bering but consisted of seven separate detachments totaling 977 men, each responsible for exploring different sections of the Arctic or Pacific coast. The vessels involved were repeatedly blocked by ice and were forced to winter in the Arctic or to return to base and try again the following year. Even after eight years of efforts, a crucial gap still remained along the north coast of the Taymyr Peninsula, which was filled by parties traveling by dog sledge. One of these, led by Semyon Chelyuskin, reached Cape Chelyuskin, the northernmost tip of Eurasia, in 1741. The other major gap (which was not traveled by either land or sea) extended from just east of the Kolyma's mouth to the Bering Strait.

Almost all the exploring parties endured extreme hardships, and there were numerous deaths from scurvy, including Bering and the leader of one of the other parties and his wife. But the entire Arctic coast was surveyed and charted from Archangel to Cape Bolshoy Baranov, quite apart from the achievements of the better-known Pacific detachment led by Bering and Aleksey Chirikov. The expedition produced 62 maps and charts of the Arctic coast and Kamchatka, generally of a very high standard, at a time when the Arctic coast of North America was totally unknown north of Hudson Bay and west of Baffin Bay.

The charts, soundings, and sailing directions compiled during the expedition were invaluable to later navigators, but the problems encountered by all the detachments owing to ice led to the conclusion in Russian government circles that the concept of a navigable Northeast Passage was totally impracticable. Indeed, the only other Russian attempt at navigating any portion of the passage in the 18th century was made by a trader, Nikita Shalaurov, although he did have government approval. He tried to sail east from the Kolyma to the Bering Strait in 1762 but was foiled by ice; trying again in 1764, he and his party disappeared. The Chukchi later told of finding the expedition's wintering site littered with skeletons.

This troublesome gap from Chaun Bay to the Bering Strait was partly filled by the English navigator James Cook in 1778 when he sailed northward through the Bering Strait and pushed as far west as Cape North (now Cape Shmidt). This initiative provoked Catherine II (the Great) of Russia to mount an expedition to explore the Chukchi Peninsula. She recruited Joseph Billings, who had been assistant astronomer with Cook. In 1791 Billings and a party of seven landed at St. Lawrence Bay and traveled west overland to Nizhnekolymsk. But it was not until 1823 that Ferdinand Petrovich Wrangel mapped the gap in the north coast of Chukchi. With orders to survey the coast east from Cape Shelagsky and to investigate rumours of land to the north, over three seasons (1821–23) he surveyed the coast to Kolyuchin Bay and attempted (unsuccessfully) to reach a landmass (now Wrangel Island) reported by the local Chukchi as being visible from Cape Yakan in clear weather. During the same period, Pyotr F. Anzhu surveyed the New Siberian Islands and made repeated efforts to locate land rumoured to lie north of that archipelago.

CONQUEST OF THE NORTHEAST PASSAGE

Later in the century a foreign attempt at the Northeast Passage, although unsuccessful, resulted in substantial new discoveries. In 1872 an Austro-Hungarian expedition aboard the *Tegetthoff* under the command of Karl

Weyprecht and Julius Payer mounted an attempt on the passage from the west, intending to winter at either Cape Chelyuskin or the New Siberian Islands. Instead, the ship was beset in the Barents Sea, and as it drifted north, it came within sight of Franz Josef Land. A sledge party led by Payer explored much of the eastern part of the archipelago in 1874.

Finally, in 1878–79 the Northeast Passage was conquered by a Swedish expedition aboard the *Vega*, led by Adolf Erik, Baron Nordenskiöld. Traveling from west to east, the *Vega* was forced by ice conditions to winter at Kolyuchin Bay, just short of the Bering Strait, and completed the passage the following spring. The first Russian traverse of the passage was not achieved until 1914–15 by the Arctic Ocean Hydrographic Expedition of 1910–15. Two small ice-breaking steamers, *Taymyr* and *Vaygach*, built expressly for the expedition at St. Petersburg in 1909, made a reconnaissance foray into the Chukchi Sea in the fall of 1910. Over the next three seasons they pushed progressively farther west along the Arctic coast of Siberia, sounding and surveying as they went, and returning each winter to Vladivostok. In 1913 they discovered an archipelago north of the Taymyr Peninsula, which was named Emperor Nicholas II Land (now Severnaya Zemlya). In 1914, under the command of Captain Boris A. Vilkitsky, the two ships set off westward intending to reach Archangel, but they were forced to winter on the west coast of Taymyr and completed the through passage in the summer of 1915.

During that period there had been two private attempts at the Northeast Passage from the west end, both starting in 1912. In one case the *Svyataya Anna*, commanded by Georgy L. Brusilov, was beset in the ice of the Kara Sea and drifted almost due north, then west past the north coasts of Franz Josef Land. There 14 men left it in the spring of 1914 to sledge south to Franz Josef Land. The fate of the ship and of the 10 people still on board is unknown; of those who left the ship, only 2 survived. In the other case, that of the geologist Vladimir A. Rusanov, the expedition vessel, *Gerkules*, entered the Kara Sea around the north end of Novaya Zemlya late in the season in 1912. None of the 11 members of the expedition survived, and remains have been found along the southeastern shores of the Kara Sea.

The first attempt at the passage mounted by the Soviet regime came in 1932. The ice-breaking steamer *Sibiryakov* (originally the Newfoundland sealing steamer *Bellaventure*) attempted the passage from west to east; after rounding the northern tip of Severnaya Zemlya and calling at Tiksi and the mouth of the Kolyma, it lost its propeller in ice just prior to reaching the Bering Strait and finally emerged through the strait under improvised sails. The following season the steamer *Chelyuskin* fared even worse; having almost reached the Bering Strait from the west, it became beset in the ice, was finally crushed, and sank in the Chukchi Sea. The first accident-free, one-season passage of the Northeast Passage was made from west to east by the icebreaker *Fedor Litke* (originally the Canadian icebreaker *Earl Grey*) in 1934. In the following season it escorted the first freighters through the passage in the opposite direction.

Since then, hundreds of vessels have completed the passage in both directions, although through passages represent only a small fraction of the total traffic in Russian Arctic waters, most of which moves between either end of the passage to transshipment ports at the mouths of the major Siberian rivers. A 12-month season has been attained for traffic moving between the west and Dudinka, the major transshipment port at the mouth of the Yenisey. The entire passage—usually called the northern sea route in Russia—is navigable from late June to late November. Since 1991 it has been open to international shipping. Although the experiment has not been repeated since, in 1978 the nuclear-powered icebreaker *Sibir* escorted a freighter from the Atlantic to the Pacific by a high-latitude variant of the Northeast Passage, north of Novaya Zemlya, Severnaya Zemlya, and the New Siberian Islands.

THE NORTHWEST PASSAGE

The search for the Northwest Passage may be said to have begun with the European discovery of America. The voyages of Jacques Cartier and his successors to the St. Lawrence and John Cabot and the brothers Gaspar and Miguel Corte-Real to Newfoundland and Labrador were all undertaken with the aim of finding the passage. The first such voyage to enter the Arctic, however, was that of the English navigator Martin (later Sir Martin) Frobisher in 1576. Frobisher set out with the *Gabriel* and *Michael* and made his North American landfall on the southeast coast of Baffin Island. In the *Gabriel*, Frobisher sailed about 60 miles (100 km) up the long inlet named for him, which he took to be a strait, and brought home a rock sample that was identified wrongly as containing gold. The Northwest Passage was forgotten, and in the next two years Frobisher made two further voyages for the sole purpose of establishing a gold mine. The last voyage was an astonishing enterprise involving 15 ships. The ships, however, were scattered by storms; at least one was sunk; and Frobisher, unable to set up his colony, loaded the remaining ships with ore and returned home, only to find that his cargo was worthless.

Next to seek the passage was another Englishman, John Davis, one of the finest of the early seamen and something of a scientist as well. In three voyages, 1585–87, Davis rediscovered Greenland (lost to Europeans since the decline of the Norse settlements); he visited the southeast coast and sailed up the west coast to beyond Disko Island (latitude 72° N). He also traced the coasts of Baffin Island and Labrador from Cape Dyer south. He explored Cumberland Sound and noted, but did not enter, Frobisher Bay and Hudson Strait.

In 1602 George Weymouth sailed a short way into Hudson Strait, and in 1610 Henry Hudson sailed into Hudson Bay and south to James Bay. Thomas (later Sir Thomas) Button in 1612–13 (with Robert Bylot, a survivor of Hudson's *Discovery* voyage, as pilot) was the first to reach the west coast of Hudson Bay, wintering near the site of York Factory and discovering Roes Welcome Sound; William Baffin, again with Bylot, sailed up the northeast coast of Southampton Island in 1615; Jens Munk, a Dane, wintered at the mouth of the Churchill River in 1619–20, where nearly all his men died of scurvy, only Munk and two others surviving to sail home; and in 1631 Luke Foxe sailed into Foxe Channel.

In the meantime, Baffin, the outstanding navigator of his day, had explored Baffin Bay (1616), but the significance of this exploration was not recognized for 200 years. With Bylot as master of his ship (Hudson's old *Discovery*), Baffin sailed up the west coast of Greenland to the head of Baffin Bay (latitude 78° N) and down the west side of the bay, discovering the three sounds that lead out of it— Smith, Jones, and Lancaster. However, he reported that all three were merely bays and that there was no passage out of Baffin Bay. Further, his map was never published, and in time the very existence of "Baffin's Bay" came to be doubted.

In 1719 James Knight sailed into Hudson Bay with two ships in search of the passage and wintered on Marble

Island, where he built a house. According to Inuit reports, all the men died, although two of them allegedly survived two winters. In 1741 Christopher Middleton also entered the bay with two vessels and wintered at the Hudson's Bay Company's post at Churchill. In the spring of 1742 he coasted north, discovered and explored Wager Bay and Repulse Bay, and then headed for home convinced that there was no Northwest Passage accessible from Hudson Bay. Almost incredibly, his sponsor, Arthur Dobbs, refused to believe this, suspecting that Middleton had found the Northwest Passage but was concealing the evidence, having been bribed to do so by his former employer, the Hudson's Bay Company. Dobbs therefore dispatched a further expedition. In 1746 William Moor and Francis Smith retraced Middleton's route almost exactly; they wintered at York Factory and in the summer of 1747 again probed the northwestern shores of the bay. Their only real addition to knowledge was to discover Chesterfield Inlet and establish that it too was not the entrance to the Northwest Passage.

19TH CENTURY ATTEMPTS AT THE PASSAGE

The end of the Napoleonic Wars had left the British navy relatively unemployed, and the British government, spurred by the enthusiasm of Sir John Barrow, second secretary to the admiralty, was persuaded to equip a series of large naval expeditions for the discovery of the Northwest Passage. The first of them, under John (later Sir John) Ross in 1818, retraced almost exactly Baffin's journey of two centuries earlier and repeated his error of mistaking the sounds for bays. Second in command to Ross was William (later Sir William) Parry. He was not convinced that no sound existed, and in 1819–20, in HMS *Hecla* and *Griper*,

he made a voyage through Lancaster Sound to Melville
Island, where he wintered. Blocked by ice in M'Clure
Strait, he next (1821–23) tried the route through Foxe
Channel, spending two winters in Foxe Basin. Again he
was stopped by ice in the narrow Fury and Hecla Strait
(named for the two ships he used on this expedition). A
number of rather unsuccessful ventures followed. Parry
on a third voyage (1824–25) explored Prince Regent Inlet;
Captain George Francis Lyon and Captain George Back
made unsuccessful attempts to reach Repulse Bay; and
John Ross, on a privately financed venture in 1829–33,
sailed down Prince Regent Inlet into the Gulf of Boothia,
passing by one of the keys to the Northwest Passage, the
narrow Bellot Strait between Somerset Island and the
Boothia Peninsula, the northernmost tip of the North
American continent. The latter expedition added greatly
to the extent of mapped territory, mostly through the
work of Ross's nephew, James (later Sir James) Clark Ross,
who established the position of the North Magnetic Pole
(then in southwestern Boothia Peninsula). After three
winters trapped in the ice, Ross had to abandon his ship,
the *Victory*, and retreat by sledge and boat, spending a
fourth winter on the way before being picked up by a
whaler in Lancaster Sound.

In the meantime, the British were also attacking the
problem from the west by both sea and land. In 1819–22
John (later Sir John) Franklin conducted an overland expe-
dition from the western shore of Hudson Bay to the Arctic
Ocean, surveying part of the coast to about 200 miles (320
km) east of the Coppermine River in northwestern Canada.
On a second overland expedition to the same region
(1825–27), Franklin led a party that explored the North
American coast westward from the mouth of the
Mackenzie River, in northwestern Canada, to Point

Beechey, now in Alaska. There Franklin almost made contact with the survey of Lieutenant Frederick William Beechey, who in 1825–26 reached Point Barrow from the west. These efforts added new knowledge of about 1,200 miles (1,932 km) of the northwest rim of the North American coastline. In 1833–35 Captain George Back discovered the Back River and mapped it to its mouth in Chantrey Inlet, and in 1837–39 Peter Warren Dease and Thomas Simpson, Hudson's Bay Company employees, made three coastal journeys by boat, filling in the gap in the Alaska coastline left by Franklin and joining Franklin's survey to Back's at Chantrey Inlet. In 1847 another Hudson's Bay Company employee, John Rae, joined Parry's Fury and Hecla Strait survey to Ross's survey in the Gulf of Boothia. Rae was a most remarkable traveler, far ahead of his time in adopting Inuit methods and living off the land.

The Franklin Expedition

Most of the continental coastline and a considerable amount of the Canadian Arctic Archipelago had now been charted, and still the Northwest Passage remained elusive. The British government sent out one last expedition: the famous and tragic last voyage of Sir John Franklin, who sailed into Lancaster Sound in 1845 and was never seen again.

Franklin's search for the Northwest Passage began on May 19, 1845, when he sailed from England with two ships, the *Erebus* and the *Terror*, carrying 128 officers and men. The vessels were last sighted by British whalers north of Baffin Island at the entrance to Lancaster Sound in late July. Although no one survived the expedition, a written account of the expedition through April 25, 1848, was found in 1859 that, along with other evidence discovered in both the 19th and 20th centuries, allowed investigators to piece together much of what had happened.

Having ascended the Wellington Channel, in the Queen Elizabeth Islands, to latitude 77° N, the *Erebus* and the *Terror* wintered at Beechey Island (1845–46). Returning southward along the western side of Cornwallis Island, they passed through Peel Sound and Franklin Strait, hitherto unnavigated. In September 1846 they became trapped in the ice in Victoria Strait, off the northern tip of King William Island (about midway between the Atlantic and Pacific oceans). By April 1848, Franklin and 23 others had perished there. The ships, still gripped by ice, were deserted on April 22, 1848, and the 105 survivors tried to head south across the North American mainland to the Back River, apparently resorting to cannibalism along the way. An old Inuit woman told McClintock of how the starving men fell down and died as they walked. Franklin himself never proved the existence of the Northwest Passage, but a small party from his expedition may have reached Simpson Strait, which connected with the western coastal waters previously visited by Franklin. Postmortems conducted on the preserved bodies of several crew members suggest that lead poisoning from eating faultily tinned food may have contributed to the mental and physical decline of the expedition.

The loss of Franklin's expedition produced a reaction of profound shock and resulted in a 12-year search that contributed tremendously to geographic knowledge. At its peak in 1850, as many as 14 ships were in the area at the same time, and a further expedition was at work from the mainland.

Rescue Attempts and Further Exploration

The first to become anxious when no word had been received from Franklin's party was Sir John Richardson, who in 1847–49 conducted a search along the northwest mainland coast, accompanied by John Rae. The first official search parties were sent out in 1848; Sir James Clark Ross, with the *Enterprise* and *Investigator*, was to enter from the east, and Captain Henry Kellett, with the *Herald* and *Plover*, had orders to stand by in the Bering Strait to meet Franklin on his way out. Ross wintered on Somerset Island and traced most of its coastline before returning in 1849 without news. In 1850–51 Captain Horatio Austin wintered with four ships off the south coast of Cornwallis Island, from which base extensive sledge trips traced many miles of coastline. Two more ships, under Captain William Penny, a whaler, were in the same area, as was also Sir John Ross, then 73 but still active. The first U.S. expedition to the Arctic, financed by Henry Grinnell and led by Edwin J. de Haven, sailed in two ships to Wellington Channel. Franklin's winter quarters at Beechey Island were found by Austin's and Penny's expeditions, but no record had been left to point the way from there.

At the same time, in 1850, Captain Richard Collinson was to enter from the west and meet Austin in a pincer movement. His two ships became separated in the Pacific, however, and operated independently. Commander Robert (later Sir Robert) McClure in the *Investigator* discovered Prince of Wales Strait, rounded Banks Island by the west, and entered Mercy Bay on the north coast, where the ship remained frozen in for two years and was finally abandoned. McClure and his men were rescued by another expedition and returned home in 1854 by the eastern route. Thus, he was the first to make the Northwest Passage, though in more than one ship and partly on foot. Collinson in the *Enterprise* spent three years on Victoria Island, reaching Victoria Strait. There he was within a short distance of the place where Franklin's ships had been abandoned, as had also been Rae, traveling by boat two years earlier. Neither found any clues. In 1852 a private expedition financed by Lady Franklin and led by a whaling captain, William Kennedy, discovered Bellot Strait, named for a French volunteer in the search.

After this the search moved north, which was generally thought to be the most likely direction; in 1852 Captain Edward Inglefield in the *Isabel* sailed north up Smith Sound to 78°35′N, and another large expedition, under Sir Edward Belcher and Henry Kellett, sailed into Lancaster Sound with Austin's four ships plus a supply vessel, the *North Star*. Splitting into an eastern and a western party and spending two winters in the Arctic, this expedition mapped many miles of new coastline north of Lancaster Sound, rescued the survivors of McClure's expedition, and then without apparent justification abandoned all four ships in the ice and sailed home in the *North Star*. One ship, the *Resolute*, was found drifting in good condition in Davis Strait in September 1855 by an American whaler, who took the vessel south to New England. The U.S. government purchased the ship, refitted it, and presented it to the British government.

In 1853 an American, Elisha Kane, sailed in the *Advance* to Kane Basin, wintering twice and searching northward to Kennedy Channel. In the same year, Rae was sent by the Hudson's Bay Company to complete the charting of the mainland coast between Chantrey Inlet and Boothia. It was this expedition that brought back the first real news of Franklin's party, obtained by Rae from Inuit in Pelly Bay and backed by identifiable relics. The British government considered the search closed, but Lady Franklin was yet not satisfied; she financed a final expedition in the *Fox* under Captain Francis Leopold McClintock. He traveled around the coasts of King William Island in 1859, finding many bodies and relics of the expedition and also the only record left by it, at Victory Point. Subsequent expeditions, particularly since 1990, have found more human remains and artifacts on King William Island.

TRAVERSES OF THE NORTHWEST PASSAGE SINCE 1900

Thus, the Northwest Passage was at last found to be a reality, and official recognition went to McClure as its discoverer, though Franklin too had proved its existence and should share the honour. An unsuccessful attempt to navigate it was made by Allen Young in the *Pandora* in 1875. In 1903 the great Norwegian explorer Roald Amundsen sailed down Peel Sound in his tiny yacht *Gjöa* and passed around the east side of King William Island, where he spent two winters taking magnetic and other scientific observations. After a third winter spent west of the Mackenzie, he passed through the Bering Strait in 1906, becoming the first to navigate the Northwest Passage. It was navigated again in 1940–42 and 1944 by Henry A. Larsen of the Royal Canadian Mounted Police in the *St. Roch*, west-east by way of Bellot Strait and east-west in one season by Prince of Wales Strait. In 1954 the first passage by a deep-draught vessel was made by HMCS *Labrador*, a Canadian naval icebreaker. In 1969 the *Manhattan*, the largest and most powerful commercial ship ever built in the United States to that time, smashed through some 650 miles (1,050 km) of ice between Baffin Bay and Point Barrow, Alaska, to assess the commercial feasibility of the passage. Some tours are now conducted through all or sections of the Northwest Passage, but it has not been used as a regular commercial route.

THE NORTH POLE

The North Pole did not become in itself a goal of exploration until the 17th century. Early expeditions that tried to reach the pole were looking for a polar route to the East rather than for the pole itself. After Hudson's first attempt in 1607, nearly two centuries elapsed before the next one. The initiator of this attempt was Mikhail Vasilyevich Lomonosov, who, like so many others at the time (and for the following 100 years), firmly believed in the existence of an open polar sea. Implementing Lomonosov's plan, in 1764 the Russian Admiralty dispatched an expedition to establish an advance base at Bellsund in Svalbard under the command of Vasily Yakovlevich Chichagov. The next year, with three ships, Chichagov pushed north to latitude 80°26' N before being forced by ice to retreat. Seven years later Captain John Constantine Phipps of the Royal Navy, in two ships, *Racehorse* and *Carcass*, tried to reach the pole from the same starting point but fared no better. In 1818 David Buchan and John Franklin in *Dorothea* and *Trent* were no more successful.

All these attempts had been in the area between Greenland and Svalbard, which actually was not the accessible route to the Arctic Ocean that it appeared to be, owing to the strong southerly drift of the ice. The Franklin search opened a new route, up the west coast of Greenland. In 1860 American Isaac Israel Hayes attempted to reach the pole by this route in the schooner *United States*. Hayes was a firm believer that the polar sea was ice-free and that it could be reached by breaking through the fringing belt of pack ice. Ironically, he met with unusually heavy ice conditions and got only as far as Etah on the coast of Smith Sound. In 1871 Charles Francis Hall, another American, with more luck and a better ship, reached 82°11' N and charted both sides of the channel to its northern end at the entrance to the Lincoln Sea. Hall himself died during the winter, and his ship, the *Polaris*, was caught in the ice on the voyage south and drifted to Smith Sound, where it was almost wrecked. A party of 19, including an Inuit mother with a two-month-old baby, became separated from the ship and drifted all winter on an ice floe before being picked up by a whaler off the coast of Labrador in April 1873.

In 1875–76 a British expedition under Captain George Strong Nares in the *Alert* and *Discovery* reached the Lincoln Sea by ship, the *Alert* wintering near Cape Sheridan on the north coast of Ellesmere Island and the *Discovery* farther south at Lady Franklin Bay. Sledge parties in the spring traced the coasts of Ellesmere Island and Greenland to Yelverton Bay and Sherard Osborn Fjord, respectively, and one, under Cdr. Albert Hastings Markham, reached 83°20′N over the pack ice, a new record northing.

In the meantime, the Svalbard route was not neglected. In 1869–70 a German expedition under Karl Koldewey in the *Germania* sailed up the east coast of Greenland to 72°30′N and traced it by sledge to Cape Bismarck. A second ship, the *Hansa*, became separated and was crushed in the ice, and the crew drifted south on a floe around Cape Farewell, reaching the settlement of Frederiksdal in safety. Baron Nordenskiöld made two journeys toward the pole from Svalbard, in 1868 by ship and in 1873 by reindeer sledge.

THE *FRAM* EXPEDITION

An entirely new approach was tried in 1879 by a U.S. expedition in the *Jeannette*, led by George Washington De Long. In the belief that Wrangel Island was a large landmass stretching far to the north, De Long hoped to sail north as far as possible along its coast and then sledge to the pole, but his ship was caught in the ice near Herald Island and drifted west for 22 months, passing north of Wrangel Island and revealing its limited extent. The *Jeannette* sank near the New Siberian Islands, and the crew traveled by boat and sledge to the Lena River delta, where many of them died, including De Long himself. A search expedition under Robert Mallary Berry surveyed Wrangel Island in 1881.

Wreckage from the *Jeannette* was found later on the southwest coast of Greenland, having apparently drifted right across the Arctic Ocean. Norwegian explorer Fridtjof Nansen conceived the daring idea that a ship might be made to do the same, thus providing a base for scientific investigation of the Arctic Ocean and incidentally a means of reaching the pole. In 1890 Nansen presented his idea before the Norwegian Geographical Society. Having collected evidence showing that the ice of the polar sea drifted from Siberia toward Spitsbergen, he proposed to build a ship of such a shape that it would be lifted but not crushed when caught by the ice. He proposed to let this ship "freeze in" off eastern Siberia in order to be carried from there across the Arctic Ocean to Spitsbergen by the currents. Though his plan was severely criticized by contemporary Arctic explorers, the necessary funding was raised. His ship, *Fram* ("Forward"), was built according to his ideas.

With a complement of 13 men, the *Fram* sailed from Kristiania (Oslo) on June 24, 1893. On September 22 it was enclosed by the ice at latitude 78°50′ N, longitude 133°37′ E; it froze in, and the long drift began. The ship bore the pressure of the ice perfectly. On March 14, 1895, Nansen, being satisfied that the *Fram* would continue to drift safely, left it in 84°4′ N, 102°27′ E, and started northward with dogsleds and kayaks, accompanied by Hjalmar Johansen. On April 8 they turned back from 86°14′ N, the highest latitude then yet reached by humans, and headed toward Franz Josef Land. As they approached the northern islands, progress was hampered by open water and, because of the advanced season, they wintered on Frederick Jackson Island (named by Nansen for the British Arctic explorer), where they stayed from Aug. 26, 1895, to May 19, 1896.

FRIDTJOF NANSEN

Fridtjof Nansen (1861–1930) first attained fame as an explorer, although scientific work (zoology, and later, oceanography) was always closest to his heart, and he became equally renowned as a statesman and humanitarian. In 1882, when he joined the crew of a sealing ship for a voyage to the Greenland waters, he saw the Greenland ice cap, and it occurred to him that it ought to be possible to cross it. Gradually he developed a plan, which he announced in 1887. Instead of starting from the inhabited west coast, he would start from the east coast and, by cutting off his means of retreat, would force himself to go forward. The expedition of six from Norway started the crossing on Aug. 15, 1888. After enduring storms and intense cold, they reached the highest point of the journey (8,920 feet [2,719 metres]) on September 5 and struck the west coast at Ameralik fjord on September 26. They were forced to winter at the settlement of Godthåb (Nuuk), where Nansen took the opportunity to study the Inuit there. The party returned home in triumph in May 1889.

Likewise, after Nansen had rejoined his companions onboard the *Fram* in 1896, they were given a rousing welcome, which reached its climax on their arrival in Kristiania on September 9. His two-volume account of the expedition, *Fram over Polhavet* (*Farthest North*), appeared in 1897. In 1900 he joined a cruise in the Norwegian Sea and in 1910 made a cruise through the northeastern North Atlantic. In 1912 he visited the Spitsbergen waters onboard his own yacht, and two years later he joined an oceanographic cruise to the Azores. In 1913, Nansen traveled through the Barents Sea and the Kara Sea to the mouth of the Yenisey River and back through Siberia. His lasting contributions to oceanography comprise improvement and design of instruments, explanation of the wind-driven currents of the seas, discussions of the waters of the Arctic, and explanation of the manner in which deep- and bottom-water is formed.

After 1900 Nansen became increasingly involved with international diplomacy and relief work. Shortly after the end of World War I (1914–18), he supervised the repatriation of troops from the former German and Austria-Hungary armies. In 1921, he directed famine-relief efforts in Russia. For these efforts, he was awarded the Nobel Prize for Peace in 1922.

They built a hut of stone and covered it with a roof of walrus hides and lived during the winter mainly on polar bear and walrus meat, using the blubber as fuel.

On their way to Spitsbergen the two explorers were lucky enough to encounter Frederick Jackson and his party of the Jackson-Harmsworth expedition, on June 17, and returned to Norway in his ship *Windward*, reaching Vardø on August 13. The *Fram* also reached Norway safely, having drifted north to 85°57′ and collected a formidable amount of scientific data. Jackson had been investigating Franz Josef Land as a possible stepping-stone to the pole but, on hearing Nansen's account, gave up the polar attempt. In his three-year stay (1894–97), however, Jackson revolutionized the map of this complicated collection of islands and did a great deal of valuable work.

THE RACE FOR THE POLE

Until the end of the 19th century, the desire to reach the pole had been coupled with that of mapping unexplored territory and collecting scientific data; after the *Fram* expedition there was no longer any doubt that the central part of the polar basin was an ice-covered sea and that any land still to be discovered would be peripheral. The race for the pole then degenerated into an international sporting event. Several expeditions, following in Jackson's footsteps, tried to reach the pole from Franz Josef Land. Three were American: Walter Wellman in 1898–99, the Baldwin-Ziegler expedition in 1901–02, and the Fiala-Ziegler expedition in 1903–06. An Italian expedition led by the duke d'Abruzzi set a new record in 1900, when Captain Umberto Cagni reached latitude 86°34′ N.

Peary's and Cook's Rival Claims

American Arctic explorer Robert E. Peary (1856–1920) traditionally has been credited with leading the first expedition to reach the North Pole (1909). Another American, physician and explorer Frederick A. Cook (1865–1940), claimed that he had discovered the North Pole in 1908; this was denounced by Peary.

Peary entered the U.S. Navy in 1881 and pursued a naval career until his retirement, with leaves of absence granted for Arctic exploration. In 1886, with his associate Matthew Henson, he traveled inland from Disko Bay over the Greenland ice sheet for 100 miles (161 km), reaching a point some 7,500 feet (2,287.5 metres) above sea level. In 1891 Peary returned to Greenland with seven companions, including his wife and Cook, who in 1909 would claim to have reached the North Pole before Peary. On this expedition Peary sledged 1,300 miles (2,100 km) to northeastern Greenland, discovered Independence Fjord, and found evidence of Greenland's being an island. He also studied the "Arctic Highlanders," an isolated Inuit tribe who helped him greatly on later expeditions.

Robert E. Peary dressed in polar expedition gear aboard the Roosevelt.
Library of Congress, Washington, D.C.

During his expedition of 1893–94 Peary again sledged to northeastern Greenland—this time in his first attempt to reach the North Pole. On summer trips in 1895 and 1896 he was mainly occupied in transporting masses of meteoric iron from Greenland to the United States. Between 1898 and 1902 he reconnoitred routes to the pole from Etah, in Inglefield Land, northwestern Greenland, and from Fort Conger, Ellesmere Island, in the Canadian Northwest Territories. On a second attempt to reach the pole he was provided with a ship built to his specifications, the *Roosevelt*, which he sailed to Cape Sheridan, Ellesmere Island, in 1905. But the sledging season was unsuccessful owing to adverse weather and ice conditions, and his party reached only latitude 87°06′N. Peary returned to Ellesmere in 1908 for his third attempt and early the following March left Cape Columbia on his successful journey to the pole. On the last stage of the trek he was accompanied by Henson and four Inuit. Peary and his companions purportedly reached the North Pole on April 6, 1909. Peary returned to civilization only to discover that his former colleague, Cook, was claiming to have reached the North Pole independently in April 1908. Cook's claim, though subsequently discredited, marred Peary's enjoyment of his triumph. In 1911 Peary retired from the navy with the rank of rear admiral. His published works include *Northward over the "Great Ice"* (1898), *The North Pole* (1910), and *Secrets of Polar Travel* (1917).

Peary's claim to have reached the North Pole was almost universally accepted, but in the 1980s the examination of his 1908–09 expedition diary and other documents newly released cast doubt on whether he had actually reached the pole. Through a combination of navigational mistakes and record-keeping errors, Peary may actually have advanced only to a point 30–60 miles (50–100 km) short of the pole. The truth remains uncertain.

MATTHEW HENSON

African American explorer Matthew Henson (1866–1955) accompanied Robert E. Peary on most of his expeditions, including the famous one in 1909 that traditionally is believed to have reached the North Pole.

Orphaned as a youth, Henson went to sea at the age of 12 as a cabin boy on the sailing ship *Katie Hines*. Later, while working in a store in Washington, D.C., he met Peary, who hired him as a valet for his next expedition to Nicaragua (1888). Peary, impressed with Henson's ability and resourcefulness, employed him as an attendant on his seven subsequent expeditions to the Arctic (1891–92; 1893–95; 1896; 1897; 1898–1902; 1905–06; 1908–09). In 1909 Peary and Henson, accompanied by four Inuit, made their dash for the pole. Henson's account of the journey, *A Negro Explorer at the North Pole*, appeared in 1912. The following year, by order of Pres. William Howard Taft, Henson was appointed a clerk in the U.S. Customs House in New York City, a post he held until his retirement in 1936. Henson received the Congressional medal awarded all members of the Peary expedition (1944).

Cook began practicing medicine after graduating from New York University in 1890. He soon achieved fame as an explorer, serving as surgeon on Peary's first Arctic expedition (1891–92) and leading others to explore and climb Mount McKinley (1903–06). Cook's claim that he had reached the North Pole on an expedition in 1908 was immediately disputed by Peary. Cook's Inuit companions on his journey later asserted that he had stopped short hundreds of miles south of the Pole, and that the photographs of his expedition were actually shot at locations far distant from the North Pole. The controversy between Cook and Peary lasted until World War I, after which time public support for Cook's claim disappeared.

Land and Sea Attempts after Peary and Cook

In part inspired by the weakness of Peary's and Cook's rival claims, the Russian naval officer Georgy I. Sedov mounted an expedition aiming for the pole in 1912 aboard *Svyatoy Foka*. The expedition, blocked by ice in the Barents Sea, wintered on the northwest coast of Novaya Zemlya and reached Franz Josef Land only in 1913. Sedov made a forlorn attempt at sledging to the pole from a base at Tikhaya Bay in the southern part of Franz Josef Land in 1914, but he died before even reaching the northern tip of the archipelago.

The first surface expedition confirmed as having reached the pole was an American effort under Ralph Plaisted, which reached it from northern Ellesmere Island by snowmobile in 1968 (the team was airlifted off the ice-cap). The following year the British Transarctic Expedition, led by Wally Herbert, was the first to reach the pole by dog team while en route from Point Barrow, Alaska, across the pole to Svalbard. The first ships to visit the pole were the U.S. nuclear submarines *Nautilus* (1958), which remained submerged, and *Skate* (1959), which surfaced through the ice. The first surface vessel to reach the pole was the Soviet nuclear icebreaker *Arktika*, which in 1977 approached from the direction of the New Siberian Islands. The first landing made by an aircraft at (or near) the pole was by the Soviet pilot Mikhail Vasilevich Vodopyanov when he deposited Ivan Dmitrievich Papanin's party at the start of the drift of the first Soviet drifting station, North Pole I, in 1937.

Byrd's Polar Flight

The first attempt to fly to the pole was made in 1897, when the Swedish scientist Salomon August Andrée and two companions left Spitsbergen in a balloon. They did not return, and their fate did not become known until 1930, when their bodies and diaries were found on Kvit Island. In 1909 Walter Wellman made an unsuccessful attempt by dirigible, and in 1925 Roald Amundsen, with two Dornier-Wal flying boats, reached 87°44′ N.

American Richard E. Byrd's experience of flying over sea ice and glaciers in western Greenland in 1924 had inspired him to attempt a flight over the pole. On May 9, 1926, Byrd, acting as navigator, and Floyd Bennett as pilot made what they claimed to be the first airplane journey over the North Pole, flying from King's Bay, Spitsbergen, Nor., to the Pole and back. The flight lasted 15 1/2 hours, with no mishaps beyond an oil leak from the starboard engine of their Fokker trimotor airplane. For this feat they were both awarded the U.S. Congressional Medal of Honor and were acclaimed as national heroes. Some doubt always lingered over whether their plane had actually reached the North Pole, and one of Byrd's early associates, Bernt Balchen, even claimed after Byrd's death that the flight to the North Pole had been a hoax. The discovery in 1996 of the diary that Byrd had kept on his famous flight shed new light on this question. Byrd's diary entries suggest that the airplane was still about 150 miles (240 km) short of the North Pole when Byrd decided to turn back because of his concern over the oil leak. Three days later, on May 12, Roald Amundsen, with Lincoln Ellsworth and Umberto Nobile, set off from the same base in a semirigid airship and, in a well-documented journey, flew across the pole to Alaska, thus becoming

NAUTILUS AND SKATE

The name *Nautilus* was chosen for the U.S. Navy vessel launched Jan. 21, 1954, as the first submarine capable of prolonged, instead of temporary, submersion. Powered by propulsion turbines that were driven by steam produced by a nuclear reactor, the *Nautilus* was capable of traveling submerged at speeds in excess of 20 knots and furthermore could maintain such a speed almost indefinitely. Much larger than the diesel-electric submarines used during World War II, the *Nautilus* was 319 feet (97 metres) long and displaced 3,180 tons. On Aug. 1–5, 1958, the *Nautilus* made a historic underwater cruise from Point Barrow, Alaska, to the Greenland Sea, passing completely beneath the thick ice cap of the North Pole. The *Nautilus* set many standards for future nuclear submarines, including extensive protection against possible radiation contamination and auxiliary diesel-electric power. The vessel was decommissioned in 1980 and went on exhibit, beginning in 1985, at the USS *Nautilus* Memorial and Submarine Force Museum in New London, Conn.

The *Skate* was the first production-model nuclear-powered attack submarine of the U.S. Navy. Launched and commissioned in 1957, it was similar to the *Nautilus* but smaller, displacing only 2,360 tons. Like the *Nautilus*, the *Skate* and the three other boats in its class incorporated nuclear propulsion into a streamlined "Guppy"-style hull that had been adapted from advanced German designs of World War II. This combination enabled them to maintain underwater speeds in excess of 20 knots indefinitely. In addition to being one of the first vessels to surface at the North Pole, the *Skate* was the first submarine to make a completely submerged transatlantic crossing, in 1958. It was decommissioned in 1986.

the first to definitively reach the pole as well as the first
to traverse the polar region.

SCIENTIFIC EXPLORATION

An important secondary motive in much of the exploration so far discussed was pure scientific curiosity, the desire
to add to the general store of knowledge of the world. In
1875 German Explorer Karl Weyprecht made an important proposal for international cooperation in collecting
scientific data, and the suggestion led to the establishment of the first International Polar Year, 1882–83, during
which stations throughout the Arctic took observations
and pooled the results. The countries participating
were Norway, Sweden, Denmark, Finland, Russia, The
Netherlands, Germany, Austria, the United States, and
Great Britain. The 11 stations, reading eastward from
Svalbard, were Isfjord (Ice Fjord), Svalbard; Bossekop,
north Norway; Sodankylä, Finland; west coast of Novaya
Zemlya; Sagastyr Island, Lena Delta; Point Barrow,
Alaska; Great Slave Lake; Lady Franklin Bay, Ellesmere
Island; Cumberland Sound, Baffin Island; Godthåb
(Nuuk), Greenland; and Jan Mayen Island. A Dutch expe-
dition, scheduled to winter at Dikson at the mouth of the
Yenisey River, spent the winter adrift in the ice of the Kara
Sea but nevertheless made a useful scientific contribution.
In 1932–33 a similar pattern was followed by the second
International Polar Year, but with more stations, and the
technique was extended to cover the whole world in
the International Geophysical Year of 1957–58.

SVALBARD

Starting in 1827 a series of expeditions, most of them
Swedish, surveyed the Svalbard archipelago and studied

the islands' geology and natural history. Among those who carried out this work were Balthazar Mathias Keilhau, Otto Torell, and Baron Nordenskiöld. Sir Martin Conway crossed the interior of Spitsbergen in 1896–97, and in 1898 Alfred Gabriel Nathorst explored the east coast and adjacent islands. Oceanographic and other work was done by the Dutch in the *Willem Barents* after 1878, by the prince of Monaco and William Spiers Bruce (1898–1914), and by the Russian admiral Stepan Osipovich Makarov in the icebreaker *Yermak* (1899). Coal mining was begun in Isfjord at the turn of the 20th century, and this led to further survey activity by Norwegian government expeditions and others. In 1924 a British expedition from the University of Oxford under George Binney was the first scientific expedition to make extensive use of an aircraft.

THE RUSSIAN ARCTIC

Between 1821 and 1824 Fyodor Petrovich Litke of the Russian navy made four voyages to Novaya Zemlya, surveying the west coast and improving the mapping of Matochkin Shar Strait and the White Sea coast, and in 1832–35 Pyotr Kuzmich Pakhtusov surveyed much of the east coast of Novaya Zemlya. In 1880 the Englishman Leigh Smith made the first of two voyages to Franz Josef Land and was the first to sail a ship there under its own power. On his second voyage his ship, the *Eira*, was nipped by ice and sank. Smith built a hut on the shore and wintered there, surveying the south coast and collecting scientific data. In the spring the party sailed to Novaya Zemlya in small boats. In 1886 and again in 1893 and 1900–02, Baron Eduard von Toll, a Russian explorer, worked in the New Siberian Islands. On the last of these expeditions, he and his men made useful contributions to the exploration and mapping of the northwest coast of

the Taymyr Peninsula and of the New Siberian Islands
from the successive wintering sites of their ship, *Zarya*.
Toll perished in an attempt to find Sannikov Land, an
island reported north of the New Siberian Islands, which,
like many similar "lands" in the Arctic, probably does not
exist. Some coordinated hydrographic work was done by
the Russians in the Barents Sea from 1898 to 1908, in the
Kara Sea from 1894 to 1904, and east of Cape Chelyuskin
from 1910 to 1915. The major contribution of the Russian
navy's icebreakers *Taymyr* and *Vaygach* was the discovery
of Severnaya Zemlya in 1913, but they also discovered
Zhokov Island (in the De Long Islands), surveyed hundreds of miles of coastline, and completed thousands of
miles of sounding traverses between 1910 and 1915.

In 1918 Roald Amundsen set out in the *Maud* to emu-
late Fridtjof Nansen's drift in the *Fram* but with the hope
of getting into a more northerly latitude by starting the
drift nearer to Bering Strait. He took three seasons to sail
east through the Northeast Passage, and it was not until
1922 that the *Maud* began its drift, under the scientific
leadership of Harald Ulrik Sverdrup. In two years it was
carried back to the New Siberian Islands, duplicating the
path of the *Jeannette* rather than the *Fram*, but useful scientific work was done throughout both phases of the
expedition.

After the Russian Revolution in 1917, the scale and
scope of exploration increased greatly as part of the work
of developing the northern sea route. Polar stations, of
which five already existed in 1917, increased in number,
providing meteorologic, ice reconnaissance, and radio
facilities. By 1932 there were 24 stations, by 1948 about 80,
and by the 1970s more than 100. The use of icebreakers
and, later, aircraft as platforms for scientific work was
developed. In 1929 and 1930 the icebreaker *Sedov* carried
groups of scientists to Franz Josef Land and also to

Severnaya Zemlya, the last major piece of unsurveyed territory in the Soviet Arctic; the archipelago was completely mapped under Georgy Alekseyevich Ushakov between 1930 and 1932.

The one-season voyage of the *Sibiryakov* through the passage in 1932 accomplished much scientific work and was the first to use the route north of Severnaya Zemlya. It gave a further stimulus to developing the sea route, and icebreaker operations to study sea and ice became annual. Particularly worth noting are three cruises of the *Sadko*, which went farther north than most. In 1935 and 1936 the last unexplored areas in the northern Kara Sea were examined and the little Ushakova Island discovered; and in 1937 the ship was caught in the ice with two others and forced to winter in the Laptev Sea, adding valuable winter observations to the usual summer ones.

GREENLAND

Greenland has received a great deal of study. The west and north coasts became fairly well known during the 19th century. The east coast was less easily explored because of severe ice conditions that make it hard to approach by ship. In 1806–13 Karl Ludwig Giesecke, a German mineralogist, used the native umiak (a kayaklike boat) to study the southeast coast, and so did Lieutenant Wilhelm A. Graah in 1829–30. In 1823 Capts. Douglas Clavering and Edward Sabine, following in the steps of William Scoresby the year before, carried the survey north to latitude 76° N and took pendulum observations. In 1876 the Danish Committee for the Geographical and Geological Investigation of Greenland was formed, and since then a consistent program of research has been carried out. The gaps in the southeast coast were filled in by naval expeditions under L.A. Mourier (1879), Gustav Holm (1883 and

1885), and C.H. Ryder (1891–92), and the rest by Lt. G.C.
Amdrup in the *Antarctica* (1898–1900), the duke d'Orléans
in the *Belgica* (1905), and Ludvig Mylius-Erichsen in the
Danmark (1906–08). On the latter expedition, long
sledge journeys by J.P. Koch and Mylius-Erichsen traced
the entire northeast corner of the island, but Mylius-
Erichsen and two companions were lost. The last details
were recorded in 1910–12 by Ejnar Mikkelsen, who traced
the route followed by Mylius-Erichsen and his companions and found their records. A series of expeditions,
known as the Thule Expeditions because they were based
on the little trading settlement of Thule (Dundas) in
northwestern Greenland, did considerable work in north
Greenland between 1912 and 1921 under Knud Rasmussen
and Lauge Koch.

The Greenland ice cap presented a formidable barrier
to travelers and at the same time a challenge to both
adventurer and scientist. Early attempts to penetrate it
from the west coast settlements were made by Edward
Whymper in 1867, by Baron Nordenskiöld in 1870 and
1883, by J.A.D. Jensen in 1878, and by Robert E. Peary in
1886. Peary, the most successful, penetrated 100 miles (160
km) from the coast. In 1888 Fridtjof Nansen with five companions, using snowshoes and skis, crossed the ice cap
from 64°23′ N on the east coast to Godthåb on the west.
Peary was the first to cross the northern part, from
Inglefield Gulf to Independence Fjord in 1892. Other
crossings were made by Knud Rasmussen and by A. de
Quervain in 1912, by J.P. Koch in 1913, by Lauge Koch in
1921, and by others.

In 1930–31 three simultaneous but independent expeditions maintained stations on the ice cap throughout
the winter, securing meteorologic data vital to the study
of world air circulation. They were the British Arctic
Air Route Expedition led by H.G. Watkins, the German

Greenland Expedition under Alfred Wegener, and the University of Michigan Expedition under W.H. Hobbs. After World War II this work was continued on a larger scale by the French explorer Paul Emile Victor (1947–53) and the British North Greenland Expedition under Commander C.J.W. Simpson (1952–54). Since 1950 numerous core samples have been taken from the Greenland ice cap and used to study climatic changes over tens of thousands of years. Two of the deepest, drilled in 1989–92 and 1996–2003, have exceeded depths of 9,800 feet (3,000 metres), the latter reaching 10,121 feet (3,085 metres).

THE NORTH AMERICAN ARCTIC

By the beginning of the first Polar Year in 1882, most of the coastlines of the North American Arctic were known except for the islands west of Ellesmere Island and the south and west coasts of Ellesmere itself. The U.S. Polar Year station at Lady Franklin Bay, in addition to its scientific program, explored a considerable amount of new terrain on Ellesmere Island and reached 83°24' N on the north coast of Greenland, a record northing at the time. Led by Lt. Adolphus Washington Greely, the expedition set up its station, Fort Conger, in 1881. In 1883, as no supply vessel had arrived, Greely started south in five small boats, according to instruction, and reached Cape Sabine in Smith Sound. There a quite inadequate depot awaited him, together with a record to the effect that the supply ship *Proteus* had sunk in Kane Basin. After a terrible winter, the survivors—7 from an expedition of 25—were rescued by Captain Winfield Scott Schley aboard the *Thetis*.

Three earlier expeditions by Americans in search of Sir John Franklin's records are worth noting. Charles Francis Hall, having failed in a plan to reach King William Island by boat from Baffin Island, spent the years 1860–62

in Frobisher Bay, which only then, three centuries after
its discovery, was proved not to be a strait; he found interesting relics of Martin Frobisher's visits. From 1864 to
1869 Hall lived among the Inuit at Repulse Bay and made
an overland trip to the south coast of King William Island.
In 1878 Lt. Frederick Schwatka traveled overland from
Hudson Bay and made the first summer search in the
area, returning by a remarkable winter journey to Hudson
Bay. Franklin's scientific records were not found, nor have
any been discovered on subsequent attempts. Further
exploration of the interior was carried out by the
Geological Survey of Canada, notably by the journeys of
Joseph B. Tyrrell, Albert P. Low, and Robert Bell. Between
1884 and 1897 four Canadian-government expeditions
studied conditions in Hudson Strait and Hudson Bay
with a view to establishing a sea route, and after 1903 a
series of voyages into the archipelago by Low and Capt.
Joseph-Elzéar Bernier visited many of the islands and
did some survey and geologic work. Two Germans—
anthropologist Franz Boas (in 1883–84) and Bernhardt
Hantzsch (in 1909–11)—contributed to the geography of
Baffin Island.

In 1898–1902 a Norwegian scientific expedition in the
Fram under Otto Sverdrup did a tremendous amount of
work in south and west Ellesmere Island and north Devon
Island and discovered three islands to the west—Axel
Heiberg Island and the Ringnes Islands. The last gaps in
the outline of Ellesmere Island were filled in by Walter
Elmer Ekblaw, a geologist and botanist with the Crocker
Land Expedition (1913–17) under Donald Baxter MacMillan.
Crocker Land, which Peary in 1906 had conjectured to be
north of Axel Heiberg Island, proved to be nonexistent;
MacMillan failed to find it in a 200-mile (320-km) journey
over the ice.

The last large-scale expedition in the old tradition in the North American Arctic was the Canadian Arctic Expedition, 1913–18, led by Vilhjalmur Stefansson. It was divided into two parties, of which the southern one, under Rudolf Martin Anderson, did survey and scientific work on the north mainland coast from Alaska to Coronation Gulf and in southern Victoria Island, while the northern traveled extensively in the northwest, discovering the last remaining islands in that area. Stefansson, a magnificent hunter, successfully adopted Inuit methods and was able to travel long distances by living off the land, avoiding the necessity of carrying large quantities of supplies. In 1921–24 the fifth Danish Thule Expedition under Rasmussen worked in Melville Peninsula and Baffin Island, and Rasmussen journeyed overland to King William Island and on to Alaska, studying the Inuit. In the 1930s a number of British expeditions under Noel Humphreys, J.M. Wordie, and T.H. Manning worked in the Canadian Arctic. Manning completed the mapping of the west coast of Baffin Island, the last major gap on the map of Canada. The last new land, however, was not added until 1948, when a Royal Canadian Air Force photo-survey aircraft found three islands in Foxe Basin—one of them, Prince Charles Island, about 3,500 square miles (9,100 square km) in area.

The exploration of Alaska after its purchase by the United States in 1867 proceeded slowly at first but later at a rapid speed. Coastal surveys by the Coast and Geodetic Survey were started immediately; among others, inland journeys were made by I. Petrof (1880); by Frederick Schwatka (1883) and H.T. Allen (1885), both of the U.S. cavalry; and by G.M. Stoney, U.S. Navy (1883–85), one of whose party made the first overland journey to Point Barrow. After the Yukon gold strike of 1897, the U.S. Geological Survey began a large-scale systematic study of all Alaska that has continued along with work in other fields of natural science. Outstanding in the early days of the project were A.H. Brooks, chief geologist of the Geological Survey in Alaska, 1903–17, and E. de K. Leffingwell, who worked on the North Coastal Plain between 1906 and 1914.

THE ARCTIC OCEAN

It is a comment on the unimportance of the North Pole as an incentive to exploration that hardly any of the real exploration of the Arctic Ocean can be credited to the pole seekers. The great exception is Nansen, whose work in the *Fram* stood alone until the 1930s. Although Nansen made a bid to reach the pole, his primary aim was rather to study the waters and bottom contours of the Arctic Ocean and the drift of the ice and to find out whether there were new lands still to be discovered in the centre of the polar basin. In accord with popular opinion, Nansen expected to find only shallow water in the North Polar Basin. In reality, soundings gave depths ranging from about 11,000 to 13,000 feet (3,300 to 4,000 metres), which showed that there was a deep basin under at least part of the North Polar Sea. These deep soundings mark the true discovery of the Arctic Ocean.

The advent of the airplane revolutionized exploration techniques. Following the polar flights of Byrd and Amundsen, George Hubert (later Sir Hubert) Wilkins and Carl Ben Eielson made the first flight by airplane across the Arctic Ocean in 1928, from Point Barrow to Svalbard, and in 1937 two long-distance transpolar flights were made by Soviet flyers, Valery Pavlovich Chkalov and Mikhail Mikhailovich Gromov. A third Soviet flight in the same year made a large but tragic contribution to exploration. A four-engined aircraft piloted by Sigizmund Aleksandrovich Levanevsky disappeared in the Arctic Ocean and set in motion a large-scale, though unsuccessful, search that covered vast areas hitherto unexplored and added tremendously to flying experience.

Also in 1937 the Soviet Union set up the first floating scientific station, using four-engined aircraft based on Franz Josef Land to land a four-man party under Papanin at the North Pole in late May. The station, now known as North Pole 1, drifted south for nine months and was taken off its melting ice floe in the Greenland Sea. In the same year, the icebreaker *Georgy Sedov* (originally *Beothic*), under the command of Konstantin Sergeyevich Badigin, was caught in the ice in the Laptev Sea and began a 27-month drift across the Arctic basin that almost duplicated that of the *Fram* and yielded useful comparative data. In 1941 an aircraft carrying a team of scientists made three landings on the ice at about 80° N, 175° E.

After World War II, scientific work in the Arctic Ocean increased greatly; today there remain no unexplored areas. After 1947 the United States carried out routine weather-reporting flights over the Arctic Ocean from Alaska and used icebreakers and aircraft to conduct oceanographic work in the Beaufort Sea. In 1952 a weather station was established on the ice island T-3; it was maintained for two years and was reoccupied briefly in 1955 and on a more permanent basis as an International Geophysical Year station in 1957. From that time there was continuous occupation of stations, usually two at any given time.

The Russians explored the Arctic Ocean on a large scale by means of floating scientific stations and extensive airborne expeditions that made numerous landings on the ice to take observations. Station North Pole 2 was established in 1950 north of Wrangel Island and was maintained for one year. After 1954 a continuous succession of stations, generally two at a time, were each occupied for one or two years or longer, until they drifted into a region where they either ceased to be of interest or joined the drift to the Greenland Sea. The last of these, North Pole 31, operated from 1988 to 1991.

The discovery phase of Arctic exploration is over; there is no longer any possibility of finding new lands. Photo surveys have provided reasonably accurate maps, and improved aircraft and base facilities are making the once formidable "frigid zone" increasingly accessible. Commercial aircraft routinely fly across or near the North Pole. The bed of the Arctic Ocean has been the subject of increasingly intensive studies since 1970. For example, it was one of many objectives of the Arctic Ice Dynamics Joint Experiment (AIDJEX), a collaborative effort between Canadian and American scientists. After several pilot projects, during the main experiment in 1975 four manned stations drifted for 15 months in the Beaufort Sea. Subsequently, the nature and configuration of the seabed was the main objective of two multidisciplinary Canadian expeditions, which involved the establishment and occupation of temporary stations on the sea ice in locations chosen so that the drift of the ice would take them across features on the seabed of particular interest. These were LOREX 79 (Lomonosov Ridge Experiment, 1979) and CESAR 83 (Canadian Expedition to Study the Alpha Ridge), mounted in April–May 1983. More recently, a considerable amount of research has focused on the relationship between the Arctic regions and global warming and climate change. Much of this work has been coordinated by the Arctic System Science program of the U.S. National Science Foundation.

Chapter 6: Exploration of Antarctica

A great many countries, large and small, played important roles in the discovery and exploration of
Antarctica. Who first saw the continent is controversial.
The Russian expedition leader Fabian Gottlieb von
Bellingshausen (1778–1852), the English naval officer
Edward Bransfield (c. 1795–1852), and the American
Nathaniel Palmer (1799–1877) all claim first sightings in
1820. Bellingshausen sighted a shelf edge of continental
ice on January 27; three days later Bransfield caught sight
of land that the British later considered to be a mainland
part of the Antarctic Peninsula; and on November 18
Palmer unequivocally saw the mainland-peninsula side of
Orleans Strait.

About 650 CE, however, long before European geographers of the Middle Ages and the Renaissance were to
conjecture about the mythical Terra Australis, Maori legend tells of a New Zealand Polynesian war canoe, under
the command of one Ui-te-Rangiora, that sailed at least as
far south as the frozen ocean. The legendary vast size of
the continent shrank to nearly its present one when in
1772–75 the Englishman James Cook circumnavigated the
globe in high southern latitude, proving that Terra Australis,
if it existed at all, lay somewhere beyond the ice packs that
he discovered between about latitudes 60° and 70° S.

The period from the 1760s to about 1900 was one
dominated by exploitation of Antarctic and subantarctic
seas, particularly along Scotia Ridge. Sealing vessels of many
nations, principally American and British, but including
Argentine, Australian, South African, New Zealand, German,
and Norwegian, participated in hunting that eventually

led to near extinction of the southern fur seal. Many also hunted whales, and the less profitable whaling industry climaxed in the 1920s following World War I after the decline of sealing. Among the few geographic and scientific expeditions that stand out during this period are those of Bellingshausen in 1819–21; Bransfield in 1819–20; the Frenchman Jules-Sébastien-César Dumont d'Urville (1790–1842) in 1837–40; the American Charles Wilkes (1798–1877) in 1838–42; and the British naval officer James Clark Ross (1800–62) in 1839–43.

VOYAGES OF BELLINGSHAUSEN, BRANSFIELD, AND PALMER

Bellingshausen's journey of 1819–21 was the second expedition to circumnavigate Antarctica but was notable for being the first close-in circumnavigation. Commanding the *Vostok* and *Mirny*, sloops of about 500 tons each, on his Antarctic voyage, he sighted the Antarctic ice sheet (Jan. 27, 1820) and discovered Peter I (Jan. 22, 1821) and Alexander I (January 29), islands in the South Sandwich Island group. These were among the first sightings of land within the Antarctic Circle, thought at first to be part of the mainland. His account of the voyage was translated into English in 1945. The Bellingshausen Sea, an area of the Antarctic waters, was named for him.

Bransfield's British expedition charting part of the Antarctic Peninsula in 1819–20 is believed to have been the first to sight the Antarctic mainland and to chart a portion of it. Master aboard HMS *Andromache* at Valparaiso, Chile, Bransfield was appointed to sail the *Williams* in order to chart the recently sighted South Shetland Islands, which lie near the Antarctic Peninsula. With William Smith, he arrived at the South Shetlands in January 1820, landed on King George Island to take formal possession, and coasted to Deception Island. Turning southward, he sighted and charted "high mountains, covered with snow," possibly Mounts Bransfield and Jacquinot on the Antarctic mainland (Jan. 30, 1820). The charts survive in the hydrographic department of the British Admiralty.

Palmer began explorations of the Cape Horn region and western Antarctic in 1819 and the following year reported a landfall along a stretch of the western coast of Antarctica; he called the area Palmer Land, which has remained its name. Although the reported sightings of Bellingshausen and Bransfield came earlier in 1820, that of Palmer's expedition was the first to be definitively of the mainland. On these and subsequent voyages Palmer discovered the Gerlache Strait and Orleans Channel in Antarctica as well as the South Orkney Islands.

PALMER LAND

The broad southern part of the Antarctic Peninsula, about 400 miles (640 km) east of Peter I Island (in the Bellingshausen Sea), Palmer Land is claimed by Britain as part of the British Antarctic Territory. It is named for its discoverer, Nathaniel Palmer, who led an expedition to Antarctica in 1819–20. Palmer Land is mountainous, attaining elevations varying between 6,600 and 13,800 feet (2,000 and 4,200 metres), and covered by thick glaciers except for its most precipitous peaks and cliffs, some of which form stretches of the coastline along the Weddell Sea. A number of minerals have been identified in Palmer Land, including magnetite, hematite, limonite, chalcopyrite, pyrite, azurite, and traces of gold and silver. The Siple research station (United States) is located in Palmer Land.

VOYAGES OF DUMONT D'URVILLE, WILKES, AND ROSS

Dumont d'Urville, already renowned for his voyage to the South Pacific in 1826–29, set sail in September 1837 from Toulon on a voyage to Antarctica. He hoped to travel beyond the 74°15′ S reached by James Weddell in 1823. After surveying in the Straits of Magellan, d'Urville's ships reached the pack ice at 63°29′ S, 44°47′ W, but they were ill-equipped for ice navigation. Unable to penetrate the pack, they coasted it for some 300 miles (480 km) to the east. Heading westward, they visited the South Orkneys and the South Shetlands and discovered Joinville Island and Louis Philippe Land before scurvy forced them to stop at Talcahuano, Chile. After proceeding across the Pacific to the Fiji and Pelew (now Palau) islands, New Guinea, and Borneo, they returned to the Antarctic, hoping to discover the magnetic pole in the unexplored sector between longitudes 120° and 160° E. In January 1840 they sighted the coast of Adélie Land, south of Australia; naming it for his wife, d'Urville claimed it for France. The expedition returned to France late in 1841.

Charles Wilkes commanded the American naval exploring and surveying expedition of 1838–42 that took him ultimately into the Antarctic Ocean and along the eastern Antarctic coast. There, he reported land at a number of points in the region subsequently known as Wilkes Land. He visited islands in the Pacific, explored the West Coast of the United States, then recrossed the Pacific and reached New York in June 1842, having sailed completely around the world. From 1844 to 1861 he prepared the report of his expedition, writing himself 7 of its 19 volumes.

Prior to his Antarctic expedition of 1839–43, James (later Sir James) Clark Ross participated in a number of

Arctic voyages. On the second Arctic expedition of his uncle, Sir John Ross, he located the north magnetic pole (June 1, 1831). His goal in 1839 was to conduct magnetic observations and to reach the south magnetic pole. Commanding the *Erebus* and *Terror*, he discovered the Ross Sea and Ross Ice Barrier (now called Ross Ice Shelf) in 1841 and, while sailing toward the position assigned to the magnetic pole, also discovered Victoria Land. He wintered at Hobart, Tas., and in November 1841 sailed again for Antarctica. He charted part of the coast of Graham Land and sailed around the Weddell Sea ice. Knighted following his return to England (1843), he published *A Voyage of Discovery and Research in the Southern and Antarctic Regions* in 1847.

ROSS ICE SHELF

The world's largest body of floating ice, the Ross Ice Shelf lies at the head of Ross Sea, an enormous indentation in the continent of Antarctica. The ice shelf lies between about longitudes 155° W and 160° E and about latitudes 78° S and 86° S. The current estimate of its area is about 182,000 square miles (472,000 square km), making it roughly the size of the Yukon Territory in Canada. The shelf has served as an important gateway for explorations of the Antarctic interior, including those carried out by many of the most famous expeditions.

The great white barrier wall of the shelf's front, first seen in 1841 by James Clark Ross, rises in places to 160 or 200 feet (50 or 60 metres) high and stretches about 500 miles (800 km) between fixed "anchor points" on Ross Island to the west and the jutting Edward VII Peninsula on the east. With its immense, gently undulating surface reaching back nearly 600 miles (950 km) southward into the heart of Antarctica, the Ross Ice Shelf provides the best surface approach into the continental interior. The McMurdo Sound region on the shelf's western edge thus became the headquarters for Robert Falcon Scott's 1911–12 epic sledging trip to the South Pole and also served several Antarctic research programs later in the century. The eastern barrier regions of the ice shelf were headquarters for Roald Amundsen's first attainment of the South Pole on Dec. 14, 1911; for Richard E. Byrd's three U.S. expeditions of 1928–41 at Little America I–III stations; and for several subsequent expeditions and research programs.

The Ross Ice Shelf is fed primarily by giant glaciers, or ice streams, that transport ice down to it from the high polar ice sheet of East and West Antarctica. The ice shelf has been likened to a vast triangular raft because it is relatively thin and flexible and is only loosely attached to adjoining lands. Giant rifts develop behind the ice shelf's barrier wall and occasionally rupture completely to spawn the huge tabular icebergs that are so characteristic of the Antarctic Ocean. Thus, although the barrier's position appears almost stationary, it actually undergoes continual change by calving and melting that accompany northward movement of the shelf ice. The shelf's mean ice thickness is about 1,100 feet (330 metres) along a line at about latitude 79° S. In a southward direction along about longitude 168° W, the ice shelf's thickness gradually increases to more than 2,300 feet (700 metres). Estimates suggest that at distances of 100 to 200 miles (160 to 320 km) inland from the barrier, 15 to 20 inches (380 to 500 mm) of ice may be added to the shelf each year by bottom freezing. Melting on the bottom of the ice shelf also occurs, and oceanographic data suggest that the net effect is the dissolution of the ice shelf by about 47–87 inches (120–220 cm) per year.

THE "HEROIC AGE" OF EXPLORATION

During the first two decades of the 20th century, commonly called the "heroic era" of Antarctic exploration, great advances were made in not only geographic but also scientific knowledge of the continent. The Englishmen Robert Falcon Scott and Ernest Henry Shackleton led three expeditions between 1901 and 1913, pioneering routes into the interior and making important geologic, glaciological, and meteorologic discoveries that provided a firm foundation for present-day scientific programs. This era was preceded by two events that proved the feasibility of Antarctic overwintering: (1) the Belgian ship *Belgica*, under command of Adrien de Gerlache, became the first vessel to winter in Antarctic waters when, from March 1898 to March 1899, it was trapped and drifted in pack ice of the Bellingshausen Sea, and (2) a scientific party under Carsten E. Borchgrevink spent the next winter camped at Cape Adare, for the first planned overwintering on the continent.

Sledge probes deep into the interior were made by Scott on the British National Antarctic *Discovery* Expedition (1901–04) and by Shackleton on the British Antarctic *Nimrod* Expedition (1907–09) from base camps on Ross Island. New southing records were set by Scott, in company with Shackleton and E.A. Wilson, who reached 82° 16′ 33″ S on Ross Ice Shelf on Dec. 30, 1902, and by Shackleton in a party of five, which reached 88°23′ S, a point about 97 nautical miles from the pole, on Jan. 9, 1909. The aerial age in Antarctica was presaged in 1902 by Scott, who went aloft in a captive balloon for aerial reconnaissance, and the mechanical age by Shackleton in 1908, who used an automobile at Cape Royds, Ross Island. The experimental use of hardy Manchurian ponies and the pioneering of a route up the great Beardmore Glacier to the polar plateau by Shackleton paved the way for the epic sledging trip of Scott in 1911–12 to the South Pole.

DISCOVERY OF THE ANTARCTIC POLES

National and personal prestige in attaining Earth's poles, as well as territorial acquisition and scientific inquiry, provided strong motivation for polar exploration in the early 1900s. The south magnetic pole, the point of vertical orientation of a magnetic dip needle, which was predicted by the German physicist Carl Friedrich Gauss to lie at 66° S, 146° E, inspired the unsuccessful quest, about 1840, of the seafarers Wilkes, d'Urville, and Ross (Ross had earlier discovered the north magnetic pole). The point was later reached, on Jan. 16, 1909, at 72°25′ S, 155°16′ E, on the high ice plateau of Victoria Land by T.W.E. David and Douglas Mawson on a sledge journey from Cape Royds. The pole has migrated more than 550 miles (885 km) since then to its present location near the Adélie Land coast. The South Pole of Earth's rotation was the unattained goal of Shackleton in 1908–09 but was eventually reached on Dec. 14, 1911, by Amundsen, and, a month later, on Jan. 17, 1912, by Scott. Whereas Amundsen's party of skiers and dog teams, using the Axel Heiberg Glacier route, arrived back at Framheim Station at Bay of Whales with little difficulty, Scott's man-hauling polar party, using the Beardmore Glacier route, perished on the Ross Ice Shelf.

Two other related discoveries were accomplished several decades later during the International Geophysical Year (IGY), a worldwide program of geophysical research that was conducted from July 1957 to December 1958. The south geomagnetic pole, the theoretical pole of Earth's magnetic field, on the East Antarctic Ice Sheet at

SOUTH POLE

The South Pole, the southern end of Earth's axis, lies in Antarctica, about 300 miles (480 km) south of the Ross Ice Shelf. This geographic South Pole does not coincide with the magnetic South Pole, from which magnetic compasses point and which lies on the Adélie Coast (at about 66°00′ S, 139°06′ E; the magnetic pole moves about 8 miles [13 km] to the northwest each year). Nor does it coincide with the geomagnetic South Pole, the southern end of Earth's geomagnetic field (this pole also moves; during the early 1900s it was located about 79°13′ S, 108°44′ E). The geographic pole, at an elevation of some 9,300 feet (2,830 metres; the elevation also changes constantly) above sea level, has six months of complete daylight and six months of total darkness each year. Ice thickness is 8,850 feet (2,700 m). The South Pole is the site of a U.S. station and landing strip (Amundsen-Scott); owing to the movement of the polar ice cap, a new location of the exact rotational pole is marked periodically by station personnel.

78°28′ S, 106°48′ E, was reached by a Soviet IGY tractor traverse on Dec. 16, 1957. The pole of relative inaccessibility, the point most remote from all coasts at 82°06′ S, 54°58′ E, was reached by a Soviet IGY tractor traverse on Dec. 14, 1958.

SHACKLETON AND SCOTT'S ILL-FATED ATTEMPTS

The British Antarctic explorer Ernest (later Sir Ernest) Henry Shackleton (1874–1922) led the first major British expedition that attempted to reach the South Pole in 1907–09. Earlier, he had been on Robert Falcon Scott's

British National Antarctic (*Discovery*) Expedition (1901–04) and took part, with Scott and Edward Wilson, in the sledge journey over the Ross Ice Shelf. In January 1908 he returned to Antarctica as leader of the new British expedition. The explorers, prevented by ice from reaching the intended base site in Edward VII Peninsula, wintered on Ross Island, McMurdo Sound. A sledging party, led by Shackleton, reached within 97 miles (156 km) of the South Pole, and another, under T.W. Edgeworth David, reached the area of the South Magnetic Pole. Victoria Land Plateau was claimed for the British crown. On his return Shackleton was knighted and was made a companion of the Royal Victorian Order. He wrote about the experience in *The Heart of the Antarctic* (1909).

The British naval officer and explorer Robert Falcon Scott (1868–12) led the famed, ill-fated second British attempt to reach the South Pole (1910–13). While commanding an Antarctic expedition on the HMS *Discovery* (1901–04), he proved to be a competent scientific investigator and leader, and he embarked on his second Antarctic expedition in June 1910. Its aims were to study the Ross Sea area and reach the South Pole. Equipped with motor sledges, ponies, and dogs, he and 11 others started overland for the pole from Cape Evans on Oct. 24, 1911. The motors soon broke down, the ponies had to be shot before reaching 83°30' S, and from there also the dog teams were sent back. On December 10 the party began to ascend Beardmore Glacier with three man-hauled sledges. By December 31 seven men had been returned to the base. The remaining polar party—Scott, E.A. Wilson, H.R. Bowers, L.E.G. Oates, and Edgar Evans—reached the pole on Jan. 18, 1912. Exhausted by their 81-day trek, they were bitterly disappointed to find evidence that Amundsen had preceded them to the pole by about a month.

Robert Falcon Scott. © Photos.com/Jupiterimages

The weather on the return journey was exceptionally bad. Evans died at Beardmore (February 17). Food and fuel supplies were low. At the end of his strength and hoping to aid his companions by his own disappearance, Oates crawled out into a blizzard on March 17 at 79°50′ S. The three survivors struggled on for 10 miles (16 km) but then were bound to their tent by another blizzard that lasted for nine days. With quiet fortitude they awaited their death—11 miles (18 km) from their destination. On March 29 Scott wrote the final entry in his diary:

Every day we have been ready to start for our depot 11 miles away but outside the door of the tent it remains a scene of whirling drift . . . We shall stick it out to the end, but we are getting weaker, of course, and the end cannot be far. It seems a pity, but I do not think I can write more.

Robert F. Scott's camp in Antarctica, c. *1912.* Library of Congress, Washington, D.C.

On Nov. 12, 1912, searchers found the tent with the frozen bodies, geological specimens from Beardmore, and Scott's records and diaries, which gave a full account of the journey. After his death Scott was regarded as a national hero for his courage and patriotism, and his widow was given the knighthood that would have been conferred on her husband had he survived.

Amundsen's Successful Expedition

Despite these repeated British attempts, it was Norwegian explorer Amundsen (1872–1928) who was the first to reach the South Pole. Also the first to make a ship voyage through the Northwest Passage and one of the first to cross the Arctic by air, he was one of the greatest figures in the field of polar exploration.

After several years of Arctic exploration, Amundsen had intended to drift across the North Pole in Nansen's old ship, the *Fram*, but this plan was affected by the news that Robert Peary had reached the North Pole in April 1909. Nonetheless, Amundsen continued his preparations, and when he left Norway in June 1910 no one but his brother knew that he was heading for the South Pole instead of the North. The base he set up at the Bay of Whales in Antarctica was 60 miles (100 km) closer to the pole than that of the rival expedition headed by Scott. An experienced polar traveler, Amundsen prepared carefully for the coming journey, making a preliminary trip to deposit food supplies along the first part of his route to the pole and back. To transport his supplies, he used sled dogs, while Scott depended on Siberian ponies.

Amundsen set out with 4 companions, 52 dogs, and 4 sledges on Oct. 19, 1911, and, after encountering good weather, arrived at the South Pole on December 14, more

Roald Amundsen, 1923. UPI/Bettmann

than a month ahead of Scott. The explorers recorded scientific data at the pole before beginning the return journey on December 17, and they safely reached their base at the Bay of Whales on Jan. 25, 1912. Amundsen wrote about the experience in *The South Pole* (1912).

EXPLORATION SINCE 1920

After Amundsen and Scott attained the South Pole, the idea that particularly haunted people's minds was that of an overland crossing of the continent. Conceived earlier by the Scotsman W.S. Bruce and the German Wilhelm Filchner to test the thought that a channel might exist connecting the Ross and Weddell seas, a trans-Antarctic expedition was organized in 1914 by Shackleton. His ship, the *Endurance*, was caught and crushed, however, in pack ice of the Weddell Sea, thus aborting one of the most ambitious polar expeditions theretofore planned. The dramatic escape and rescue of the expedition party—which included an 800-mile (1,300-km) voyage in an open whaling boat—was captured in Shackleton's *South*, published in 1919.

The idea of a cross-Antarctic journey lay dormant for several decades and came to fruition during IGY with the British Commonwealth Trans-Antarctic Expedition led by Vivian Fuchs. Using tracked vehicles and aided by aerial flights, the party left Shackleton Base on Filchner Ice Shelf on Nov. 24, 1957, and by way of the South Pole reached the New Zealand Scott Base on Ross Island on March 2, 1958. The continent was again crossed (1979–81) as part of the British Transglobe Expedition that undertook the first polar circumnavigation of Earth. Antarctica again was crossed in 1989–90, on a 3,741-mile (6,020-km) trek by ski and dog team, supported by aircraft, on the privately financed international Trans-Antarctica Expedition led by the American Will Steger.

ANN BANCROFT

The American explorer Ann Bancroft (1955–) was the first woman to participate in and successfully finish several arduous expeditions to the Arctic and Antarctic. She participated in the 1986 Steger International North Pole Expedition, led by Will Steger. After 56 days she and five other team members arrived at the North Pole by dogsled without benefit of resupply. She thus became the first woman to reach the North Pole by sled and on foot. She was also the first woman to ski across Greenland. In 1992–93 she led three other women on the American Women's Expedition to Antarctica. After successfully completing their 67-day, 660-mile (1,060-km) expedition, they became the first women's team to reach the South Pole on skis.

Technological
Advancements in Exploration

The period between World Wars I and II marks the beginning of the mechanical, particularly the aerial, age of Antarctic exploration. Wartime developments in aircraft, aerial cameras, radios, and motor transport were adapted for polar operation. On Nov. 16, 1928, the first heavier-than-air flight in Antarctica was made by the Alaskan bush pilot C.B. Eielson and George Hubert Wilkins in a wheel-equipped Lockheed Vega monoplane. Polar explorer Richard E. Byrd, already famous for his 1926 polar flight, followed the effort of Eielson and Wilkins with better-equipped, aircraft-supported expeditions (1928–30, 1933–35, 1939–41, and 1946–47), in which progressively greater use was made of ski-planes and aerial photography. Byrd, on Nov. 29, 1929, was first to fly over the South Pole.

Meanwhile, the courageous flight of Lincoln Ellsworth, an American, and Herbert Hollick-Kenyon, a Canadian pilot, across uncharted lands and icefields on the first aerial crossing of the continent from Nov. 23 to Dec. 5, 1935, clearly demonstrated the feasibility of aircraft landings and takeoffs for inland exploration. These early aerial operations and the extensive use of ship-based seaplanes in Norwegian explorations of coastal Queen Maud Land during the 1930s were forerunners of present-day aerial programs.

Byrd's Antarctic Expeditions

In 1928 Byrd announced his intentions to explore the unknown regions of Antarctica by air. His first expedition (1928–30) there, the largest and best-equipped that had ever set out for that continent, sailed south in October 1928. A substantial and well-supplied base, called Little America, was built on the face of the Ross Ice Shelf, a wide plain of shelf ice fronting the Ross Sea near an indentation in the ice cliff named the Bay of Whales. Flights were made from this base over the Antarctic continent. A range of high mountains, named the Rockefeller Mountains, was discovered; and a large tract of hitherto unknown territory beyond them was named Marie Byrd Land, for Byrd's wife. On Nov. 29, 1929, Byrd, as navigator, and three companions made the first flight over the South Pole, flying from Little America to the Pole and back in 19 hours with no mishap.

In 1933–35 a second Byrd expedition visited Little America with the aim of mapping and claiming land around the Pole; he extended the exploration of Marie Byrd Land and continued his scientific observations.

During the winter of 1934 (from March to August) Byrd
spent five months alone in a hut at a weather station
named Bolling Advance Base, buried beneath the ice shelf
face 123 miles (196 km) south of Little America, enduring
temperatures between -58 and -76 °F (-50 and -60 °C) and
sometimes much lower. He was finally rescued in a desper-
ately sick condition, suffering from frostbite and carbon
monoxide poisoning. This was perhaps his most controversial exploit.

At the request of Pres. Franklin D. Roosevelt, Byrd took
command of the U.S. Antarctic service and led a third
expedition to Antarctica in 1939–41, this one financed and
sponsored by the U.S. government. Bases were located at
Little America and Stonington Island, off the Antarctic
Peninsula. Byrd's discovery of Thurston Island greatly
decreased the length of unexplored coast of the continent.

After World War II Byrd was placed in charge of the
U.S. Navy's Operation High Jump. This Antarctic expedition, his fourth, was the largest and most ambitious
exploration of that continent yet attempted and involved
4,700 men, 13 ships (including an aircraft carrier), and 25
airplanes. Operation High Jump's ship- and land-based
aircraft mapped and photographed some 537,000 square
miles (1,390,000 square km) of the Antarctic coastline and
interior, much of it never seen before. Some 49,000 aerial
photographs were added to thousands more taken on land.
Byrd flew into Little America from the deck of the aircraft
carrier *Philippine Sea* north of the ice pack, about 700 miles
(1,100 km) from the camp. He made a second flight over
the South Pole and took part in several other flights.

In 1955 Byrd was made officer in charge of the United
States' Antarctic programs and became the senior authority for government Antarctic matters. In this capacity he
helped supervise Operation Deep Freeze, a major scientific

and exploratory expedition sent to the Antarctic under navy auspices as part of the program of the International Geophysical Year in 1957–58. Byrd accompanied the expedition aboard the icebreaker *Glacier* and took his last exploratory flight over the South Pole on Jan. 8, 1956.

Byrd's Accomplishments

Byrd was one of the world's foremost aviators and displayed extraordinary gifts in organizing successful expeditions to Antarctica. His major achievement was to apply the airplane, radio, camera, and other modern technical resources to these polar explorations. His five Antarctic expeditions made progressively greater use of ski-planes, ship-based seaplanes, and even helicopters (in 1946–47) to transport men and equipment and to carry out systematic reconnaissance and mapping programs using aerial photography. The expeditions yielded a wealth of new information about the continent, and operations High Jump and Deep Freeze in particular were milestones in the history of sustained, permanent scientific polar research. The aerial sextant and wind-drift instruments that Byrd invented in the years following World War I considerably advanced the science of aerial navigation and were of great use in his own explorations. In addition to his heavy use of airplanes in Antarctica, other innovations by Byrd included the use of an autogiro in 1933–34 and several helicopters in 1946–47.

Byrd wrote several books about his adventures. His first book, *Skyward* (1928), contains descriptions of his 1928–30 expedition to Antarctica, his flight to the North Pole, and his flight across the Atlantic. *Little America* (1930) is an official account of his aerial exploration in the Antarctic and his flight to the South Pole, and *Alone* (1938) describes his experiences at Bolling Advance Base.

LITTLE AMERICA

The principal American base in Antarctica, Little America lies on the northeastern edge of Ross Ice Shelf near Kainan Bay. First set up in 1928 as the headquarters for Byrd's polar explorations, it was reused and enlarged by him on his return expedition in 1933–35. In 1940 Byrd established a camp 7 miles (11 km) northeast, later named Little America III, that served as the western base for a government-sponsored exploration of Marie Byrd Land before World War II. After the war Little America IV, consisting of an airstrip and 60 tents, was set up nearby as a headquarters for the Operation High Jump expedition (1946–47).

When an expedition next returned (1956) in preparation for the International Geophysical Year (1957–58), parts of the earlier Little America camps were found to have vanished because of calving of the ice shelf. Consequently, Little America V was set up several miles northeast, near Kainan Bay, to serve as a supply base and terminus of a 630-mile- (1,014-kilometre-) long "highway" to Byrd Station in the continent's interior.

NATIONAL RIVALRIES AND CLAIMS

The early discoveries led to a few controversies not only for territorial claims but also in geographic nomenclature. The struggle for national influence in Antarctica was especially acute in the slender peninsular landmass south of Scotia Sea that became known as O'Higgins Land (Tierra O'Higgins) to Chileans and San Martin Land (Tierra San Martín) to Argentines, named for national heroes who helped in gaining independence from Spain. To the English it was known as Graham Land, for a former first lord of the admiralty, and to Americans as Palmer Peninsula, for the sealer and explorer Nathaniel Palmer. By international agreement, the region is now known simply as the Antarctic Peninsula, Graham Land its northern half and Palmer Land its southern half.

The first half of the 20th century is the colonial period in the history of Antarctica. Between 1908 and 1942, seven nations decreed sovereignty over pie-shaped sectors of the continent. Many nations—including the United States, the Soviet Union, Japan, Sweden, Belgium, and Germany—carried out Antarctic exploration without lodging formal territorial claims, even though claims may have been announced by some of their exploratory parties. The U.S. government, for example, has never taken up the claims made in 1929 by Richard Byrd's expedition in the Ford Ranges of Marie Byrd Land (an area presently unclaimed), nor those made by Lincoln Ellsworth on aerial landings on Nov. 23, 1935, in Ellsworth Land (an area now claimed by Chile) and on Jan. 11, 1939, in the American Highland near the Amery Ice Shelf of East Antarctica (an area now claimed by Australia). The German Antarctic Expedition of 1939 aerially photographed an extensive segment of the Princess Astrid and Princess Martha coasts of western Queen Maud Land and, dropping metal swastikas over the region, claimed it for the Nazi government (the area is now claimed by Norway). Other claims were transferred, such as that made in 1841 by James Ross, who, after discovering and naming the coastal Ross Sea region for Queen Victoria, claimed it for the British crown; the area was later transferred to, and is now claimed by, New Zealand.

After the French claim of Adélie Land caused Americans to demand retaliatory action, the United States' official

position was announced in 1924 by Secretary of State
Charles Evans Hughes:

*It is the opinion of this Department that the discovery of lands
unknown to civilization, even when coupled with a formal
taking of possession, does not support a valid claim of sovereignty, unless the discovery is followed by an actual settlement
of the discovered country.*

This policy has been reiterated many times since.

Few combative activities have marred the history of
Antarctica. World War II brushed the continent lightly,
only in that its nearby seas were used by Nazi commerce
raiders. The threat of increased activity, however, prompted
British warships to keep the northern Antarctic Peninsula
under surveillance. On one visit to Deception Island in
January 1943, it was discovered that Argentine visitors had
been there the year before, leaving a brass cylinder with
notice of claim to the peninsular region. The British oblit-
erated the Argentine signs, hoisted the Union Jack, posted
a notice of crown ownership, and returned the cylinder to
the Argentine government. Reaction was swift. In London,
growing concern that the territory might possibly be lost
and that a pro-German Argentine government might control both sides of the vital Drake Passage linking Atlantic
and Pacific sea routes resulted in a secret military plan,
code-named "Operation Tabarin," to establish a base on
Deception Island for closer watch. When the British
returned to the island in February 1944, they found their
earlier sign gone and an Argentine flag painted in its place.
This they soon replaced with their own flag, and their base
was established to back up the British claims to the region.
Several other stations were built, and, with the conclusion
of the war, the United Kingdom decided to maintain a
continued presence in Antarctica.

Argentina and Chile both were stimulated to increase activities to back up their claims to the Antarctic Peninsula as a result of the British occupancy. (Chile had expressed a claim in 1940.) The Argentines had maintained a weather station in the South Orkney Islands continuously since 1903, and after 1947 they and the Chileans constructed bases at several sites. With the coming of the U.S. Ronne Antarctic Research Expedition (RARE) in 1947–48 to the old U.S. Antarctic Service East Base camp on Marguerite Bay, the peninsula protagonists — British, Argentine, and Chilean — became concerned that the United States might rejuvenate its claims. Any antagonism was soon overcome, and the Americans and British joined forces for an arduous sledging journey down the east side of the peninsula.

Military violence has flared on two occasions in the region and in both instances has involved Argentina and the United Kingdom. The first incident took place in 1952, when Argentine navy small-arms fire chased a British meteorologic party that had landed at Hope Bay (at the northern end of the Antarctic Peninsula) back to its ship. The matter was resolved when the Argentine government agreed not to interfere with the party. The second, much more serious confrontation took place in 1982 in the Falkland Islands, a British colony that is also claimed by Argentina (called the Islas Malvinas by the Argentines). Argentine forces invaded the Falklands and South Georgia Island in early April. The British responded by sending a military task force, reoccupying the islands, and forcing the Argentines to surrender on June 14.

By the mid-1950s, many nations had active Antarctic interests, some commercial and some scientific but generally political. In 1947–48 Australia had established stations on Heard and Macquarie islands and in 1954 built Mawson Station on the mainland coast of Mac. Robertson Land as a basis for its vast territorial claim. South Africans raised their flag over Prince Edward and Marion islands. France established permanent bases by 1953 in the Kerguelen and Crozet islands and surveyed much of the Adélie Land coast. In 1955, with icebreaker aid, Argentina established General Belgrano Station on the Filchner Ice Shelf. A profusion of British, Chilean, and Argentine bases had been built in such proximity to one another on the peninsula and nearby islands that their purpose seemed more for intelligence activities than for science. The international Norwegian-British-Swedish Expedition of 1949–52 carried out extensive explorations from Maudheim Base on the Queen Maud Land coast in the territory claimed in 1939 by Norway. The United States had shown little interest in Antarctica since the Ronne expedition and the U.S. naval Operation Windmill, both in 1947–48 (the latter expedition was to obtain ground checks on the aerial photography of the previous season's Operation High Jump), but it continued its policy of nonrecognition of any claims. The Soviet Union had shown little interest, other than whaling, in Antarctica since Bellingshausen's pioneer voyage. On June 7, 1950, however, the Soviet government sent a memorandum to other interested governments intimating that it could not recognize any decisions on the regime for Antarctica taken without its participation. Such was the political climate on the continent during the organizational years for the coming International Geophysical Year of 1957–58.

SCIENTIFIC EXPLORATION

The importance of coordinating polar science efforts was recognized in 1879 by the International Polar Commission meeting in Hamburg, Ger., and thus the 11 participating nations organized the First International Polar Year of

1882–83. Most work was planned for the better-known Arctic, and, of the four geomagnetic and meteorologic stations scheduled for Antarctic regions, only the German station on South Georgia materialized. The decision was made at that time to organize similar programs every 50 years. In 1932–33 the Second International Polar Year took place, with 34 nations participating, but no expeditions were mounted to Antarctica.

THE DEVELOPMENT OF IGY

The idea for more frequent programs was born in 1950, when it was proposed that scientists take advantage of increasing technological developments, interest in polar regions, and, not the least, the maximum sunspot activity expected in 1957–58. (The earlier, second polar year was a year of sunspot minimum.) The idea quickly germinated and grew: a formalized version was adopted by the International Council of Scientific Unions (ICSU), and in 1952 ICSU appointed a committee that was to become known as the Comité Spécial de l'Année Géophysique Internationale (CSAGI) to coordinate IGY planning. Plans widened to include the scientific study of the whole Earth, and eventually 67 nations showed interest in joining. Plans were laid for simultaneous observations, at all angles, of the Sun, weather, the aurora, the magnetic field, the ionosphere, and cosmic rays. Whereas in the first polar year observations were confined to ground level and in the second to about 33,000 feet by balloon, during IGY satellites were to be launched by the United States and the Soviet Union for exploration of space. Several international data centres were established to collect all observations and make them freely available for analysis to scientists of any nation.

Two programs, outer space and Antarctica, were especially emphasized at an ICSU committee meeting in Rome
in 1954. Antarctica was emphasized because very few geophysical studies had yet been made on the continent,
because the south geomagnetic pole focuses auroral and
cosmic-ray activity in the Southern Hemisphere, and
because on the eve of IGY almost half the continent had
not yet even been seen by humans. The First Antarctic
Conference was held in Paris in July 1955 to coordinate
plans for expeditions, the advance parties of which were
soon to set sail for the continent. Early tensions, due in
part to overlapping political claims on the continent, were
relaxed by the conference president's statement that over-
all aims were to be entirely scientific. Plans were laid for
extensive explorations: 12 nations were to establish more
than 50 overwintering stations on the continent and subantarctic islands; the first regular aircraft flights to the
continent were to be inaugurated (by the United States);
massive tractor traverses were to be run in order to establish inland stations in West Antarctica (Byrd Station for
the United States), at the south geomagnetic pole (Vostok
Station for the Soviet Union), and the pole of relative inaccessibility (also for the Soviet Union); and an airlift by
giant cargo aircraft was to be established in order to set up
a station at the South Pole itself (Amundsen–Scott Station
for the United States). Several major scientific programs
were scheduled for Antarctica, dealing with the aurora
and airglow, cosmic rays, geomagnetism, glaciology, grav-
ity measurement, ionospheric physics, meteorology,
oceanography, and seismology. Biology and geology were
not primary studies of IGY.

Coastal bases were established in the summer of
1955–56 and inland stations the next summer for the official opening of IGY on July 1, 1957. For 18 months, until

the end of IGY on Dec. 31, 1958, a frenzy of activity not only in Antarctica but all over the world and in space resulted in a multitude of discoveries that revolutionized concepts of the Earth and its oceans, landmasses, glaciers, atmosphere, and gravitational and geomagnetic fields. Perhaps the greatest contribution was the political moratorium by the governments and the cooperative interchange between scientists of participating nations.

POST-IGY RESEARCH

In order to continue and coordinate the international Antarctic scientific effort in the post-IGY period, ICSU in September 1957 organized the Special Committee on Antarctic Research, or SCAR. (In 1961 the word *Scientific* was substituted for *Special*.) The foundations for the committee were laid at its first meeting in The Hague in 1958. SCAR, a nonpolitical body, coordinates not only research activities in Antarctica itself but also, through ICSU, those Antarctic programs that relate to worldwide projects, such as the International Years of the Quiet Sun, the World Magnetic Survey, the Upper Mantle Project, the International Biological Program, and the International Hydrological Decade. Member nations send representatives to periodic meetings of "working groups" for the various scientific disciplines. International scientific symposia are organized by SCAR for exchange of latest research results, on a timetable depending upon progress in the discipline. The great success of the political venture of the Antarctic Treaty depends in no small way on the achievements of SCAR and of the scientific and support teams in the field and laboratory.

Scientific knowledge of Antarctica has increased steadily. Many important problems relating to knowledge of the entire Earth are best resolved in the polar region, such as studying the stratosphere's apparently endangered ozone layer. About half the topics of modern polar research could not even have been guessed at in the early 20th century. At that time no one could have foreseen the advent of jet aircraft, turbine-powered helicopters, ski-planes, data-recording machines powered by radioactive isotopes, and polar-orbiting satellites that automatically collect meteorologic and upper atmosphere data across the continent and transmit it to a base collection station. The polar knowledge gained in the decades during and after IGY have far outweighed that learned in the preceding millennia. The incredible advances in modern Antarctic science have only been possible by adapting to polar operation the great technological advances in aircraft, oceanographic technique, and remote data acquisition and telemetry systems (unmanned weather stations, satellite surveillance, and the like). For example, advances in airborne radio-echo sounding methods now allow routine mapping of Antarctica's ice-covered bedrock surface by aircraft, a task that previously required laborious seismic surveys from tracked vehicles across the ice sheets.

During the period of the Antarctic Treaty there has been a steady growth in the number and nature of cooperative international scientific projects (the International Antarctic Glaciological Project, Dry Valley Drilling Project, Biomass [Biological Investigations of Antarctic Systems and Stocks], International Weddell Sea Oceanographic Expedition); of the various SCAR working groups; and, notably, of projects at the interface of astronomy and atmospheric physics (the International Magnetospheric Study, Antarctic and Southern Hemisphere Aeronomy Year).

In addition to these internationally supported programs, there have been major increases in individual national programs, mostly among those countries with territorial interests in the continent but also among countries that had not for decades (or never) supported programs there. This latter group includes Italy, which mounted its first expedition during 1975–76; Uruguay, which made its first land expedition in 1975; Poland, which established marine and land programs during 1976–77; West Germany, which first undertook large-scale operations in 1980–81; India, which began work in the early 1980s; and China, which established its first station in 1984.

Virtually all the physical sciences are represented in the studies carried out under these programs, often having direct impact on such disparate fields as meteoritics and planetary geology, continental drift, geophysics, astrophysics, meteorology and climate history, or biology and population studies. The biological programs reflect both the inherent interest of the Antarctic subjects themselves and the interest elsewhere in the world in ecology and conservation. The history of Antarctic whaling had made apparent to scientists the necessity of conserving biological populations, and the area below latitude 60° S had long contained nature reserves of greater or lesser extent, but the Convention on the Conservation of Antarctic Marine Living Resources (1982) gave special impetus to the principle.

As noted above, geologic and geophysical studies led to an expectation that Antarctica probably has a mineral and petroleum potential similar to that of other continents, though nothing of possible economic interest has ever been found. Environmental and political concerns over the commercial exploration and eventual development of such resources if found led, after six years of arduous negotiations, to the June 1988 signing in New Zealand of a new Convention on the Regulation of Antarctic Mineral

Resource Activities (CRAMRA), also known as the Wellington Convention, by the representatives of 33 nations. CRAMRA was designed to manage the exploitation and development of Antarctica's nonrenewable resources, a subject not covered under the original 1959 Antarctic Treaty. Several nations soon raised strong objections, and the convention was short-lived. Ensuing consultative party meetings on the Antarctic Treaty in Paris (1989) and Chile (1990) overturned the CRAMRA agreements and called for a complete and permanent ban on all mineral-resource activities in Antarctica. An October 1991 meeting in Madrid finalized CRAMRA's defeat. Article VII of a new Protocol on Environmental Protection to the Antarctic Treaty states simply, "Any activity relating to mineral resources, other than scientific research, shall be prohibited." The protocol has been accepted by Treaty member nations. Treaty nations now plan for the protection of Antarctica under some regime such as a world park. In the United States, for example, the U.S. Congress proposed the Antarctica World Park and Protection Act of 1990. With the elimination of the threat of mineral resource exploitation, the regime of an Antarctica World Park seems assured, though many political hurdles remain for its establishment.

Chapter 7: The Quest for Everest

$\mathbf{M}$ount Everest is a mountain peak on the crest of the Great Himalayas of southern Asia that lies on the border between Nepal and the Tibet Autonomous Region of China, at 27°59′ N, 86°56′ E. Reaching an elevation of 29,035 feet (8,850 metres), it is the highest mountain in the world, the highest point on Earth.

Like other high peaks in the region, Mount Everest has long been revered by local peoples; its most common Tibetan name, Chomolungma, means "Goddess Mother of the World" or "Goddess of the Valley"; its Chinese (Pinyin) name, Zhumulangma (or Qomolangma) Feng, is based on the Tibetan one. The Sanskrit name Sagarmatha means literally "Ocean Mother." Its identity as the highest point on the Earth's surface was not recognized, however, until 1852, when the governmental Survey of India established that fact. In 1865 the mountain—previously referred to as Peak XV—was renamed for Sir George Everest, British surveyor general of India from 1830 to 1843. As one of the world's great physical extremes, the mountain has long been a principal focus for exploration, mountaineering, and high-altitude studies. An intense campaign ensued to climb it, which was accomplished on May 29, 1953, by New Zealander Edmund (later Sir Edmund) Hillary and Tibetan Tenzing Norgay.

EARLY EXPEDITIONS

In the 1890s British army officers Sir Francis Younghusband and Charles (C.G.) Bruce, who were stationed in India, met and began discussing the possibility of an expedition to Everest. The officers became involved with two British exploring organizations—the Royal Geographical Society (RGS) and the Alpine Club—and these groups became instrumental in fostering interest in exploring the mountain. Bruce and Younghusband sought permission to mount an Everest expedition beginning in the early 1900s, but political tensions and bureaucratic difficulties made it impossible. Though Tibet was closed to Westerners, British officer John (J.B.L.) Noel disguised himself and entered it in 1913; he eventually got within 40 miles (65 km) of Everest and was able to see the summit. His lecture to the RGS in 1919 once again generated interest in Everest, permission to explore it was requested of Tibet, and this was granted in 1920. In 1921 the RGS and the Alpine Club formed the Mount Everest Committee, chaired by Younghusband, to organize and finance the expedition. A party under Lt. Col. C.K. Howard-Bury set out to explore the whole Himalayan range and find a route up Everest. The other members were G.H. Bullock, A.M. Kellas, George Mallory, H. Raeburn, A.F.R. Wollaston, Majors H.T. Morshead and O.E. Wheeler (surveyors), and A.M. Heron (geologist).

During the summer of 1921 the northern approaches to the mountain were thoroughly explored. On the approach to Everest, Kellas died of heart failure. Because Raeburn also fell ill, the high exploration devolved almost entirely upon Mallory and Bullock. Neither had Himalayan experience, and they were faced with the problem of acclimatization besides the difficulty of the terrain.

The first object was to explore the Rongbuk valley. The party ascended the Central Rongbuk Glacier, missing the narrower opening of the eastern branch and the possible line up Everest. They returned eastward for a rest at Kharta Shekar. From there they discovered a pass at 22,000 feet (6,700 metres), the Lhakpa (Lhagba), leading to the head of the East Rongbuk Glacier. The saddle north of Everest, despite its forbidding appearance, was climbed on September 24 by Mallory, Bullock, and Wheeler and named the North Col. A bitter wind prevented them from going higher, but Mallory had from there traced a potential route to the summit.

ATTEMPT OF 1922

Members of the expedition were Brig. Gen. C.G. Bruce (leader), Capt. J.G. Bruce, C.G. Crawford, G.I. Finch, T.G. Longstaff, Mallory, Capt. C.J. Morris, Maj. Morshead, Edward Norton, T.H. Somervell, Col. E.I. Strutt, A.W. Wakefield, and John Noel. It was decided that the mountain must be attempted before the onset of the summer monsoon. In the spring, therefore, the baggage was carried by Sherpas across the high, windy Plateau of Tibet.

Supplies were carried from Base Camp at 16,500 feet (5,030 metres) to an advanced base at Camp III. From there, on May 13, a camp was established on the North Col. With great difficulty a higher camp was set at 25,000 feet (7,620 metres) on the sheltered side of the North Ridge. On the next morning, May 21, Mallory, Norton, and Somervell left Morshead, who was suffering from frostbite, and pushed on through trying windy conditions to 27,000 feet (8,230 metres) near the crest of the Northeast Ridge. On May 25 Finch and Captain Bruce set out from Camp III using oxygen. Finch, a protagonist of oxygen, was justified by the results. The party, with the Gurkha Tejbir Bura, established Camp V at 25,500 feet (7,772 metres). There they were stormbound for a day and two nights, but the next morning Finch and Bruce reached 27,300 feet (8,320 metres) and returned the same day to Camp III. A third attempt during the early monsoon snow ended in disaster. On June 7 Mallory, Crawford, and Somervell, with 14 Sherpas, were crossing the North Col slopes. Nine Sherpas were swept by an avalanche over an ice cliff, and seven were killed. Mallory's party was carried down 150 feet (45 metres) but not injured.

ATTEMPT OF 1924

Members of the expedition were Brig. Gen. Bruce (leader), Bentley Beetham, Captain Bruce, J. de V. Hazard, Maj. R.W.G. Hingston, Andrew Irvine, Mallory, Norton, Noel Odell, E.O. Shebbeare (transport), Somervell, and Noel (photographer). Noel devised a novel publicity scheme for financing this trip by buying all film and lecture rights for the expedition, which covered the entire cost of the venture. To generate interest in the climb, he designed a commemorative postcard and stamp; sacks of postcards were then mailed from Base Camp, mostly to schoolchildren who had requested them. This was the first of many Everest public relations ventures.

On the climb itself, because of wintry conditions, Camp IV on the North Col was established only on May 22 by a new and steeper though safer route; the party was then forced to descend. General Bruce had to return because of illness, and under Norton Camp IV was reestablished on June 1. At 25,000 feet (7,620 metres), Mallory and Captain Bruce were stopped when the Sherpas became exhausted. On June 4 Norton and Somervell, with three Sherpas, pitched Camp VI at 26,800 feet (8,170 metres); the next day they reached 28,000 feet (8,535 metres). Norton went on to 28,100 feet (8,565 metres), a documented height unsurpassed until 1953. Mallory and Irvine, using oxygen, set out from the North Col on June 6. On June 8 they started for the summit. Odell, who had come up that morning, believed he saw them in early afternoon high up between the mists.

Initially, Odell claimed to have seen them at what became known as the Second Step (more recently, some have claimed that Odell was describing the Third Step), though later he was less certain exactly where it had been. On the Northeast Ridge there are three "steps"—steep rock barriers—between the elevations of 27,890 and 28,870 feet (8,500 and 8,800 metres) that make the final approach to the summit difficult. The First Step is a limestone vertical barrier about 110 feet (34 metres) high. Above that is a ledge and the Second Step, which is about 160 feet (50 metres) high. (In 1975 a Chinese expedition from the north affixed an aluminum ladder to the step that now makes climbing it much easier.) The Third Step contains another sheer section of rock about 100 feet (30 metres) high that leads to a more gradual slope to the summit. If Odell actually saw Mallory and Irvine at the Third Step at about 12:50 PM, then they would have been some 500 feet (150 metres) below the summit at that point. However, there has long been great uncertainty and considerable debate about all this, especially whether the pair made it to the top that day and if they were ascending or descending the mountain when Odell spotted them. The next morning Odell went up to search and reached Camp VI on June 10, but he found no trace of either man.

When Mallory was asked why he wanted to climb Everest, he replied with the famous line, "Because it's there." The British public had come to admire the determined climber over the course of his three expeditions, and they were shocked by his disappearance. The fate of Mallory remained a mystery for 75 years until, in May 1999, members of an American-led team found his body lying on a scree terrace at about 26,700 feet (8,140 metres).

ATTEMPT OF 1933

Members of the expedition were Hugh Ruttledge (leader), Captain E. St. J. Birnie, Lt. Col. H. Boustead, T.A. Brocklebank, Crawford, C.R. Greene, Percy Wyn-Harris, J.L. Longland, W.W. McLean, Shebbeare (transport), Eric Shipton, Francis S. Smythe, Lawrence R. Wager, G. Wood-Johnson, and Lieutenants W.R. Smyth-Windham and E.C. Thompson (wireless).

High winds made it extremely difficult to establish Base Camp in the North Col, but it was finally done on May 1. Its occupants were cut off from the others for several days. On May 22, however, Camp V was placed at 25,700 feet (7,830 metres); again storms set in, retreat was ordered, and V was not reoccupied until the 28th. On the 29th Wyn-Harris, Wager, and Longland pitched Camp VI at 27,400 feet (8,350 metres). On the way down, Longland's party, caught in a blizzard, had great difficulty.

On May 30, while Smythe and Shipton came up to Camp V, Wyn-Harris and Wager set off from Camp VI. A short distance below the crest of the Northeast Ridge, they found Irvine's ice ax. They reckoned that the Second Step was impossible to ascend and were compelled to follow Norton's 1924 traverse to the Great Couloir splitting the face below the summit. They crossed the gorge to a height about the same as Norton's but then had to return. Smythe and Shipton made a final attempt on June 1. Shipton returned to Camp V. Smythe pushed on alone, crossed the couloir, and reached the same height as Wyn-Harris and Wager. On his return the monsoon ended operations.

Also in 1933 a series of airplane flights were conducted over Everest, which permitted the summit and surrounding landscape to be photographed. In 1934 Maurice Wilson, an inexperienced climber who was obsessed with the mountain, died above Camp III attempting to climb Everest alone.

RECONNAISSANCE OF 1935

In 1935 an expedition led by Shipton was sent to reconnoitre the mountain, explore the western approaches, and discover more about monsoon conditions. Other members were L.V. Bryant, E.G.H. Kempson, M. Spender (surveyor), H.W. Tilman, C. Warren, and E.H.L. Wigram. In late July the party succeeded in putting a camp on the North Col, but dangerous avalanche conditions kept them off the mountain. One more visit was paid to the North Col area in an attempt on Changtse (the north peak). During the reconnaissance Wilson's body was found and buried; his diary was also recovered.

ATTEMPTS OF 1936 AND 1938

Members of the 1936 expedition were Ruttledge (leader), J.M.L. Gavin, Wyn-Harris, G.N. Humphreys, Kempson, Morris (transport), P.R. Oliver, Shipton, Smyth-Windham (wireless), Smythe, Warren, and Wigram. This expedition had the misfortune of an unusually early monsoon. The route up to the North Col was finished on May 13, but the wind had dropped, and heavy snowfalls almost immediately after the camp was established put an end to climbing the upper part of the mountain. Several later attempts to regain the col failed.

Members of the 1938 expedition were Tilman (leader), P. Lloyd, Odell, Oliver, Shipton, Smythe, and Warren. Unlike the two previous parties, some members of this expedition used oxygen. The party arrived early, in view of the experience of 1936, but they were actually too early and had to withdraw, meeting again at Camp III on May

ROYAL GEOGRAPHICAL SOCIETY (RGS)

The Royal Geographical Society is a British group founded as the Geographical Society of London in 1830. Its headquarters are in the borough of Westminster, next to Royal Albert Hall. It originated in the Raleigh Travellers' Club (formed in 1827) and was incorporated in 1859 under its present name. Soon after its foundation it absorbed the African Association, founded in 1788.

In the 19th century the society promoted or supported explorations in British Guiana (now Guyana; led by Sir Robert Schomburgk), in Africa (David Livingstone, Sir Richard Burton, John Hanning Speke, James Augustus Grant, and Joseph Thomson), and in the Arctic (Sir John Franklin and Sir George Strong Nares). Activities during the 20th century include Robert Falcon Scott's first Antarctic expedition, Sir Ernest Shackleton's Imperial Trans-Antarctic Expedition, consecutive Mount Everest expeditions culminating in Sir Edmund Hillary's successful ascent of 1953, the Norwegian-British-Swedish Antarctic expedition (1949–52), Sir Vivian Ernest Fuchs's British Commonwealth Trans-Antarctic Expedition (1957–58), and major expeditions to various tropical regions.

The society absorbed the smaller Institute of British Geographers in 1995. The objectives of the combined organization are to advance geographic knowledge through lectures and publications (Geographical Journal, Geographical Magazine, Area, and others), through its libraries and map collections, and through instruction in surveying and the support of exploration and research. The British sovereign annually awards two gold medals for exploration on the council's recommendation. The society's membership was about 15,000 in the early 21st century.

20. The North Col camp was pitched under snowy conditions on May 24. Shortly after, because of dangerous snow, the route was changed and a new one made up the west side of the col. On June 6 Camp V was established. On June 8, in deep snow, Shipton and Smythe with seven Sherpas pitched Camp VI, at 27,200 feet (8,290 metres), but the next day they were stopped above it by deep powder. The same fate befell Tilman and Lloyd, who made their attempt on the 11th. Lloyd benefited from an open-circuit oxygen apparatus that partly allowed him to breathe the outside air. Bad weather compelled a final retreat.

GOLDEN AGE OF EVEREST CLIMBS

After 1938, expeditions to Everest were interrupted by World War II and the immediate postwar years. In addition, the Chinese takeover of Tibet in 1950 precluded using the northern approach. In 1951 permission was received from the Nepalese for a reconnaissance of the mountain from the south. Members of the expedition were Shipton (leader), T.D. Bourdillon, Edmund Hillary, W.H. Murray, H.E. Riddiford, and M.P. Ward. The party marched through the monsoon, reaching Namche Bazar, the chief village of Solu-Khumbu, on September 22. At Khumbu Glacier they found it possible to scale the great icefall seen by Mallory from the west. They were stopped at the top by a huge crevasse but traced a possible line up the Western Cwm (cirque, or valley) to the South Col, the high saddle between Lhotse and Everest.

SPRING ATTEMPT OF 1952

Expedition members were E. Wyss Dunant (leader), J.J. Asper, R. Aubert, G. Chevalley, R. Dittert (leader of climbing party), L. Flory, E. Hofstetter, P.C. Bonnant, R. Lambert, A. Roch, A. Lombard (geologist), and A. Zimmermann (botanist). This strong Swiss party first set foot on the Khumbu Icefall on April 26. After considerable difficulty with the route, they overcame the final crevasse by means of a rope bridge. The 4,000-foot (1,220-metre) face of Lhotse, which had to be climbed to reach the South Col, was attempted by a route running beside a long spur of rock christened the Éperon des Genevois. The first party, Lambert, Flory, Aubert, and Tenzing Norgay (sirdar, or leader of the porters), with five Sherpas, tried to reach the col in one day. They were compelled to bivouac quite a distance below it (May 25) and the next day reached the summit of the Éperon, at 26,300 feet (8,016 metres), whence they descended to the col and pitched camp. On May 27 the party (less the five Sherpas) climbed up the Southeast Ridge. They reached approximately 27,200 feet (8,290 metres), and there, Lambert and Tenzing bivouacked. The next day they pushed on up the ridge and turned back at approximately 28,000 feet (8,535 metres). Also on May 28 Asper, Chevalley, Dittert, Hofstetter, and Roch reached the South Col, but they were prevented by wind conditions from going higher and descended to the base.

AUTUMN ATTEMPT OF 1952

Members of this second Swiss expedition were Chevalley (leader), J. Buzio, G. Gross, Lambert, E. Reiss, A. Spöhel, and Norman Dyhrenfurth (photographer). The party found the icefall easier to climb than in the spring and had brought poles to bridge the great crevasse. Camp IV was occupied on October 20. Higher up, however, they were constantly harassed by bitterly cold winds. On the ice slope below the Éperon one Sherpa was killed, and the party took to the glaciated face of Lhotse on the right. The South Col was reached on November 19, but the summit party climbed only 300 feet (90 metres) higher before being forced to withdraw.

THE HISTORIC ASCENT OF 1953

Members of the expedition, which was sponsored by the Royal Geographical Society and the Alpine Club, were Col. John Hunt (leader; later Baron Hunt), G.C. Band, Bourdillon, R.C. Evans, A. Gregory, Edmund Hillary, W.G. Lowe, C.W.F. Noyce, M.P. Ward, M.H. Westmacott, Maj. C.G. Wylie (transport), T. Stobart (cinematographer), and L.G.C. Pugh (physiologist). After three weeks' training on neighbouring mountains, a route was worked out up the Khumbu Icefall, and it was possible to start ferrying loads of supplies to the Western Cwm head. Two forms of oxygen apparatus, closed- and open-circuit types, were tried. As a result of a reconnaissance of Lhotse in early May, Hunt decided that Bourdillon and Evans, experts on closed-circuit, should make the first attempt from the South Col. Hillary and Tenzing Norgay, as sirdar, were to follow, using open-circuit and a higher camp.

Lowe spent nine days, most of them with the Sherpa Ang Nyima, working at the lower section of the Lhotse face. On May 17 a camp was pitched on it at 24,000 feet (7,315 metres). The route on the upper part of the face, over the top of the Éperon, was first made by Noyce and the Sherpa Annullu on May 21. The next day 13 Sherpas led by Wylie, with Hillary and Tenzing ahead, reached the col and dumped loads. The fine weather continued from May 14 but with high winds. On May 24 the first summit party, with Hunt and two Sherpas in support, reached the col. On the 26th Evans and Bourdillon climbed to the South Summit of Everest, but by then it was too late in the day to go farther. Meanwhile Hunt and the Sherpa Da Namgyal left loads for a ridge camp at 27,350 feet (8,335 metres).

On the 28th the ridge camp was established at 27,900 feet (8,500 metres) by Hillary, Tenzing, Lowe, Gregory, and Ang Nyima, and Hillary and Tenzing passed the night there. The two set out early on the morning of May 29, reaching the South Summit by 9:00 AM. The first challenge on the final approach to the summit of Everest was a fairly level ridge of rock some 400 feet (120 metres) long flanked by an ice "cornice"; to the right was the East (Kangshung) Face, and to the left was the Southwest Face, both sheer drop-offs. The final obstacle, about halfway between the South Summit and the summit of Everest, was a steep spur of rock and ice—now called the Hillary Step. Though it is only about 55 feet (17 metres) high, the formation is difficult to climb because of its extreme pitch and because a mistake would be deadly. Climbers now use fixed ropes to ascend this section, but Hillary and Tenzing had only ice-climbing equipment. First Hillary and then Tenzing tackled the barrier much as one would climb a rock chimney—i.e., they inched up a little at a time with their backs against the rock wall and their feet wedged in a crack between the rock and ice.

They reached the summit of Everest at 11:30 AM. Hillary turned to Tenzing, and the men shook hands; Tenzing then embraced Hillary in a hug. Hillary took photos, and the two searched for but did not find signs that Mallory and Irvine had been to the summit. Tenzing, a Buddhist, made an offering of food for the mountain; Hillary left a crucifix Hunt had given him. The two men ate some sweets and then headed down. They had spent about 15 minutes on the top of the world.

They were met on the slopes above the South Col that afternoon by Lowe and Noyce. Hillary is reputed to have

said to Lowe, "Well, George, we knocked the bastard off."
By June 2 the whole expedition had reassembled at the
Base Camp.

A correspondent for the *Times*, James (later Jan) Morris,
had hiked up to Camp IV to follow the story more closely
and was on hand to cover the event. Worried that other
papers might scoop him, Morris wired his story to the
paper in code. It reached London in time to appear in the
June 2 edition. A headline from another London paper published later that day, "All this, and Everest too!" referred to
the fact that Queen Elizabeth II was being crowned on the
same day on which the news broke about the success on
Everest. After years of privation during and after World
War II and the subsequent loss of empire, the effect of the
successful Everest ascent was a sensation for the British
public. The feat was also celebrated worldwide, but nowhere
like in Britain and the Commonwealth, whose climbers
had been so closely associated with Everest for more than
30 years. As Walt Unsworth described it in *Everest*,

> *And so, the British, as usual, had not only won the last battle
> but had timed victory in a masterly fashion. Even had it not
> been announced on Coronation Day it would have made world
> headlines, but in Britain the linking of the two events was
> regarded as almost an omen, ordained by the Almighty as a
> special blessing for the dawn of a New Elizabethan Age. It is
> doubtful whether any single adventure had ever before received
> such universal acclaim: Scott's epic last journey, perhaps, or
> Stanley's finding of Livingstone—it was of that order.*

The expedition little expected the fanfare that awaited
them on their return to Britain. Both Hillary and Hunt
were knighted in July (Hunt was later made a life peer),
and Tenzing was awarded the George Medal. All members

of the expedition were feted at parties and banquets for
months, but the spotlight fell mostly on Hillary and
Tenzing as the men responsible for one of the defining
events of the 20th century.

EVEREST-LHOTSE, 1956

In 1956 the Swiss performed the remarkable feat of get-
ting two ropes up Everest and one up Lhotse, using oxygen.
Members of the expedition were A. Eggler (leader), W.
Diehl, H. Grimm, H.R. von Gunten, E. Leuthold, F.
Luchsinger, J. Marmet, F. Müller, Reiss, A. Reist, and E.
Schmied. They followed roughly the British route up the
icefall and the Lhotse face. From their Camp VI Reiss and
Luchsinger reached the summit of Lhotse on May 18.
Camp VI was moved to the South Col, and the summit of
Everest was reached from a camp at 27,500 feet (8,380
metres) by Marmet and Schmied (May 23) and Gunten and
Reist (May 24).

ATTEMPTS OF 1960

In 1960 an Indian expedition with Sherpas, led by Brig.
Gyan Singh, attempted to scale Everest from the south.
Camp IV was established in the Western Cwm on April
19. Bad weather followed, but a party using oxygen
reached the South Col on May 9. On May 24 three members pitched a tent at 27,000 feet (8,230 metres) on the
Southeast Ridge but were turned back by wind and
weather at about 28,300 feet (8,625 metres). Continued
bad weather prevented the second summit party's leaving
the South Col.

Also that spring it was reported that a Chinese expedition led by Shi Zhanzhun climbed Everest from the north.
By their account they reached the North Col in April, and

on May 24 Wang Fuzhou, Qu Yinhua, Liu Lianman, and a Tibetan mountaineer, Konbu, climbed the slab by a human ladder, reaching the top at 4:20 AM to place the Chinese flag and a bust of Mao Zedong. The credibility of their account was doubted at the time but later was generally accepted.

THE U.S. ASCENT OF 1963

The first American expedition to Everest was led by the Swiss climber Norman Dyhrenfurth, who selected a team of 19 mountaineers and scientists from throughout the United States and 37 Sherpas. The purpose was twofold: to reach the summit and to carry out scientific research programs in physiology, psychology, glaciology, and meteorology. Of particular interest were the studies on how the climbers changed physiologically and psychologically under extreme stresses at high altitudes where oxygen deprivation was unavoidable. These studies were related to the U.S. space program, and among the 400 sponsors of the expedition were the National Geographic Society, the U.S. State Department, the National Science Foundation, the Office of Naval Research, the National Aeronautics and Space Administration, the U.S. Army Quartermaster Corps, the Atomic Energy Commission, and the U.S. Air Force.

On February 20 the expedition left Kathmandu, Nepal, for Everest, 180 miles (290 km) away. More than 900 porters carried some 26 tons of food, clothing, equipment, and scientific instruments. Base Camp was established at 17,800 feet (5,425 metres) on Khumbu Glacier on March 20, one month earlier than on any previous expedition. For the next five weeks the team selected a route toward the summit and established and stocked a series of camps up the mountain via the traditional South

Col route. They also explored the more difficult and untried West Ridge route. On May 1 James W. Whittaker and the Sherpa Nawang Gombu, nephew of Tenzing Norgay, reached the summit despite high winds. On May 22 four other Americans reached the top. Two of them, William F. Unsoeld and Thomas F. Hornbein, made mountaineering history by ascending the West Ridge, which until then had been considered unclimbable. They descended the traditional way, along the Southeast Ridge toward the South Col, thus also accomplishing the first major mountain traverse in the Himalayas. On the descent, Unsoeld and Hornbein, along with Barry C. Bishop and Luther G. Jerstad (who had also reached the summit that day via the South Col), were forced to bivouac in the open at 28,000 feet (8,535 metres). All suffered frostbite, and Bishop and Unsoeld later lost their toes; the two had to be carried out of Base Camp on the backs of Sherpas. On July 8 Dyhrenfurth and all members of the expedition were presented the National Geographic Society's Hubbard Medal by Pres. John F. Kennedy.

THE INDIAN ASCENT OF 1965

In 1965 a 21-man Indian expedition, led by Lt. Cdr. M.S. Kohli, succeeded in putting nine men on the summit of Everest. India thus became the fourth country to scale the world's highest mountain. One member of the group, Nawang Gombu, became the first person ever to climb Mount Everest twice, having first accomplished the feat on the U.S. expedition.

DEVELOPMENTS 1965 TO 1980

From 1966 to 1969 the government of Nepal banned mountaineers from climbing in the Nepalese Himalayas.

When the ranges were reopened in 1969, the world's top mountaineers—following the American example of 1963—set their eyes on new routes to Everest's summit.

THE SOUTHWEST FACE

With Tibet still closed and only the southern approach available, the obvious challenge was the huge Southwest Face rising from the Western Cwm. The crux of the problem was the Rock Band—a vertical cliff 2,000 feet (600 metres) high starting at about 26,250 feet (8,000 metres). A Japanese reconnaissance expedition reached the foot of the Rock Band in the autumn of 1969 and returned in spring 1970 for a full-scale attempt led by Matsukata Saburō. Failing to make further progress on the Southwest Face, the expedition switched to the easier South Col route, getting the first Japanese climbers, including the renowned Japanese explorer Uemura Naomi, to the summit.

Expeditions continued to lay "siege" to the Southwest Face. The most publicized of these climbs was the 1971 International Expedition led by Norman Dyhrenfurth; however, internationalist ideals were savaged by the stresses of high altitude, and the expedition degenerated into rancour between the British and non-British climbers. In the spring of 1972 a European expedition led by the German Karl Herrligkoffer was equally inharmonious.

The battle for the Southwest Face continued in a predictable pattern: large teams, supported by Sherpas acting as high-altitude porters, established a succession of camps in the broad, snow-covered couloir leading to the foot of the intractable Rock Band. Success finally came in the autumn of 1975 to a British expedition led by Chris (later Sir Chris) Bonington, who got the full team and its meticulously prepared equipment to Base Camp by the end of

August and made the most of the mainly calm weather during the September time window.

Climbing equipment had changed significantly since 1953. In the mid-1970s rigid box-shaped tents were bolted to aluminum alloy platforms dug into the 45° slope. Smooth-sheathed nylon ropes were affixed to the rock face to make a continuous safety line, which climbers could ascend and descend very efficiently. The 1975 expedition was a smooth operation that utilized a team of 33 Sherpas and was directed by some of the world's best mountaineers. Unlike previous expeditions, this team explored a deep gully cutting through the left side of the Rock Band, with Paul Braithwaite and Nick Estcourt breaking through to establish Camp VI at about 27,000 feet (8,230 metres). From there Doug Scott and Dougal Haston made a long, bold traverse rightward, eventually gaining the South Summit and continuing over the Hillary Step to the Everest summit, which they reached at 6:00 PM. Rather than risk descending in the dark, they bivouacked in a snow cave close to the South Summit—at 28,750 feet (8,750 metres), this was the highest bivouac in climbing history until the Sherpa Babu Chiri bivouacked on the summit itself in 1999. Their oxygen tanks were empty, and they had neither tent nor sleeping bags, but both men survived the ordeal unharmed and returned safely to Camp VI in the morning. Two days later Peter Boardman and the Sherpa Pertemba reached the summit, followed by Mick Burke heading for the top in deteriorating weather. Burke never returned; he is presumed to have fallen to his death in the whiteout conditions.

THE FIRST ASCENT BY A WOMAN

When Scott and Haston reached the summit of Everest in September 1975, they found a metal surveying tripod left the previous spring by a Chinese team—definitive proof of the first uncontested ascent from the north. The Chinese team included a Tibetan woman, Phantog, who reached the summit on May 27. The honours for the first woman to summit Everest, however, belong to the Japanese climber Tabei Junko, who reached the top from the South Col on May 16. She was climbing with the first all-women expedition to Everest (although male Sherpas supported the climb.)

THE WEST RIDGE DIRECT ASCENT

With the Southwest Face climbed, the next obvious—and harder—challenge was the complete West Ridge direct ascent from Lho Pass (Lho La). Just getting to Lho Pass from Base Camp is a major climb. The West Ridge itself then rises 9,200 feet (2,800 metres) over a distance of 3.5 miles (5.5 km), much of it over difficult rock. In 1979 a Yugoslav team, led by Tone Skarja, made the first ascent, fixing ropes to Camp V at an elevation of about 26,750 feet (8,120 metres), with one rope fixed farther up a steep rock chimney (a crack or gorge large enough to permit a climber to enter). On May 13 Andrej Stremfelj and Jernej Zaplotnik set out from Camp V for the summit. Above the chimney there were two more hard pitches of rock climbing. With no spare rope to fix in place, the climbers realized that they would not be able to descend via these difficult sections. After reaching the summit in midafternoon, they descended by the Hornbein Couloir, bypassing the hardest part of the West Ridge to regain the safety of Camp IV late that evening.

CLIMBING WITHOUT SUPPLEMENTAL OXYGEN

Beginning in the 1920s and '30s, the received wisdom had been that an Everest climb needed a team of at least 10 climbers supported by Sherpas and equipped with supplemental oxygen for the final stages. In 1978 that belief was shattered by the Italian (Tyrolean) climber Reinhold Messner and his Austrian climbing partner Peter Habeler. They had already demonstrated on other high Himalayan peaks the art of Alpine-style climbing—moving rapidly, carrying only the barest essentials, and sometimes not even roping together for safety—as opposed to the standard siege style. Another innovation was their use of plastic boots, which were much lighter than the leather equivalent. In 1978 Messner and Habeler attached themselves as a semiautonomous unit to a large German-Austrian expedition led by Oswald Ölz. At 5:30 AM on May 8, the two men left their tent at the South Col and started up the summit ridge carrying nothing but ice axes, cameras, and a short rope. The only external assistance was from the Austrians at their top camp, above the South Col, where the two stopped briefly to melt snow for drinking water. (In those days it was still common practice to place a top camp higher than the South Col; nowadays virtually all parties start their final push from the col, some 3,100 feet [950 metres] below the summit). Maintaining a steady ascent rate of about 325 feet (100 metres) per hour, they reached the summit at 1:15 PM. Habeler was terrified of possibly suffering brain damage from the lack of oxygen and made a remarkable descent to the South Col in just one hour. Messner returned later that afternoon. Exhausted—and in Messner's case snow-blind from having removed his goggles—the two were escorted back down to the Western Cwm the next morning by the Welsh climber Eric Jones.

Messner and Habeler had proved that human beings could climb to the top of the world without supplemental oxygen; the German Hans Engl and the Sherpas Ang Dorje and Ang Kami were among several climbers who duplicated this feat in the autumn of 1978. However, for

Messner, climbing Everest without supplemental oxygen was not enough: he now wanted to reach the summit completely alone. To do that unroped over the treacherous crevasses of the Western Cwm was considered unthinkable, but it was possible on the less-crevassed northern approach through Tibet; by the late 1970s Tibet was again becoming an option.

THE NORTH APPROACH

After China occupied Tibet in 1950, permission was denied to any expeditions from noncommunist countries wishing to climb Everest. In 1960 the Chinese army built a road to the Rongbuk Base Camp, then claimed to have made the first ascent of Everest from the north, following the North Col–North Ridge–Northeast Ridge route earlier explored by prewar British expeditions. Many in the West doubted the Chinese assertion, mainly because the official account—which included the claim that Qu Yinhua had scaled the notorious vertical cliff of the Second Step barefoot and which also made constant references to party solidarity and the inspiration of Chairman Mao Zedong—was deemed so improbable. Not for the last time, Everest was used as a vehicle for propaganda.

Since that time, however, people in the West have seen Qu's feet, mutilated by frostbite, and experts have reexamined the 1960 photos and film—many now believe that Qu, Wang Fuzhou, Liu Lianman, and the Tibetan, Konbu, did indeed reach the summit on May 25, 1960. What none can doubt is the Chinese repeat ascent of 1975 by eight Tibetans (including Phantog) and one Chinese. On that climb the group bolted an aluminium ladder to the Second Step, which has remained there and greatly aided all subsequent ascents on what has become the standard route from the north.

THE 1980S

In 1979 the Chinese authorities announced that noncommunist countries could again begin mounting Everest expeditions through Tibet. Japan was first to do so, with a joint Sino-Japanese expedition led by Watanabe Hyōrikō in the spring of 1980. Half of the 1980 team repeated the Chinese North Ridge–Northeast Ridge route, with Katō Yasuo reaching the summit alone—making him the first person to climb Everest from the south and north. Meanwhile, another team made the first complete ascent of the North Face from the Central Rongbuk Glacier. The upper face is split by the Great Couloir on the left and the Hornbein Couloir (first attained from the West Ridge in 1963) on the right. The 1980 team climbed a lower couloir (the Japanese Couloir) that led directly to the base of the Hornbein Couloir, which was then followed to the top. Shigehiro Tsuneo and Ozaki Takashi ran out of oxygen about four hours below the summit but continued without it, reaching the summit late and bivouacking on the way down. Once again, modern insulated clothing and modern psychological attitudes about what was possible on Everest had allowed climbers to push on in a manner unthinkable to the prewar pioneers.

FIRST SOLO CLIMB

Reinhold Messner arrived at Rongbuk during the monsoon in July 1980. He spent a month acclimatizing, did one reconnaissance to the North Col to cache supplies there, then set off alone from Advance Base on the East Rongbuk Glacier before dawn on August 18. After a lucky escape from a concealed crevasse into which he had fallen, he reached the North Col, collected his gear, and continued to

climb higher up the North Ridge. He then slanted diago-
nally right, as George Finch and Geoffrey Bruce had done
in 1922, traversing a full 1.2 miles (2 km) before stopping to
pitch his tent a second time, at 26,900 feet (8,200 metres).
On the third day he entered the Great Couloir, continued
up it, and achieved what had eluded Edward Norton,
Lawrence Wager, Percy Wyn-Harris, and Francis Smythe
by climbing rightward out of the couloir, onto the final
terraces, and to the summit. Messner later recounted,

> *I was in continual agony; I have never in my whole life been
> so tired as on the summit of Everest that day. I just sat and sat
> there, oblivious to everything . . . I knew I was physically at
> the end of my tether.*

Back at his tent that night he was too weak even to eat
or drink, and the next morning he jettisoned all his survival equipment, committing himself to descending all the
way to Advance Base Camp in a single day.

FURTHER EXPLORATION FROM TIBET

Messner's 1980 solo climb demonstrated just what could
be done on the world's highest mountain. With that same
bold spirit, a four-man British team came to Rongbuk in
1982 to attempt the complete Northeast Ridge from
Raphu Pass (Raphu La). While he was leading the climb of
the first of the three prominent Pinnacles that start at
about 26,900 feet (8,200 metres), Dick Renshaw suffered
a mild stroke and was invalided home. The expedition
leader, Chris Bonington, felt too tired to go back up, and
thus it was left to Peter Boardman and Joe Tasker to
attempt the final ascent. They were last seen alive between
the First Pinnacle and the Second Pinnacle on May 17.

Boardman's body was found 10 years later, sitting in the snow near that point; Tasker has not been found.

In 1981 a large American team made the first-ever attempt on Everest's gigantic East Face from Kangshung Glacier. Avalanche risk thwarted the attempt, but the team returned in autumn of 1983 to attempt again the massive central buttress of the face. This produced some spectacularly hard climbing, led by George Lowe. Above the buttress, the route followed a broad spur of snow and ice to reach the Southeast Ridge just below the South Summit. Carlos Buhler, Lou Reichardt, and Kim Momb reached the Everest summit on October 8, followed the next day by Jay Cassell, Lowe, and Dan Reid.

In 1984 the first Australians to attempt Everest chose a new route up the North Face, climbing through the huge central snowfield, dubbed "White Limbo," to gain the Great Couloir. Then, like Messner in 1980, the Australians cut out right, with Tim Macartney-Snape and Greg Mortimer reaching the summit at sunset before making a difficult descent in the dark.

The most remarkable achievement of this era was the 1986 ascent by the Swiss climbers Jean Troillet and Erhard Loretan. Like Messner, they snatched a clear-weather window toward the end of the monsoon for a lightning dash up and down the mountain. Unlike Messner, they did not even carry a tent and sleeping bags. Climbing by night, resting during the comparative warmth of the day, they took just 41.5 hours to climb the Japanese and Hornbein couloirs up the North Face; then, sliding most of the way on their backsides, they descended in about 4.5 hours.

DEVELOPMENTS IN NEPAL

While the most dazzling deeds were being done on the Tibetan side of Everest, there was still much activity in

Nepal during the 1980s, with the boldest pioneering expeditions coming from eastern European countries. For dogged teamwork, nothing has surpassed the first winter ascent of Everest. Completed in 1980 by a team of phenomenally rugged Polish climbers, this ascent was led by Andrzej Zawada; expedition members Leszek Cichy and Krzysztof Wielicki reached the summit on February 17. To crown this success, Zawada then led a spring expedition to make the first ascent of the South Pillar (left of the South Col), getting Andrzej Czok and Jerzy Kukuczka to the summit. Kukuczka, like Messner, would eventually climb all of the world's 26,250-foot (8,000-metre) peaks, nearly all by difficult new routes.

Several teams attempted to repeat the Yugoslav West Ridge direct route without success, until a Bulgarian team did so in 1984. The first Bulgarian to reach the summit, Christo Prodanov, climbed without supplemental oxygen, was forced to bivouac overnight during the descent, and died—one of four summiteers who climbed without oxygen in the 1980s and failed to return.

The first Soviet expedition to Everest, in 1982, climbed a new route up the left-hand buttress of the Southwest Face, involving harder climbing than the original 1975 route. Led by Evgeny Tamm, the expedition was highly successful, putting 11 Soviet climbers on the summit.

THE END OF AN ERA

The last of the great pioneering climbs of the decade was via a new route up the left side of the East Face to the South Col. Led by American Robert Anderson, it included just four climbers who had no Sherpa support and used no supplemental oxygen. British climber Stephen Venables was the only member of this expedition to reach the summit, on May 12, 1988. After a harrowing descent, during which Venables was forced to bivouac overnight without a tent, all four members of the team made it back to the Base Camp.

During the same period, more than 250 members of the "Asian Friendship Expedition" from China, Nepal, and Japan staged a simultaneous traverse of the mountain from north and south, which was recorded live on television. Also in 1988 the Sherpas Sungdare and Ang Rita both made their fifth summit of the mountain. (By 2002 the Sherpa Apa had made a then-record 12 summits). That autumn the ace French climber, Marc Boivin, made the first paragliding descent from the summit; New Zealander Russell Brice and Briton Harry Taylor climbed the infamous Pinnacles on the Northeast Ridge; and four Czech climbers disappeared in a storm after making an Alpine-style climb of the Southwest Face without supplemental oxygen. The following year five Poles were lost in an avalanche on the West Ridge.

The increasing activity on Everest in 1988 foreshadowed what was to come. At the start of the spring season that year fewer than 200 individuals had summited Everest. However, by the 2003 season, a half century after the historic climb by Hillary and Tenzing, that number exceeded 1,200, and more than 200 climbers had summited Everest two or more times. It became increasingly common for dozens of climbers to reach the summit on a single day; on May 23, 2001, nearly 90 accomplished the feat.

NOTABLE CLIMBERS

Reaching the summit of Everest is now possible for a great many people—including those who are visually or physically impaired. However, before the current era of commercial climbing expeditions, those who ventured onto the mountain constituted a unique group of individuals who often captured the public's imagination. Below are profiles of several of the more notable climbers.

GEORGE MALLORY

The British explorer and mountaineer George Mallory (1886–1924) was a leading member of early expeditions to Mount Everest. His disappearance on that mountain in 1924 became one of the most celebrated mysteries of the 20th century.

Mallory had been a longtime member of Britain's prestigious Alpine Club. When the club began assembling members for the first major expedition to Mount Everest, Mallory was a natural choice. The 1921 Everest expedition was mainly for reconnaissance, and the team had to first locate Everest before it could trek to and then around the mountain's base. Mallory and his old school friend Guy Bullock mapped out a likely route to the summit of Everest from the northern (Tibetan) side. In September the party attempted to climb the mountain, but high winds turned them back at the valley that came to be called the North Col.

Mallory also was part of the second expedition, mounted in 1922, which featured the major innovation of using supplemental (bottled) oxygen on some of the ascents. Mallory and his team climbed without supplemental oxygen and reached a height of 27,300 feet (8,230 metres) but could go no farther. A second attempt a few days later ended disastrously when his party was caught in an avalanche that killed seven porters.

In 1924 Mallory was selected for the third expedition, though he was less certain about returning. Before he left he was asked why climbers struggled to scale Everest, to which he gave the famous reply, "Because it's there." The expedition had a difficult time with high winds and deep snows. On June 6 he and a young and less-experienced climber, Andrew Irvine, set off for an attempt on the summit. The two started out from their last camp at 26,800 feet (8,170 metres) on the morning of June 8. Another member of the expedition claimed to have caught a glimpse of the men climbing in the early afternoon when the mists briefly cleared. Mallory and Irvine were never seen again. The British public was shocked at Mallory's loss.

The mystery of their fateful climb has been debated since that day, especially whether Mallory and Irvine had reached the summit. In the 1930s Irvine's ice axe was found at about 27,700 feet (8,440 metres), and in 1975 a Chinese climber discovered a body that he described as being that of an Englishman. In addition, an oxygen canister from the 1920s was found in 1991. With these clues, an expedition set out in 1999 to search for the two. Mallory's body was found at 26,760 feet (8,155 metres), and it was determined that he had died after a bad fall; Irvine was not found. It was hoped that the camera Mallory had with him would be recovered and that it might reveal if he and Irvine had made it to the top. Effects such as an altimeter, pocketknife, and letters were found but no camera. His body was buried where it had been discovered.

JOHN HUNT

The British army officer, mountaineer, and explorer John Hunt (1910–98) led the expedition on which Edmund Hillary and Tenzing Norgay reached the summit of Mount Everest. He described the venture in *The Ascent of Everest* (1953).

While serving in India and Burma (Myanmar) in the 1930s, Hunt became acquainted with the Karakoram

Range in northern Kashmir (1935) and with the Himalayas in Sikkim (1937 and 1939). An army officer during and after World War II, he was recalled from active duties in 1952 to lead the 1953 British Everest expedition. Hunt retired from the army in 1956 and later served as rector of the University of Aberdeen from 1963 to 1966. He was made a life peer, Baron Hunt of Llanfair Waterdine, in 1966.

EDMUND HILLARY

The New Zealand mountain climber and Antarctic explorer Edmund Hillary (1919–2008) was, with the Tibetan mountaineer Tenzing Norgay, the first person to reach the summit of Mount Everest (29,035 feet [8,850 metres]), the highest mountain in the world.

Hillary began climbing in New Zealand's Southern Alps while in high school. After military service in World War II, he resumed climbing and became determined to scale Everest. In 1951 he joined a New Zealand party to the central Himalayas and later that year participated in a British reconnaissance expedition of the southern flank of Everest. He was subsequently invited to join the team of mountaineers planning to climb the peak.

The well-organized expedition was launched in the spring of 1953, and a high camp from which to mount attempts at the summit was established by mid-May. After a pair of climbers failed to reach the top on May 27, Hillary and Tenzing set out for it early on May 29; by late morning they were standing on the summit. The two shook hands, then Tenzing embraced his partner. Hillary took photographs, and both searched for signs that George Mallory, a British climber lost on Everest in 1924, had been on the summit. Hillary left behind a crucifix, and Tenzing, a Buddhist, made a food offering. After spending about 15 minutes on the peak, they began their descent. They were met back at camp by their colleague W.G. Lowe, to whom Hillary reputedly said, "Well, George, we knocked the bastard off." Hillary described his exploits in *High Adventure* (1955). He made other expeditions to the Everest region during the early 1960s but never again tried to climb to the top.

Between 1955 and 1958 Hillary commanded the New Zealand group participating in the British Commonwealth Trans-Antarctic Expedition led by Vivian Fuchs. He reached the South Pole by tractor on Jan. 4, 1958, and recorded this feat in *The Crossing of Antarctica* (1958; with Fuchs) and *No Latitude for Error* (1961). On his Antarctic expedition of 1967, he was among those who scaled Mount Herschel (10,941 feet [3,335 metres]) for the first time. In 1977 he led the first jet boat expedition up the Ganges River and continued by climbing to its source in the Himalayas. His autobiography, *Nothing Venture, Nothing Win*, was published in 1975.

Hillary never anticipated the acclaim that would follow the historic ascent. He was knighted in 1953, shortly after the expedition returned to London. From 1985 to 1988 he served as New Zealand's high commissioner to India, Nepal, and Bangladesh. Over the years numerous other honours were bestowed on him, including the Order of the Garter in 1995. Throughout it, however, he maintained a high level of humility, and his main interest came to be the welfare of the Himalayan peoples of Nepal, especially the Sherpas. Through the Himalayan Trust, which he founded in 1960, he built schools, hospitals, and airfields for them. This dedication to the Sherpas lasted into his later years and was recognized in 2003, when, as part of the observance of the 50th anniversary of his and Tenzing's climb, he was made an honorary citizen of Nepal.

TENZING NORGAY

The Tibetan mountaineer Tenzing Norgay (1914–86) was, with Edmund Hillary, the first person to set foot on the summit of Mount Everest, the world's highest peak (29,035 feet [8,850 metres]).

It is not known exactly when, how, or under what conditions Norgay (whose name in Nepali means "Wealthy-Fortunate Follower of Religion") came to live in Nepal as a young boy. At age 19, having married a Sherpa, he was chosen as a porter for his first expedition; in 1935 he accompanied Eric Shipton's reconnaissance expedition of Everest. In the next few years he took part in more Everest expeditions than any other climber. After World War II he became a sirdar, or organizer of porters, and in this capacity accompanied a number of expeditions. In 1952 the Swiss made two attempts on the southern route up Everest, on both of which Tenzing was sirdar. He went as sirdar of the British Everest expedition of 1953 and formed the second summit pair with Hillary. From a tent at about 27,900 feet (8,500 metres) on the Southeast Ridge, they reached the summit at 11:30 AM on May 29. He spent 15 minutes there "taking photographs and eating mint cake," and, as a devout Buddhist, he left an offering of food. After his feat he was regarded as a legendary hero by many Nepalese and Indians. His many honours included Britain's George Medal and the Star of Nepal (Nepal Tara). *Man of Everest* (1955; also published as *Tiger of the Snows*), written in collaboration with James Ramsey Ullman, is an autobiography. *After Everest* (1978), as told to Malcolm Barnes, tells of his travels after the Everest ascent and his directorship of the Field Training Himalayan Mountaineering Institute in Darjeeling, which the Indian government established in 1954. *Tenzing: Hero of Everest* (2003), a biography of Tenzing Norgay by mountaineer and journalist Ed Douglas, is a sensitive appreciation of his life, achievements, and disappointments.

REINHOLD MESSNER

The Italian (Tyrolian) mountain climber and polar trekker Reinhold Messner (1944–) was renowned for his pioneering and difficult ascents of the world's highest peaks. In 1978 he and Austrian Peter Habeler were the first to climb Mount Everest (29,035 feet [8,850 metres]), the highest mountain in the world, without the use of contained oxygen for breathing, and two years later he completed the first solo ascent of Everest, also without oxygen. He was the first person to climb all 14 of the world's mountains that exceed an elevation of 26,250 feet (8,000 metres).

Messner was raised in a German-speaking region of the Dolomite Alps of northern Italy. His father introduced him to mountaineering, and from the age of 13 he made numerous difficult climbs, first on mountains in the Eastern Alps and later on other Alpine peaks. During the 1960s Messner became one of the earliest and strongest proponents of what came to be called the "Alpine" style of mountaineering, which advocates the use of minimal amounts of lightweight equipment and little or no outside support (e.g., the Sherpa porters typically employed in the Himalayas). He was joined in this philosophy by his younger brother Günther and by Habeler, whom Messner met on an expedition to the Peruvian Andes in 1969.

He made his first trip to the Himalayas in 1970, when he and Günther scaled Nanga Parbat (26,660 feet [8,126 metres]) and were the first to ascend by way of its Rupal (south) face; his brother died during the descent, and Reinhold barely survived the ordeal, losing several toes to frostbite. In 1975 Messner and Habeler made their first

Alpine-style ascent of an 8,000-metre mountain without supplemental oxygen when they climbed the northwestern face of Gasherbrum I (Hidden Peak; 26,470 feet [8,068 metres]) in the Karakoram Range.

For their historic oxygen-free climb of Mount Everest in 1978, Messner and Habeler accompanied a large German-Austrian conventional expedition to the mountain. Setting out on their own from about 26,200 feet (7,985 metres) on the morning of May 8, the two reached the summit in the early afternoon. Habeler, fearing the effects of oxygen deprivation, descended quickly, with Messner following more slowly. Messner recounted the adventure in *Everest: Expedition zum Endpunkt* (1978; *Everest: Expedition to the Ultimate*, 1979). Messner's landmark solo ascent of Everest in 1980 was equally remarkable. After three days of exhausting climbing on the north side of the mountain (which included a fall into a crevasse), on August 20 he stood on the summit.

Messner continued tackling lofty peaks, usually by untried routes. In 1978 he had again climbed Nanga Parbat, reaching the summit alone by a new route, and in 1979 he had led a team of six to the top of K2 (28,251 feet [8,611 metres]), the world's second highest mountain. In 1983 he led a party on a notable ascent of Cho Oyu (26,906 feet [8,201 metres]) using a new approach, the southwest face, and the following year made the first traverse between two 8,000-metre peaks: Gasherbrum I and II. By 1986 he had climbed all of the world's 8,000-metre mountains, many of them twice. In 1990 he and German Arved Fuchs became the first people to traverse Antarctica via the South Pole by foot without either animals or machines. Their journey, which covered 1,740 miles (2,800 km), is described in Messner's *Antarktis: Himmel und Hölle zugleich* (1990; *Antarctica: Both Heaven and Hell*, 1992). His autobiography, *Die Freiheit, aufzubrechen, wohin ich will: ein Bergsteigerleben* (*Free Spirit: A Climber's Life*), appeared in 1989.

Chapter 8:
Reaching for Great Heights and Depths

Just as Everest and other great mountains have exerted an irresistible pull on adventurers, so, too, have the highest and lowest reaches on Earth. Since the advent of the first lighter-than-air vessels or primitive diving apparatuses, people have sought to reach these great extremes. The technological advances made in the 20th century finally made it possible for individuals to reach these goals.

AUGUSTE PICCARD AND EARLY ASCENTS INTO THE STRATOSPHERE

Unmanned sounding balloons for high-altitude scientific investigations were introduced in 1893, but manned ballooning was limited to moderate altitudes until the 1930s. The Swiss-born Belgian physicist Auguste Piccard (1884–1962) became interested in balloon ascents as a means of making experiments. He participated in many important research studies, and when the University of Brussels created a chair for applied physics in 1922, Piccard, who was also a mechanic and an engineer, readily accepted the post. Having studied cosmic rays, he conceived of an experiment for observing them at ascents above 52,500 feet (16,000 metres). Previous ascents had shown that the stratosphere could be fatal and that to penetrate the isothermal layer, with its low pressure, a revolutionary balloon would be necessary.

Piccard built such a balloon in 1930, with Belgian financing. Its main innovative feature was an airtight aluminum cabin, devised by him and his twin brother, Jean-Felix Piccard (1884–1963), equipped with pressurized air; this technique later became commonplace on airplanes. Another innovation was the design of a very large lightweight rubberized-cotton netless hydrogen balloon having sufficient ascent strength so that, on departure, it need not be completely filled. This would make possible the first successful stratosphere flight. On May 27, 1931, it carried Auguste and his assistant, Paul Kipfer, to 51,775 feet (15,781 metres), where the atmospheric pressure is about one-tenth that at sea level. Upon returning to the surface, the scientist-adventurers were received triumphantly in Zürich and then Brussels. In 1932, in a new cabin equipped with a radio, Piccard was able to reach an altitude of 55,800 feet (17,008 metres).

On Oct. 23, 1934, Jean-Felix Piccard and his wife, Jeannette, went to 57,579 feet (17,550 metres), with a slightly larger duplicate that used a magnesium-alloy cabin. The official project was completed earlier when U.S. Navy Lt. Cdr. Thomas G.W. Settle achieved a world-record flight of 18,665 metres 61,237 feet (18,665 metres) in the same balloon on Nov. 20, 1933. Jean and Jeannette Piccard's balloon had several novel advances, the most significant being the remote-control pyrotechnic ballasting system. Contrary to conventional designs, they used blasting caps and trinitrotoluene (TNT) to cut cords outside the sealed capsule.

The Piccard 57,579-foot flight was followed by long-time *National Geographic* magazine contributor Capt. A. Stevens and Capt. Orville Anderson, both of the U.S. Army Air Corps, going to 72,395 feet (22,066 metres) on Nov. 11, 1935. The flight was sponsored by the National

Geographic Society and the U.S. Army Air Corps. Stevens and Anderson used a 3,700,000-cubic-foot (100,000-cubic-metre) rubberized-cotton balloon carrying a large magnesium-alloy cabin. That balloon, the *Explorer II*, was seven times the size of Piccard's, but still with very similar fabric. The stress in the skin of the giant balloon was formidable, resulting in repeated failures. On one occasion the crew, this time including Maj. William E. Kepner, barely escaped by parachute.

SUBSEQUENT STRATOSPHERIC FLIGHTS

Jean-Felix Piccard realized that the giant single-cell balloon had reached the end of its practical development. Larger balloons would require heavier fabric with diminishing returns. Small latex balloons were routinely carrying light loads to much greater heights, and Piccard postulated that with a cluster of these he could extend the limits of ballooning. Thomas H. Johnson of the Franklin Institute suggested using fewer but larger cellophane balloons. Piccard, working with Johnson, designed a netless film balloon that substituted a conical skin section for the suspension system. The payload was attached directly to the base of the cone. By 1937 Piccard and his students at the University of Minnesota, including Robert Gilruth (later head of NASA's Project Mercury), had flown one of these unmanned balloons about 600 miles (1,000 km), carrying an automatic ballast-releasing device and radio instrumentation.

Piccard dreamed of a stratosphere flight with a cluster of film balloons, but there was concern that they would become tangled. To test the concept, he made a successful solo flight in the *Pleiades* with an ensemble of 92 latex balloons on July 18, 1937.

After World War II, General Mills, Inc., accepted a contract from the U.S. Office of Naval Research to advance the theory of ballooning. The DuPont Company's new polyethylene film was chosen for the envelope. Launches of individual test balloons were finally successful, but there was little faith that the complicated task of rigging 80 of these at once would work, and the project was abandoned. However, the plastic balloon had been created, and they constantly grew larger and more acceptable as polyethylene films improved.

The conversion of the seam tapes—from their original simple joining task to backup use over heat-welded seams and, finally, with reinforcing filaments, to the primary structural load-bearing factor—enabled further size increases and advanced reliability. Their use also enabled the abandonment of the load ring in the mouth of the balloon. This facilitated the development of the natural shape.

In December 1955 the U.S. Air Force established Project Man High to obtain scientific data on the stratosphere and to test equipment for exploring above Earth's atmosphere. Three pilots, Capt. Joseph W. Kittinger, Maj. David Simmons, and Lt. Clifton M. McClure, in *Manhigh I* (June 2, 1957), *Manhigh II* (Aug. 19, 1957), and *Manhigh III* (Oct. 8, 1958), respectively, each ascended to about 19 miles (30 km) aboard a single-cell plastic balloon. Unmanned flights, generally carrying scientific research payloads of more than 5,000 pounds (2,250 kg), have reached altitudes above 26 miles (42 km) with balloons as big as some 40,000,000 cubic feet (1,000,000 cubic metres).

SUPERPRESSURE BALLOONS

Polyester film at a tensile strength of 20,000 pounds per square inch (1,400 kg per square cm)—compared with

A weather balloon is released at a weather station at the South Pole.
NOAA

polyethylene at a tensile strength of about 600 pounds per square inch (40 kg per square cm)—finally made it possible to produce superpressure balloons, which do not expand or contract as the enclosed gas heats up or cools down. A series of contracts were awarded to the G.T. Schjeldahl Company by the U.S. Air Force in the late 1950s to develop polyester balloons. After repeated failures, Donald Piccard (son of Jean and Jeannette Piccard) was assigned the project. He theorized that the failures were caused by the self-destructive tendencies of the stiff film. By laminating two layers of very thin Mylar, he produced a more flexible film that resulted in the first successful superpressure balloon. These balloons have been used by the U.S. National Center for Atmospheric Research to carry instrumentation aloft for months at a time, continually circumnavigating Earth. Manned superpressure balloons have had some success but have not yet been able to carry on through diurnal heating cycles.

INTRODUCTION OF THE BATHYSPHERE

The bathysphere was a spherical steel vessel for use in undersea observation that was provided with portholes and was suspended by a cable from a boat. Built by the American zoologist William Beebe and the American engineer Otis Barton, the bathysphere made its first dives in 1930. On June 11, 1930, it reached a depth of about 1,300 feet (400 metres), and in 1934 Beebe and Barton reached a then-record depth of 3,028 feet (923 metres). Through these dives, the bathysphere proved its qualities but also revealed weaknesses. It was difficult to operate and involved considerable potential risks. A break in the suspension cable would have meant certain death for the observers. Surface waves and resulting movement of the boat could have produced such a fatal strain. Because of these disadvantages, the bathysphere was supplanted by the safer, more maneuverable mesoscaphe and bathyscaphe.

WILLIAM BEEBE

William Beebe (1877–1962) combined careful biological research with a rare literary skill. He was the coinventor of the bathysphere.

Beebe was curator of ornithology at the New York Zoological Gardens from 1899 and director of the department of tropical research of the New York Zoological

Society from 1919. He led numerous scientific expeditions abroad and in 1934 with Otis Barton descended in his bathysphere to a then-record depth of 3,028 feet (923 metres) in Bermuda waters. A noted lecturer, he received numerous prizes and honours for scientific research and for his books, both technical and popular. His books include *Jungle Days* (1925), *Pheasants, Their Lives and Homes* (1926), *Beneath Tropic Seas* (1928), *Half Mile Down* (1934), *High Jungle* (1949), *The Edge of the Jungle* (1950), and *Unseen Life of New York* (1953).

William Beebe (left) and John T. Vann with Beebe's bathysphere, 1934.
Encyclopædia Britannica, Inc.

AUGUSTE PICCARD AND THE DEVELOPMENT OF THE BATHYSCAPHE

As a child, Auguste Piccard had been fascinated by accounts of marine fish and thought that humans should also descend into the depths. Now, after his successes with high-altitude balloon flight, he wanted to build a device capable of resisting the pressures of the ocean depths, the bathyscaphe.

Depth-resistant cabins are, of necessity, heavier than water. Before Piccard, they had been suspended from a cable, but at great depths this procedure was not dependable. Piccard revolutionized the dive by the principle of the balloon. Just as a lighter-than-air balloon carried the nacelle, or balloon gondola, a lighter-than-water float would support the cabin. Thus, the bathyscaphe consists of two main components: a steel cabin, heavier than water and resistant to sea pressure, to accommodate the observers; and a light container called a float, filled with a petroleum product (e.g., gasoline), which, being lighter than water, provides the necessary lifting power. The cabin and float are closely linked. On the surface, one or more ballast tanks filled with air provide enough lift to keep the bathyscaphe afloat. When the ballast tank valves are opened, air escapes and is replaced by water, making the whole device heavy enough to start its descent. The gasoline is in direct contact with the sea water and so is compressed at a rate almost exactly in proportion to the prevailing depth. Thus, the bathyscaphe gradually loses buoyancy as it descends, and the speed of its descent tends to increase rapidly. To slow down or to begin the reascent, the pilot releases ballast that consists essentially of iron shot stored in silos and held in place by electromagnets.

World War II interrupted the construction of the first bathyscaphe, the *FNRS 2*, but it was finally built in Belgium between 1946 and 1948. On Oct. 26, 1948, an unpiloted trial dive with the bathyscaphe was conducted successfully in shallow waters of 80 feet (24 metres). On Nov. 3, 1948, in a deeper dive of approximately 4,600 feet (1,400 metres), the cabin withstood the pressure perfectly, but the float was severely damaged by a heavy swell of water that it encountered after the dive. The bathyscaphe project was subsequently troubled by various difficulties until Auguste's son, Jacques Piccard (1922–2008), intervened.

JACQUES PICCARD AND THE MESOSCAPHE

In addition to his work on bathyscaphes, Jacques Piccard, along with his father, Auguste Piccard, also invented the mesoscaphe, an undersea diving vessel for exploring middle depths that suspended itself automatically at predetermined depths. Four mesoscaphes were built. His first mesoscaphe, the *Auguste Piccard*, capable of carrying 40 passengers, transported some 33,000 tourists through the depths of Lake Geneva during the 1964 Swiss National Exhibition in Lausanne. Although it could descend to more than 2,000 feet (600 metres), most of the mesoscaphe's 1,100 descents into Lake Geneva during 1964 and 1965 reached only about 300 feet (90 metres). A second and smaller mesoscaphe, the *Ben Franklin*, was equipped to remain submerged a month or more. In 1969 Piccard drifted underwater in the *Ben Franklin* some 1,800 miles (3,000 km) along the east coast of North America from Florida to Nova Scotia in a successful study of the Gulf Stream for the U.S. Navy.

In his later career Jacques Piccard was a consultant scientist for several private American organizations for deep-sea research, including the Grumman Aircraft Engineering Corporation, New York (1966–71). In the 1970s he founded the Foundation for the Study and Protection of Seas and Lakes, based in Cully, Switz. In 1999 his son Bertrand Piccard, together with Englishman Brian Jones, completed the first nonstop circumnavigation of the globe in a balloon.

Substantially rebuilt and greatly improved, the vessel was renamed *FNRS 3* and carried out a series of descents under excellent conditions, including one of 13,000 feet (4,000 metres) into the Atlantic off Dakar, Seneg., on Feb. 15, 1954. However, Jacques—then an assistant in the economics department at the University of Geneva—received an unexpected offer from the city of Trieste, Italy, for the local shipbuilding industry there to build a new bathyscaphe. This second improved bathyscaphe, dubbed the *Trieste*, was launched on Aug. 1, 1953, and that month the two bathyscaphes competed in the Mediterranean, at Toulon, Fr., and near Naples, Italy. The French-based craft descended to about 6,900 feet (2,100 metres), and the Italian-based craft went down to about 10,300 feet (3,150 metres). Jacques abandoned economics and collaborated in future work with bathyscaphes.

In 1956 Jacques went to the United States seeking funding; two years later the U.S. Navy bought the *Trieste* and retained him as a consultant. The *Trieste* was taken to California and equipped with a new cabin designed to enable it to reach the seabed of the great oceanic trenches. Several successive descents were made into the Pacific by

MARIANA TRENCH

The Mariana Trench is a submarine trench in the floor of the western North Pacific Ocean, situated east of the Mariana Islands. It is the deepest such trench known, part of the western Pacific system of oceanic trenches coinciding with subduction zones—points where two adjacent plates collide, one descending below the other. An arcing depression, the Mariana Trench stretches for more than 1,580 miles (2,550 km) with a mean width of 43 miles (69 km). There is a smaller steep-walled valley on the floor of the main trench. In 1899 Nero Deep (31,693 feet [9,660 metres]) was discovered southeast of Guam. This sounding was not exceeded until a 32,197-foot (9,813-metre) hole was found in the vicinity 30 years later. In 1957, during the International Geophysical Year, the Soviet research ship *Vityaz* sounded a new world record depth of 36,056 feet (10,990 metres). This was later increased to 36,201 feet (11,034 metres). On Jan. 23, 1960, the Italian-built U.S. Navy-operated bathyscaphe *Trieste*, with the inventor's son, Jacques Piccard, aboard, made a record dive to 35,810 feet (10,916 metres) in the trench. In 2009 the Mariana Trench was designated a U.S. national monument.

Jacques Piccard, and on Jan. 23, 1960, Piccard, accompanied by Lt. Don Walsh of the U.S. Navy, dived to a record 35,810 feet (10,916 metres) in the Pacific Ocean's Mariana Trench. He recounted this feat in *Seven Miles Down* (1961), written with Robert Dietz.

Chapter 9: Notable Archaeological Finds

Throughout history, most exploration has been undertaken to further such goals as establishing territorial sovereignty or securing shipping lanes and trading rights. In addition, most of the scientific inquiry over the centuries has been focused on exploring the natural world—its physical properties and flora and fauna. Ancient ruins long were regarded as a source of plunder or building materials, but in the 18th century interest grew in exploring these antiquities and learning about humanity's largely forgotten ancient past. By the late 19th century, the discipline of archaeology was well established in Europe and North America, and researchers began making a wide range of fascinating discoveries. Surveyed below are seven of the more significant archaeological finds and the individuals associated with them. Each is notable as a milestone in the discipline, as well as being a find that captured the public's imagination.

POMPEII

The ancient city of Pompeii (Italian: Pompei) in Campania, Italy, lies 14 miles (23 km) southeast of Naples, at the southeastern base of Mount Vesuvius. It was built on a spur formed by a prehistoric lava flow to the north of the mouth of the Sarnus (modern Sarno) River. Pompeii was destroyed, together with Herculaneum, Stabiae, Torre Annunziata, and other communities, by the violent eruption of Mount Vesuvius in 79 CE. The circumstances of their preservation make their remains a unique document of Greco-Roman life. Pompeii, Herculaneum, and Torre

Annunziata were collectively declared a World Heritage site by UNESCO in 1997.

Pompeii supported between 10,000 and 20,000 inhabitants at the time of its destruction. The modern town of Pompei lies to the east; it contains the Basilica of Santa Maria del Rosario, a pilgrimage centre.

HISTORY

It seems certain that Pompeii, Herculaneum, and nearby towns were first settled by Oscan-speaking descendants of the Neolithic inhabitants of Campania. Archaeological evidence indicates that the Oscan village of Pompeii, strategically located near the mouth of the Sarnus River, soon came under the influence of the cultured Greeks who had settled across the bay in the 8th century BCE. Greek influence was challenged, however, when the Etruscans came into Campania in the 7th century. The Etruscans' influence remained strong until their sea power was destroyed by King Hieron I of Syracuse in a naval battle off Cumae in 474 BCE. A second period of Greek hegemony followed. Then, toward the end of the 5th century, the warlike Samnites, an Italic tribe, conquered Campania, and Pompeii, Herculaneum, and Stabiae became Samnite towns.

Pompeii is first mentioned in history in 310 BCE, when, during the Second Samnite War, a Roman fleet landed at the Sarnus port of Pompeii and from there made an unsuccessful attack on the neighbouring city of Nuceria. At the end of the Samnite wars, Campania became a part of the Roman confederation, and the cities became "allies" of Rome. But they were not completely subjugated and Romanized until the time of the Social War. Pompeii joined the Italians in their revolt against Rome in this war and was besieged by the Roman general Lucius Cornelius Sulla in 89 BCE. After the war, Pompeii, along with the rest of Italy south of the Po River, received Roman citizenship; however, as a punishment for Pompeii's part in the war, a colony of Roman veterans was established there under Publius Sulla, the nephew of the Roman general. Latin replaced Oscan as the official language, and the city soon fell under the influence of Roman institutions, architecture, and culture.

A riot in the amphitheatre at Pompeii between the Pompeians and the Nucerians, in 59 CE, is reported by the Roman historian Tacitus. An earthquake in 62 CE did great damage in both Pompeii and Herculaneum. The cities had not yet recovered from this catastrophe when final destruction overcame them 17 years later.

Mount Vesuvius erupted on Aug. 24, 79 CE. A vivid eyewitness report is preserved in two letters written by Pliny the Younger to the historian Tacitus, who had inquired about the death of Pliny the Elder, commander of the Roman fleet at Misenum. Pliny the Elder had rushed from Misenum to help the stricken population and to get a close view of the volcanic phenomena, and he died at Stabiae. Site excavations and volcanological studies, notably in the late 20th century, have brought out further details. Just after midday on August 24, fragments of ash, pumice, and other volcanic debris began pouring down on Pompeii, quickly covering the city to a depth of more than 9 feet (3 metres) and causing the roofs of many houses to fall in. Surges of pyroclastic material and heated gas, known as *nuées ardentes*, reached the city walls on the morning of August 25 and soon asphyxiated those residents who had not been killed by falling debris. Additional pyroclastic flows and rains of ash followed, adding at least another 9 feet of debris and preserving in a pall of ash the bodies of the inhabitants who perished while taking shelter in their houses or trying to escape toward the coast or by the roads leading to Stabiae or Nuceria. Thus Pompeii remained buried under a layer of pumice stones and ash 19 to 23 feet (6 to 7 metres) deep. The city's sudden burial served to protect it for the next 17 centuries from vandalism, looting, and the destructive effects of climate and weather.

HISTORY OF EXCAVATIONS

The ruins at Pompeii were first discovered late in the 16th century by the architect Domenico Fontana. Herculaneum was discovered in 1709, and systematic excavation began there in 1738. Work did not begin at Pompeii until 1748, and in 1763 an inscription ("Rei publicae Pompeianorum") was found that identified the site as Pompeii. The work at these towns in the mid-18th century marked the start of the modern science of archaeology.

Under the patronage of Don Carlos, king of Naples, the military engineer Karl Weber carried out systematic studies from 1750 to 1764, but other early digging was often haphazard and irresponsible, carried out by treasure seekers or other untrained workers. Haphazard digging was brought to a stop in 1860, when the Italian archaeologist Giuseppe Fiorelli became director of the excavations. Areas lying between excavated sites were cleared and carefully documented. Pompeii was divided into nine regions; the insulae (blocks) in each region were numbered, and each door on the street was given a number so that each house could be conveniently located by three numerals. Fiorelli also developed the technique of making casts of bodies by pouring cement into the hollows formed in the volcanic ash where the bodies had disintegrated.

In 1951, after the interruption caused by World War II, intensive excavation was resumed under Amedeo Maiuri, who was in charge of the excavations from 1924 to 1961. Large areas were uncovered to the south of the Via dell'Abbondanza, in Regions I and II, and the debris piled outside the city walls was cleared away. This revealed the Porta (Gate) di Nocera and an impressive stretch of cemetery lining each side of the road leading from the gate to Nuceria. By the 1990s, about two-thirds of the city had been excavated.

In the vicinity of Stabiae and Gragnano, excavations initiated by Don Carlos of Naples discovered 12 villas between 1749 and 1782. Work was resumed there in the 20th century. The Villa of San Marco, with its two large peristyle gardens and bath, is the best preserved. Other villas have been found at nearby Scafati, Domicella, Torre Annunziata, and on the lower slopes of Vesuvius near Boscoreale and Boscotrecase. Many of these villas were reburied after excavation, but a few can be seen, notably the Villa of the Mysteries.

DESCRIPTION OF THE REMAINS

The city of Pompeii was shaped irregularly because it was built on a prehistoric lava flow. Excavations indicate that the southwestern part of the town is the oldest, but scholars do not agree on the stages by which the walls were expanded or on who the builders were. The walls are 2 miles (3 km) in circumference, and they enclose an area of about 163 acres (66 hectares). Seven city gates have been excavated. The chief street running in a southeast-northwest direction was the Via Stabiana; it connected the Porta Vesuvio, or Vesuvius Gate (144 feet [44 metres] above sea level), in the highest part of the city, with the Porta di

Stabia, or Stabiae Gate (26 feet [8 metres]), in the lowest part. Through this gate came traffic from the Sarnus River and Stabiae. This street was crossed by two other main streets, the Via dell'Abbondanza and the Via di Nola.

The public buildings are for the most part grouped in three areas: the Forum (elevation 110 feet [34 metres]), located in the large level area on the southwest; the Triangular Forum (82 feet [25 metres]), standing on a height at the edge of the south wall overlooking the bay; and the Amphitheatre and Palaestra, in the east.

The Forum was the centre of the city's religious, economic, and municipal life; it was a large rectangular area surrounded by a two-story colonnaded portico. Dominating the Forum on the north was the temple dedicated to the Capitoline triad of deities: Jupiter, Juno, and Minerva. To the east was the Macellum, or large provision market; to the south were the small sanctuary of the city Lares (guardian deities), built after the earthquake in 62 CE; the Temple of Vespasian; and the imposing headquarters of the woolen industry, erected by the wealthy patroness Eumachia. Opposite the Capitolium, on the southern end of the Forum, were the meeting place of the city council and the offices of the magistrates of the city. The large basilica, with its main room surrounded on four sides by a corridor, is the most architecturally significant building in the city; it is of considerable importance in studying the origin and development of the Christian basilica. It served as a covered exchange and as a place for the administration of justice. To the west was the Temple of Venus Pompeiana, patron deity of Pompeii. Across from the basilica was the Temple of Apollo, one of the earliest in the city.

The Triangular Forum is the site of the Doric Temple, the oldest temple in Pompeii. Between the 3rd and the 1st century BCE, a theatre, a palaestra (sports ground), and a small covered theatre were built to the east of the Triangular Forum. The temples of Zeus Meilichius and of Isis and the old Samnite palaestra were nearby. In the east corner of Pompeii was the Amphitheatre, and to the west a large palaestra was built to replace the old Samnite palaestra. Baths were scattered throughout the town: the Stabian Baths (which predate the Roman period), the Forum Baths, the Central Baths (still under construction at the time of the eruption), and many baths in luxurious private homes.

But more significant than the public buildings, examples of which have been excavated at other sites, are the hundreds of private homes. These are unique, for only at Pompeii is it possible to trace the history of Italic and Roman domestic architecture for at least four centuries. The earliest houses date from the first Samnite period (4th–3rd century BCE). The House of the Surgeon is the best-known example of the early atrium house built during this period.

The most luxurious houses were built during the second Samnite period (200–80 BCE), when increased trade and cultural contacts resulted in the introduction of Hellenistic refinements. The House of the Faun occupies an entire city block and has two atria (chief rooms), four triclinia (dining rooms), and two large peristyle gardens. Its facade is built of fine-grained gray tufa from Nuceria, the chief building material of this period. The walls are decorated in the First Pompeian, or Incrustation, style of painting, which imitates marble-veneered walls by means of painted stucco. The famous Alexander the Great mosaic found in the House of the Faun is probably a copy of a lost Hellenistic painting. Many of the houses from this period were decorated with elaborate floor mosaics. The House of the Silver Wedding, with its imposing high-columned atrium, was also built during this period, but it underwent later alterations. The handsome banquet hall and the exedra, which served as a schoolroom for children of the family, were decorated in the Second Pompeian, or Architectural, style, which was popular from 80 BCE to 14 CE.

The large number of houses built during the Samnite period made it necessary to build fewer houses in the Roman period. Those that were built were usually less imposing, with lower atria, but with more elaborate decoration. The House of Marcus Lucretius Fronto is a small but elegant house of the Roman Imperial period. The tablinum (master's office) is decorated in especially fine Third Pompeian, or Egyptianizing, style, usually dated from the early empire to the earthquake. The House of the Vettii is typical of the homes of the prosperous merchant class of the Roman period. Some of its rooms are decorated in the Fourth Pompeian, or Ornamental, style.

The atrium-peristyle house, with its handsome paintings, elegant furniture, and beautiful gardens with fountains and bronze and marble sculptures, is not as typical as has generally been supposed. There are also numerous small homes throughout the city, many of them shop houses. Excavators now preserve as completely as possible all aspects of ancient life. The homes of the humble are as informative as those of the wealthy. Many roofs, second stories, and balconies have been restored.

INFLUENCE ON EUROPEAN CULTURE

The discoveries at Pompeii and other sites buried by the Vesuvian eruption had a profound influence on European taste. News of the excavations kindled a wave of enthusiasm for antiquity that spread throughout Europe. The laudatory pronouncements of the eminent German classicist Johann Joachim Winckelmann, who made his first trip to Naples in 1755, and the etchings of Giambattista Piranesi did much to popularize the excavations. Naples, Pompeii, and Herculaneum became important stops on the European Grand Tour made by English visitors.

Artists, architects, potters, and even furniture makers drew much inspiration from Pompeii. Contemporary painted interiors were inspired by the frescoed walls found in the excavations. The stucco work popularized in England by the 18th-century architects James and Robert Adam used the same motifs. In France, the Louis XVI style incorporated Pompeian motifs, and the apartment of Louis's queen, Marie Antoinette, at Fontainebleau was decorated in this style, which became popular throughout Europe. Jacques-Louis David and his student Jean-Auguste-Dominique Ingres drew inspiration for their paintings from the excavations. Indeed, the Neoclassic style stimulated by the discoveries at Pompeii completely replaced the Rococo and became the artistic style of the French Revolution and of the Napoleonic period.

IMPORTANCE AS HISTORICAL SOURCE

The extent of the archaeological sites makes them of the greatest importance, for they provide a unique source of information about so many aspects of social, economic, religious, and political life of the ancient world. The many well-preserved house shrines give a hitherto unexpected picture of the vitality of religion in the family. The bakeries, complete with mills, kneading machines, and ovens, some still containing loaves of bread, show how this staple of everyday life was produced. Numerous fulleries (processing and cleaning plants for wool) make it possible to study this important industry. The shops of the sculptor, toolmaker, and gem cutter, as well as the factories for *garum* (fish sauce) and lamps and the many wine and food shops, document other aspects of ancient life. Pompeii was a busy port town that exported products throughout the Mediterranean region. Merchants and tradesmen found food and lodging near the city gates and the Forum. Some restaurants and inns were quite attractive and served food to guests who reclined in the garden; in the cheaper places, the rooms were small and dark, and customers sat on stools.

Inscriptions provide further information. They include monumental inscriptions on public buildings, tombs, and statue bases; the business transactions recorded in the famous wax tablets of the banker Lucius Caecilius Jucundus; announcements of gladiatorial combats; and many election notices, echoes of hotly fought contests. Preserved in the graffiti are accounts, lists of market days, insults and accusations, the exchanges of lovers, quotations from Virgil, and even the scratched alphabets of children. Epigraphical and archaeological evidence makes it possible to study the stratification of society and learn more of the freedmen, slaves, small businessmen, and aristocrats of the ancient Roman world.

Further, Pompeii offers the best opportunity for the study of city planning and land use in an ancient city. Excavations since the mid-20th century have revealed an unexpected amount of open land. The large insula across from the Amphitheatre was not the Foro Boario (Cattle Market), as had been long supposed, but a vineyard. Many vineyards, fruit trees, and gardens have been found, indicating less intensive land use and a smaller population than had been thought.

Unfortunately, the excavations are constantly endangered by the ravages of weather, tourist traffic at the site, and destructive vegetation. Reinforced concrete roofs were applied to many structures in the 1950s, but over subsequent decades this protective measure made upkeep difficult as some of the concrete deteriorated. In 1995 Pietro Giovanni Guzzo was made superintendent of the site, and existing conservation efforts were revitalized and expanded. Despite such actions, however, Pompeii continued to face numerous problems, including degradation, mismanagement, and vandalism. In July 2008 the Italian government took the unprecedented step of declaring a one-year state of emergency for the site and appointed a special commissioner to oversee Pompeii. Of first importance is the preservation, restoration, and study of the valuable evidence already uncovered before it is lost forever.

GIUSEPPE FIORELLI

The systematic excavation at Pompeii by Italian archaeologist Giuseppe Fiorelli (1823–96) helped to preserve much of the ancient city as nearly intact as possible and contributed significantly to modern archaeological methods.

Fiorelli's initial work at Pompeii was completed in 1848. Then, when he became professor of archaeology at the University of Naples and director of excavations at Pompeii (1860), he pioneered his meticulous method of studying archaeological strata; observation, recording, preservation (including building a museum), and reporting were its fundamental features. In particular he studied the materials and building methods utilized at Pompeii and published *Descrizione di Pompei* (1875; "Description of Pompeii"), among many other works. He was named director of the National Museum, Naples (1863), and director general of Italian antiquities and fine arts (1875–96).

TROY

The ancient city of Troy in northwestern Anatolia—known to the ancient Greeks and Romans as Troia—holds an enduring place in both literature and archaeology. The legend of the Trojan War is the most notable theme from ancient Greek literature and forms the basis of Homer's *Iliad*. Although the actual nature and size of the historical settlement remain matters of scholarly debate, the ruins of Troy at Hisarlık, Tur., are a key archaeological site whose many layers illustrate the gradual development of civilization in northwestern Asia Minor.

GEOGRAPHY

Ancient Troy commanded a strategic point at the southern entrance to the Dardanelles (Hellespont), a narrow strait linking the Black Sea with the Aegean Sea via the Sea of Marmara. The city also commanded a land route that ran north along the west Anatolian coast and crossed the narrowest point of the Dardanelles to the European shore. In theory, Troy would have been able to use its site astride these two lines of communication to exact tolls from trading vessels and other travelers using them; the actual extent to which this took place, however, remains unclear.

The Troad (Greek Troias; "Land of Troy") is the district formed by the northwestern projection of Asia Minor into the Aegean Sea. The present-day ruins of Troy itself occupy the western end of a low descending ridge in the extreme northwest corner of the Troad. Less than 4 miles (6 km) to the west, across the plain of the Scamander (Küçük Menderes) River, is the Aegean Sea, and toward the north are the narrows of the Dardanelles.

ARCHAEOLOGY

The Search for Troy at Hisarlık

The approximate location of Troy was well known from references in works by ancient Greek and Latin authors. But the exact site of the city remained unidentified until modern times. A large mound, known locally as Hisarlık, had long been understood to hold the ruins of a city named Ilios or Ilion by the Greeks and Ilium by the Romans that had flourished in Hellenistic and Roman times. In 1822 Charles Maclaren suggested that this was the site of Homeric Troy, but for the next 50 years his suggestion received little attention from classical scholars, most of whom regarded the Trojan legend as a mere fictional creation based on myth, not history. The German archaeologist Heinrich Schliemann deserves full credit for adopting Maclaren's identification and demonstrating to the world that it was correct. In seven major and two minor campaigns between 1870 and 1890, Schliemann conducted excavations on a large scale mainly in the central area of the Hisarlık mound, where he exposed the remains of a walled citadel. After Schliemann's death in 1890, the excavations were continued (1893–94) by his colleague Wilhelm Dörpfeld and later (1932–38) by an expedition from the University of Cincinnati headed by Carl W. Blegen. After a lapse of some 50 years, excavations resumed (1988–2005) under the leadership of University of Tübingen archaeologist Manfred Korfmann and continued after his death.

Questions of Troy's physical size, population, and stature as a trade entrepôt and regional power became subjects of intense scholarly dispute following the resumption of excavations at Hisarlık in the late 1980s. Although Homeric Troy was described as a wealthy and populous city, by this

time some scholars had come to accept the probability
of a lesser Troy—a more minor settlement, perhaps a
princely seat. Beginning in 1988, Korfmann's team investigated the terrain surrounding the citadel site in search
of wider settlement. Korfmann's findings at Hisarlık,
drawn from geomagnetic surveying and isolated excavations, led him to conclude in favour of a greater Troy—
that is, a settlement of some size and prosperity. His
presentation of this perspective in a 2001 exhibition,
accompanied by a controversial model reconstruction
of the city, sparked especially intense scholarly debate
over the city's true nature.

Findings

Before excavations began, the mound rose to a height of
105 feet (32 metres) above the plain. It contained a vast
accumulation of debris that was made up of many clearly
distinguishable layers. Schliemann and Dörpfeld identified a sequence of nine principal strata, representing nine
periods during which houses were built, occupied, and
ultimately destroyed. At the end of each period when a
settlement was destroyed (usually by fire or earthquake or
both), the survivors, rather than clear the wreckage down
to the floors, merely leveled it out and then built new
houses upon it.

The nine major periods of ancient Troy are labeled I to
IX, starting from the bottom with the oldest settlement,
Troy I. In periods I to VII Troy was a fortified stronghold
that served as the capital of the Troad and the residence of
a king, his family, officials, advisers, retinue, and slaves.
Most of the local population, however, were farmers who
lived in unfortified villages nearby and took refuge in the
citadel in times of danger. Troy I to V corresponds roughly
to the Early Bronze Age (c. 3000 to 1900 BCE). The citadel of Troy I was small, not more than 300 feet (90 metres)

HEINRICH SCHLIEMANN

The German archaeologist and excavator of Troy, Mycenae, and Tiryns, Heinrich Schliemann (1822–90) is considered to be the modern discoverer of prehistoric Greece and creator of prehistoric Greek archaeology. Schliemann's excavations helped to lengthen considerably the perspective of history and to popularize archaeology.

As a boy Schliemann loved the Homeric poems, and he eventually learned ancient and modern Greek and many other languages. He made a sufficient fortune as a military contractor during the Crimean War to retire at age 36 and to devote himself to archaeology. In 1873, at Hisarlık, Tur., he uncovered fortifications and the remains of a city of great antiquity, and he discovered a treasure of gold jewelry, which he smuggled out of Turkey. He believed the city he had found was Homeric Troy and identified the treasure as that of Priam. His discoveries and theories, at first were received skeptically by many scholars, but others, and a wide public, accepted his identification.

Because the Ottoman government prevented his return, he began excavating Mycenae in Greece, where he found more invaluable remains and treasures. Schliemann resumed work at Hisarlık in 1878–79, exposing the stratigraphy more clearly and advancing archaeological technique. He conducted a third excavation at Troy in 1882–83 and a fourth from 1888 until his death, during which time he was assisted by Wilhelm Dörpfeld. In 1884 the two men excavated the great fortified site at Tiryns (modern Tirins, Gr.), near Mycenae.

in diameter. It was enclosed by a massive wall with gateways and flanking towers and contained perhaps 20 rectangular houses. Troy II was twice as large and had higher, sloping stone walls protecting an acropolis on which stood the king's palace and other princely residences, which were built of brick in a megaron plan. This city came to an end through fire, and Schliemann mistakenly identified it with Homer's Troy. In the "burnt layer's" debris were found a trove of gold jewelry and ornaments and gold, silver, copper, bronze, and ceramic vessels that Schliemann named "Priam's treasure." The burning of Troy II seems to have been followed by an economic decline; each of the citadels of Troy III, IV, and V was fortified and somewhat larger than its predecessor, but the houses inside the walls were much smaller and more closely packed than in Troy II.

Troy VI and VII may be assigned to the Middle and Late Bronze Ages (c. 1900 to 1100 BCE). Troy at this time had new and vigorous settlers who introduced domesticated horses to the Aegean area. They further enlarged the city and erected a magnificent circuit of cut limestone walls that were 15 feet (4.5 metres) thick at the base, rose to a height of more than 17 feet (5 metres), and had brick ramparts and watchtowers. Inside the citadel, which was now about 650 feet (200 metres) long and 450 feet (140 metres) wide, great houses were laid out on ascending, concentric terraces. Troy VI was destroyed by a violent earthquake a little after 1300 BCE. Dörpfeld had identified this stage as Homeric Troy, but its apparent destruction by an earthquake does not agree with the realistic account of the sack of Troy in Greek tradition. Moreover, the city's date, as indicated by imported Mycenaean pottery found in the earthquake debris, is too early for the Trojan War.

The survivors of the earthquake quickly rebuilt the town, thus inaugurating the short-lived Troy VIIa. The ruins were leveled and covered over by new buildings, which were set close together and filled all available space inside the fortress. Almost every house was provided with

WILHELM DÖRPFELD

The German archaeologist and authority on Greek architecture Wilhelm Dörpfeld (1853–1940) excavated the Mycenaean palace at Tiryns (modern Tirins, Gr.) and continued the excavation of Heinrich Schliemann at Hisarlık, Tur., the site of ancient Troy.

After working with archaeologist Ernst Curtius on the excavation of ancient Olympia, he joined Schliemann at Troy (1882–90). Dörpfeld brought to Troy the new system and efficiency of the German classical archaeologists working in Greece, and he was able to expose the stratigraphy at Troy more clearly than before and to revolutionize Schliemann's techniques. Together they numbered the successive levels of occupation I–IX. He went with Schliemann to Tiryns in 1884 and in 1885 took charge of excavation, uncovering the first fairly well-preserved Mycenaean palace of the 2nd millennium BCE. In his own excavation of Troy (1893 and 1894), he concentrated on the edge of the site and uncovered Middle and Late Bronze Age ruins. He associated the destruction of Priam's Troy with level VI, though later study indicated it more likely was level VIIa. He prepared detailed architectural plans of level VI and in *Troja und Ilion*, 2 vol. (1902; "Troy and Ilium"), formulated a chronology for all levels of the site.

one or several huge storage jars that were sunk deep into the ground, with only their mouths above the level of the floor. Troy VIIa probably lasted little more than a generation. The crowding together of houses and the special measures to store up food supplies suggest that preparations had been made to withstand a siege. The town was destroyed in a devastating fire, and remnants of human bones found in some houses and streets strengthen the impression that the town was captured, looted, and burnt by enemies. Based on the evidence of imported Mycenaean pottery, the end of Troy VIIa can be dated to between 1260 and 1240 BCE. The Cincinnati expedition under Blegen concluded that Troy VIIa was very likely the capital of King Priam described in Homer's *Iliad*, which was destroyed by the Greek armies of Agamemnon.

The partly rebuilt Troy VIIb shows evidence of new settlers with a lower level of material culture, who vanished altogether by 1100 BCE. For about the next four centuries the site was virtually abandoned. About 700 BCE Greek settlers began to occupy the Troad. Troy was reoccupied and given the Hellenized name of Ilion; this Greek settlement is known as Troy VIII. The Romans sacked Ilion in 85 BCE, but it was partially restored by the Roman general Sulla that same year. This Romanized town, known as Troy IX, received fine public buildings from the emperor Augustus and his immediate successors, who traced their ancestry back to the Trojan Aeneas. After the founding of Constantinople (324 CE), Ilion faded into obscurity.

KNOSSOS

The city of Knossos (or Cnossus) in ancient Crete was the capital of the legendary king Minos and the principal centre of the Minoan, the earliest of the Aegean civilizations. The site of Knossos stands on a knoll between the confluence of two streams and is located about 5 miles (8 km) inland from Crete's northern coast. Excavations were begun at Knossos under the British archaeologist Arthur (later Sir Arthur) Evans in 1900 and revealed a palace and

surrounding buildings that were the centre of a sophisticated Bronze Age culture that dominated the Aegean
between about 1600 and 1400 BCE.

HISTORY

The first human inhabitants of Knossos probably came
there from Anatolia in the 7th millennium BCE and established an agricultural society based on wheat and livestock
raising. At the beginning of the Early Minoan period
(3000–2000 BCE) they began using bronze and making
glazed pottery, engraved seals, and gold jewelry. A hieroglyphic script was invented, and trade with the Egyptians
was undertaken. The first palace at Knossos was built at
the beginning of the Middle Minoan period (2000–1580
BCE). It consisted of isolated structures built around a rectangular court. Knossos produced fine polychrome pottery
on a black glazed ground during this period. About 1720
BCE a destructive earthquake leveled most of Knossos.
The palace was rebuilt, this time with extensive colonnades
and flights of stairs connecting the different buildings on
the hilly site. The remains of this palace occupy the excavated site in the present day. An elaborate system of drains,
conduits, and pipes provided water and sanitation for the
palace, and the whole urban complex was connected to
other Cretan towns and ports by paved roads. The art of
Minoan fresco painting reached its zenith at this time,
with scenes of dancing, sports, and dolphins done in a nat-
uralistic style. The Minoans also replaced their hieroglyphic
script with a linear script known as Linear A.

About 1580 BCE Minoan culture and influence began
to be extended to mainland Greece, where it was further
developed and emerged as the culture known as Mycenaean.
The Mycenaeans, in turn, achieved control over Knossos

sometime in the 15th century BCE; the Linear A script was replaced by another script, Linear B, which is identical to that used at Mycenae and is most generally deemed the prototype of Greek. Detailed administrative records in Linear B found at Knossos indicate that at this time the city's Mycenaean rulers controlled much of central and western Crete.

On the crest of Minoan prosperity came a great crash. Some time after about 1400 BCE, what Evans called the "Last Palace" of Knossos was destroyed by a fire of uncertain origin but probably an invasion; fires also destroyed many other Cretan settlements at this time. Knossos was reduced henceforth to the status of a mere town, and the political focus of the Aegean world shifted to Mycenae on the Greek mainland. Knossos continued to be inhabited through the subsequent centuries, though on a much-reduced scale.

PALACE OF MINOS

The great maritime civilization of Crete crystallized around palaces such as those at Knossos, Phaestus, Ayía Triáda, Mallia, and Tylissos. The immensely important Palace of Minos at Knossos offers evidence of unbroken architectural and artistic development from Neolithic beginnings, culminating in a brilliant display of building activity during the third phase of the Middle Minoan period and continuing until the invasion of the Achaeans in the 12th century. The palace, however, is essentially a structure of the late two Middle Minoan periods (1800–1580 BCE). It no doubt rivaled Middle Eastern and Egyptian palaces in monumentality.

Following the example of such structures, the Palace of Minos is a quadrangular complex of rooms and corridors grouped around a great central court, roughly 175 × 100 feet

(50 × 30 metres). At the northern end, toward the sea, a grand portico of 12 pilasters would have given access to the central court. At this end, also, is situated the grand theatrical area, a rectangular open-air theatre that was perhaps used for ritual performances. The east wing of the palace is divided into two parts by a long corridor running on an east–west axis; originally it rose four or five stories above the slope of the valley. The southeast portion of the palace contains domestic apartments, elaborately supplied with plumbing and flushing facilities, as well as a sanctuary. A wide stairway led to an upper story, which no longer exists. The northeast portion of the palace is occupied by offices and storerooms. The west portion is again divided by a main corridor, more than 200 feet (60 metres) long, running north and south. Behind this corridor, along the western side, was discovered a series of long narrow storerooms containing great numbers of pithoi, or human-size storage vessels for oil. On the other side of the corridor, facing toward the central court, are the rooms of state, including the throne room with its unique gypsum throne and world-famous griffin frescoes. Brilliantly hued frescoes played an important part in both the interior and the exterior decoration of the palace. Light was supplied from above by an ingenious system of light wells, and several colonnaded porticoes provided ventilation during the hot Cretan summers.

The development of the other Minoan palaces (Phaestus, Mallia, Ayía Triáda, Tylissos) roughly parallels that of Knossos. Each is notable, and Phaestus is particularly fascinating, due to extensive Italian excavations. Maritime hegemony enabled the Cretan sea kings to build these palaces in low and unprotected places; consequently there is a conspicuous absence of fortification walls, as contrasted to the great walls of Mesopotamian palaces. Since Cretan worship seems to have been conducted

SIR ARTHUR EVANS

Sir Arthur Evans (1851–1941) is renowned for excavating the ruins of Knossos in Crete and uncovering evidence of a sophisticated Bronze Age civilization there, which he named Minoan. His work was one of archaeology's major achievements and greatly advanced the study of European and eastern Mediterranean prehistory.

A distinguished scholar, Evans was curator of the Ashmolean Museum, University of Oxford, from 1884 to 1908 and became extraordinary professor of prehistoric archaeology at Oxford in 1909. His interest in ancient coins and the writing on stone seals from Crete lured him to the island for the first time in 1894. During an address in 1896 he suggested that the Mycenaean civilization of the Greek mainland had its origins in Crete. Three years later he purchased a tract of land that included the site of Knossos, and after a year's digging he had unearthed palace ruins covering 5.5 acres (2.2 hectares). The size and splendour of the findings indicated that Knossos had been an ancient cultural capital. The complex ground plan of the palace suggested the labyrinth associated with the legendary King Minos, prompting Evans to name the civilization Minoan.

Over the course of the next 25 years Evans pursued his investigations. Digging below the Bronze Age ruins, he came upon remains of a Neolithic civilization, thus helping to place Mycenae in historical perspective. His discovery of Egyptian artifacts dating from known historical periods helped him establish the periods of Minoan civilization. Later estimates, however, differ from his.

Knossos also yielded some 3,000 clay tablets bearing one form of Minoan writing, the Linear B script. Evans hoped to decipher this as well as the other forms, the Linear

A and the pictorial. He failed, but a lecture he delivered in 1936 inspired the English architect and cryptographer Michael Ventris to work on the script. (Ventris later presented evidence that Linear B was a form of Greek, and his proposal was widely accepted.) Evans received many honours for his discoveries and was knighted in 1911.

largely in the open air, there are no real temples as in the Middle East. Yet, the disposition of the various parts of the palace around the central court and the avoidance of outside windows as much as possible are characteristics that seem to indicate an early contact with the Middle East. A taste for long, straight palace corridors, as well as a highly developed water-supply system, may also have been inherited from older civilizations to the east. The column made its first European appearance in the Cretan palace, where it is often employed individually to divide an entranceway.

MACHU PICCHU

Machu Picchu (or Machupijchu) is the site of ancient Inca ruins located about 50 miles (80 km) northwest of Cuzco, Peru, in the Cordillera de Vilcabamba of the Andes Mountains. It is perched above the Urubamba River valley in a narrow saddle between two sharp peaks — Machu Picchu ("Old Peak") and Huayna Picchu ("New Peak") — at an elevation of 7,710 feet (2,350 metres). One of the few major pre-Columbian ruins found nearly intact, Machu Picchu was designated a UNESCO World Heritage site in 1983.

Machu Picchu. © Digital Vision/Getty Images

SITE AND EXCAVATION

Although Machu Picchu escaped detection by the Spaniards, the German adventurer Augusto Berns may have visited the site in 1867. However, its existence was not widely known in the West until it was "discovered" in 1911 by the Yale University professor Hiram Bingham, who was led to the site by Melchor Arteaga, a local Quechua-speaking resident. Bingham had been seeking Vilcabamba (Vilcapampa), the "lost city of the Incas," from which the last Inca rulers led a rebellion against Spanish rule until 1572. He cited evidence from his 1912 excavations at Machu Picchu, which were sponsored by Yale University and the National Geographic Society, in his labeling of the site as Vilcabamba; however, that interpretation is no longer widely accepted. (Nevertheless, many sources still follow Bingham's precedent and erroneously label Machu Picchu as the "lost city of the Incas.") Evidence later associated Vilcabamba with another ruin, Espíritu Pampa, which was also discovered by Bingham. In 1964 Espíritu Pampa was extensively excavated under the direction of the American explorer Gene Savoy. The site was much deteriorated and overgrown with forest, but Savoy uncovered remains there of some 300 Inca houses and 50 or more other buildings, as well as extensive terraces, proving that Espíritu Pampa was a much larger settlement.

Machu Picchu was further excavated in 1915 by Bingham, in 1934 by the Peruvian archaeologist Luis E. Valcarcel, and in 1940–41 by Paul Fejos. Additional discoveries throughout the Cordillera de Vilcabamba have shown that Machu Picchu was one of a series of *pucaras* (fortified sites), *tambos* (travelers' barracks, or inns), and signal towers along the extensive Inca foot highway.

The dwellings at Machu Picchu were probably built and occupied from the mid-15th to the early or mid-16th century. Machu Picchu's construction style and other evidence suggest that it was a palace complex of the ruler Pachacuti Inca Yupanqui (reigned *c.* 1438–71). Several dozen skeletons were excavated there in 1912, and, because most of those were initially identified as female, Bingham suggested that Machu Picchu was a sanctuary for the Virgins of the Sun (the Chosen Women), an elite Inca group. Technology at the turn of the 21st-century, however, identified a significant proportion of males and a great diversity in physical types. Both skeletal and material remains now suggest to scholars that Machu Picchu served as a royal retreat. The reason for the site's abandonment is also unknown, but lack of water may have been a factor.

ARCHITECTURE AND TOURISM

The high level of preservation and the general layout of
the ruin are remarkable. Its southern, eastern, and western portions are surrounded by dozens of stepped
agricultural terraces formerly watered by an aqueduct system. Some of those terraces were still being used by local
Indians when Bingham arrived in 1911. Walkways and
thousands of steps, consisting of stone blocks as well as
footholds carved into underlying rock, connect the plazas,
the residential areas, the terraces, the cemetery, and the
major buildings. The Main Plaza, partly divided by wide
terraces, is at the north-central end of the site. At the
southeastern end is the only formal entrance, which leads
to the Inca Trail.

Few of Machu Picchu's white granite structures have
stonework as highly refined as that found in Cuzco, but
several are worthy of note. In the southern part of the ruin
is the Sacred Rock, also known as the Temple of the Sun (it
was called the Mausoleum by Bingham). It centres on an
inclined rock mass with a small grotto; walls of cut stone
fill in some of its irregular features. Rising above the rock
is the horseshoe-shaped enclosure known as the Military
Tower. In the western part of Machu Picchu is the temple
district, also known as the Acropolis. The Temple of the
Three Windows is a hall 35 feet (10.6 metres) long and 14
feet (4.2 metres) wide with three trapezoidal windows (the
largest known in Inca architecture) on one wall, which is
built of polygonal stones. It stands near the southwestern
corner of the Main Plaza. Also near the Main Plaza is the
Intihuatana (Hitching Post of the Sun), a uniquely preserved ceremonial sundial consisting of a wide pillar and
pedestal that were carved as a single unit and stand 6 feet
(1.8 metres) tall. In 2000 this feature was damaged during

Machu Picchu. Mayes/FPG

the filming of a beer commercial. The Princess's Palace is a bi-level structure of highly crafted stonework that probably housed a member of the Inca nobility. The Palace of the Inca is a complex of rooms with niched walls and a courtyard. At the other end of Machu Picchu, another path leads to the famous Inca Bridge, a rope structure that crosses the Urubamba River. Many other ruined cities—like that atop the dark peak of Huayna Picchu, which is accessible by a lengthy, precipitous stairway and trail—were built in the region; Machu Picchu is only the most extensively excavated of these.

Machu Picchu is the most economically important tourist attraction in Peru, bringing in visitors from around the world. For this reason the Peruvian government wishes to repatriate the materials taken by Bingham to Yale. The ruins are commonly reached in a day trip from Cuzco by first taking a narrow-gauge railway and then ascending nearly 1,640 feet (500 metres) from the Urubamba River valley on a serpentine road. Smaller numbers of visitors arrive by hiking the Inca Trail. The portion of the trail from the "km 88" train stop to Machu Picchu is normally hiked in three to six days. It is composed of several thousand stone-cut steps, numerous high retaining walls, tunnels, and other feats of classical engineering; the route traverses a wide range of elevations between about 8,530 and 13,780 feet (2,600 and 4,200 metres), and it is lined with Inca ruins of various types and sizes. At Machu Picchu there is a hotel with a restaurant, and thermal baths are at the nearby village of Aguas Calientes. The Inca Bridge and other parts of Machu Picchu were damaged by a forest fire in August 1997, but restoration was begun immediately afterward. Concern for the damage caused by tourism was heightened by discussion of the building of a cable-car link to the site (the plan was later abandoned).

HIRAM BINGHAM

The American archaeologist and politician Hiram Bingham (1875–1956) in 1911 initiated the scientific study of Machu Picchu. Bingham may have been preceded by the German adventurer Augusto Berns, who, some scholars believe, visited the site in 1867. Whether or not he was preceded by Berns, however, Bingham and his work were the key catalysts for the archaeological investigation of sites in the Andes and other parts of South America.

As a boy, Bingham learned mountaineering from his father. This skill vastly aided his Inca research. In 1906, seeking to enhance his ability to teach Latin American history, he traveled the Andean route taken in 1819 by Simón Bolívar from Venezuela to Colombia. In 1908 he followed the old Spanish trade route through the Andes from Buenos Aires, Arg., to Lima, Peru.

Bingham was a member of the history faculty at Yale University from 1909 until 1924. In July 1911 he directed a Yale archaeological expedition whose main objective was to find Vilcabamba (Vilcapampa), which was the "lost city of the Incas," the secret mountain stronghold used during the 16th-century rebellion against Spanish rule. Prospects for locating it were poor: not even the Spanish conquistadores had discovered it. Clues from early chronicles of the Incas were scanty. It was believed to be situated somewhere near Cuzco, Peru, where the problems of crossing the Andes were formidable. The expedition owed its success largely to Bingham's steadfastness and courage. He visited several Inca sites, sometimes risking his life to do so.

After arriving in Cuzco, Bingham was urged by the prefect of Apurímac, J.J. Nuñez, to search the vicinity of the Urubamba River valley for the fabled ruins of Choquequirau ("Cradle of Gold"), and Bingham suspected that site might be Vilcabamba. On July 24 Bingham was led by a Quechua-speaking resident, Melchor Arteaga, to the ruins of Machu Picchu. There he found well-preserved stonework remains and was particularly struck by the similarity of one of the structures to the Temple of the Sun at Cuzco. In 1912 Bingham led the expedition that excavated Machu Picchu, and he returned there in 1915. He became convinced that Machu Picchu was Vilcabamba, and it wasn't until the mid-20th century that his claim was seriously disputed. Bingham's additional work in the region revealed the important sites of Vitcos and Espíritu Pampa, a larger ruin that was thoroughly excavated in 1964 by the American archaeologist Gene Savoy, who demonstrated it to be a more likely site for Vilcabamba. Bingham's publications on South America include *Inca Land* (1922), *Machu Picchu, a Citadel of the Incas* (1930), and *Lost City of the Incas* (1948).

VALLEY OF THE KINGS AND TUTANKHAMEN

The long, narrow defile just west of the Nile River in Upper Egypt is the fabled Valley of the Kings (Arabic: Wādī Al-Mulūk), also known as the Valley of the Tombs of the Kings (Wādī Bībān al-Mulūk). It was part of the ancient city of Thebes and was the burial site of almost all the kings (pharaohs) of the 18th, 19th, and 20th dynasties (1539–1075 BCE) of ancient Egypt, from Thutmose I to Ramses X. Included among these tombs is the especially celebrated one of Tutankhamen, which was discovered, largely undisturbed, in 1922. Located in the hills behind Dayr al-Baḥrī, the 62 known tombs exhibit variety both in plan and in decoration. In 1979 UNESCO designated the valley part of the World Heritage site of ancient

Thebes, which also includes Luxor, the Valley of the Queens, and Karnak.

VALLEY OF THE KINGS

The kings of the New Kingdom (*c.* 1539–1075 BCE), fearing for the safety of their rich burials, adopted a new plan of concealing their tombs in a lonely valley in the western hills behind Dayr al-Baḥrī. There, in tombs sunk deep into the heart of the mountain, pharaohs were interred, as were several queens, a few officials of high rank, and the numerous sons of Ramses II. The plan of the tombs varies considerably but consists essentially of a descending corridor interrupted by deep shafts to baffle robbers and by pillared chambers or vestibules. At the farther end of the corridor is a burial chamber with a stone sarcophagus in which the royal mummy was laid and store chambers around which furniture and equipment were stacked for the king's use in the next world.

The walls were in many cases covered with sculptured and painted scenes depicting the dead king in the presence of deities, especially the gods of the underworld, and with illustrated magical texts similar to those found in funerary papyri, designed to help him on his journey through the nether regions. There were a number of these texts; they represent differing but not necessarily conflicting views of the afterlife, in which the king had to undergo trials and surmount perils. In the "Book of That Which Is in the Underworld," for instance, he travels in the boat of the sun god through 12 divisions that represent the 12 hours of the night. In the "Book of Gates," giant serpents guard the portals through which the sun has to pass as strange demons help or hinder the boat on its way. Other funerary compositions include the "Book of Day" and the "Book of Night," which depict Nut, the sky-goddess, spread out across the heavens, as well as the "Book of the Heavenly Cow," in which Nut is transformed into a cow on whom Re ascends to the firmament. Astronomical figures decorate the ceilings of several burial chambers.

Virtually all the tombs in the valley were cleared out in antiquity. Some had been partially robbed during the New Kingdom, but all were systematically denuded of their contents in the 21st dynasty, in an effort to protect the royal mummies and to recycle the rich funerary goods back into the royal treasury. In the time of Strabo (1st century BCE), Greek travelers were able to visit 40 of the tombs. Several tombs were reused by Coptic monks, who left their own inscriptions on the walls. Only the little tomb of Tutankhamen, located on the floor of the valley and protected by a pile of rock chippings thrown down from a later tomb, escaped pillage. The longest tomb (number 20) belongs to Queen Hatshepsut (reigned *c.* 1472–58 BCE), whose burial chamber is nearly 700 feet (215 metres) from the entrance and descends 320 feet (100 metres) into the rock.

The largest and most complex tomb in the Valley of the Kings (number 5) was apparently built to contain the burial chambers of many of the sons of Ramses II (reigned 1279–13 BCE), the greatest king of the 19th dynasty. This tomb, which had been previously discovered but dismissed as insignificant, was again located in the late 1980s and partially excavated in the 1990s. The uppermost of the tomb's two levels contains a central pillared hall and various corridors leading away to dozens of chambers.

TUTANKHAMEN AND HIS TOMB

Tutankhamen, king of ancient Egypt (reigned 1333–23 BCE), is known chiefly for his intact tomb, KV 62 (tomb 62), discovered in the Valley of the Kings in 1922. During his reign, powerful advisers restored the traditional Egyptian religion and art, both of which had been set aside by his predecessor Akhenaton, who had led the "Amarna revolution."

The parentage of Tutankhaten—as he was originally known—remains uncertain, although a single black fragment originating at Akhetaton (Tell el-Amarna), Akhenaton's capital city, names him as a king's son in a context similar to that of the princesses of Akhenaton. Medical analysis of Tutankhaten's mummy shows that he shares very close physical characteristics with the mummy discovered in KV 55 (tomb 55) of the Valley of the Kings. Some scholars identify these remains as those of Smenkhkare, who seems to have been coregent with Akhenaton in the final years of his reign. Others have suggested the mummy may be Akhenaton himself.

With the death of Smenkhkare, the young Tutankhaten became king, and was married to Akhenaton's third daughter, Ankhesenpaaton (or Ankhesenamen), probably the eldest surviving princess of the royal family. Because at his accession he was still very young, the elderly official Ay, who had long maintained ties with the royal family, and the general of the armies, Horemheb, served as Tutankhaten's chief advisers.

By his third regnal year Tutankhaten had abandoned Tell el-Amarna and moved his residence to Memphis, the administrative capital, near modern Cairo. He changed his name to Tutankhamen and issued a decree restoring the temples, images, personnel, and privileges of the old gods. He also began the protracted process of restoring the sacred shrines of Amon, which had been severely damaged during his father's rule. No proscription or persecution of the Aton, Akhenaton's god, was undertaken, and royal vineyards and regiments of the army were still named after the Aton.

*King Tutankhamen and Queen Ankhesenamen, detail from the back of
the throne of Tutankhamen; in the Egyptian Museum, Cairo.* Hirmer
Fotoarchiv, Munich

In addition to a palace built at Karnak and a memorial
temple in western Thebes, both now largely vanished, the
chief extant monument of Tutankhamen is the Colonnade
of the Temple of Luxor, which he decorated with reliefs
depicting the Opet festival, an annual rite of renewal
involving the king, the three chief deities of Karnak (Amon,
Mut, and Khons), and the local form of Amon at Luxor.

Tutankhamen unexpectedly died in his 19th year without designating an heir and was succeeded by Ay. He was buried in a small tomb hastily converted for his use in the Valley of the Kings (his intended sepulchre was probably taken over by Ay). Like other rulers associated with the Amarna period—Akhenaton, Smenkhkare, and Ay—he was to suffer the posthumous fate of having his name stricken from later king lists and his monuments usurped, primarily by his former general, Horemheb, who subsequently became king. Although Tutankhamen's tomb shows evidence of having been entered and briefly plundered, the location of his burial was clearly forgotten by the time of the 20th dynasty (1190–1075 BCE), when craftsmen assigned to work on the nearby tomb of Ramses VI built temporary stone shelters directly over its entrance. The tomb was preserved until a systematic search of the Valley of the Kings by the English archaeologist Howard Carter revealed its location in 1922.

Tutankhamen's tomb (lower left) *in the Valley of the Kings, near Luxor (ancient Thebes), Egypt.* © Robert Holmes

Inside his small tomb, the king's mummy lay within a nest of three coffins, the innermost of solid gold, the two outer ones of gold hammered over wooden frames. On the king's head was a magnificent golden portrait mask, and numerous pieces of jewelry and amulets lay upon the mummy and in its wrappings. The coffins and stone sarcophagus were surrounded by four text-covered shrines of hammered gold over wood, which practically filled the burial chamber. The other rooms were crammed with furniture, statuary, clothes, chariots, weapons, staffs, and numerous other objects. But for his tomb, Tutankhamen has little claim to fame; as it is, he is perhaps better known than any of his longer-lived and better-documented predecessors and successors. His renown was secured after the highly popular "Treasures of Tutankhamun" exhibit traveled the world in the 1960s and '70s. The treasures are housed at the Egyptian Museum in Cairo.

HOWARD CARTER

The British archaeologist Howard Carter (1873–1939) made one of the richest and most celebrated contributions to Egyptology when he discovered (1922) the largely intact tomb of King Tutankhamen.

At age 17 Carter joined the British-sponsored archaeological survey of Egypt. He made drawings (1893–99) of the sculptures and inscriptions at the terraced temple of Queen Hatshepsut in ancient Thebes. He next served as inspector general of the Egyptian antiquities department. While supervising excavations in the Valley of the Tombs of the Kings in 1902, he discovered the tombs of Hatshepsut and Thutmose IV.

About 1907 he began his association with the 5th earl of Carnarvon, a collector of antiquities who had sought out Carter to supervise excavations in the valley. On Nov. 4, 1922, Carter found the first sign of what proved to be Tutankhamen's tomb, but it was not until November 26 that a second sealed doorway was reached, behind which were the treasures. Carter's diary captured the drama of the moment. After making a tiny hole in the doorway, Carter, with candle in hand, peered into the tomb.

Howard Carter.
Encyclopædia
Britannica, Inc.

It was sometime before one could see, the hot air escaping caused the candle to flicker, but as soon as one's eyes became accustomed to the glimmer of light the interior of the chamber gradually loomed before one, with its strange and wonderful medley of extraordinary and beautiful objects heaped upon one another.

For the next 10 years Carter supervised the removal of its contents, most of which are housed in the Egyptian Museum in Cairo. He published *Thoutmôsis IV* (1904) and *The Tomb of Tut-ankh-Amen* (1923–33) with, respectively, P.E. Newberry and A.C. Mace. An account of the Tutankhamen excavation may be found in C.W. Ceram's *Gods, Graves & Scholars* (2nd rev. and enlarged ed., 1994).

EASTER ISLAND

Easter Island (Spanish: Isla de Pascua), a Chilean depend-
ency in the eastern Pacific Ocean, is the easternmost
outpost of the Polynesian island world. It is famous for its
giant stone statues. The island stands in isolation some
1,200 miles (1,900 km) east of Pitcairn Island and 2,200
miles (3,500 km) west of Chile. Forming a triangle 14 miles
long by seven miles wide, it has an area of 63 square miles
(163 square kilometres). Its highest point, Mount Terevaka,
is 1,969 feet (600 metres) above sea level.

To its original inhabitants the island is known as Rapa
Nui ("Great Rapa") or Te Pito te Henua ("Navel of the
World"). The first European visitors, the Dutch, named
it Paaseiland ("Easter Island") in memory of their own
day of arrival. Its mixed population is predominantly of
Polynesian descent; almost all live in the village of Hanga
Roa on the sheltered west coast.

ARCHAEOLOGY

Easter Island is famous for its gigantic stone statues, of
which there are more than 600, and for the ruins of giant
stone platforms (*ahus*) with open courtyards on their land-
ward sides, some of which show masterly construction.
Archaeological surveys were carried out in 1886, 1914, and
1934; archaeological excavations were initiated in 1955.
The excavations revealed that three distinct cultural periods are identifiable on the island. The early period is
characterized by *ahus* at Tahai, Vinapu, and Anakena, carbon dated to about 700–850 CE. The first two were
admired and described by Capt. James Cook. The wall in
Anakena remained hidden below ground until it was
excavated archaeologically in 1987. The excavations in

Moai *statues on Easter Island.* © Goodshoot/Jupiterimages

Anakena have revealed that a variety of statues were carved in the early period, among them a smaller proto-type of the middle-period busts, which mainly differ from the latter by their rounded heads and stubby bodies. Another type was a realistic sculpture in full figure of a kneeling man with his buttocks resting on his heels and his hands on his knees, in one case with his ribs exposed, all features characteristic of pre-Inca monuments at Tiwanaku in South America. In the middle period (*c.* 1050–1680), statues were deliberately destroyed and dis-carded, and all *ahus* were rebuilt with no regard for solar orientation or masonry fitting. The sole desire seems to have been to obtain strong platforms capable of support-ing ever taller and heavier busts, the classical *moai* of the middle period.

Burial chambers also were constructed within the *ahus* in the middle period. The sizes of the statues made were increased until they reached stupendous dimen-sions; the slim and lofty busts also had huge cylindrical *pukao* (topknots) of red tuff placed on top of their slender heads. Most middle-period statues range from about 10 to 20 feet (3 to 6 metres) in height, but the biggest among those formerly standing on top of an *ahu* was about 32 feet tall (9.75 metres), consisted of a single block weighing about 82 tons, and had a *pukao* of about 11 tons balanced on its apex. The largest statue still standing partly buried in the deep silt below the quarries is about 37 feet (11.25 metres) tall, and the largest unfinished one with its back attached to the rock is about 68 feet (21 metres) tall. Traditions, supported by archaeology, suggest that the images represented important personalities who were deified after death.

Statues of the middle period were all quarried from the special yellow-gray tuff found in the crater walls of Rano

Raraku. Inside and outside the crater bowl numerous unfinished statues and thousands of crude stone picks are scattered about, bearing witness to a sudden interruption of the sculptors' work. The unfinished images show that each statue had its front and sides completed to a polish before the back was detached from the bedrock. The image was then slid away to be raised at random in the rubble below the quarries to have the back finished before being moved to some distant *ahu*. Eye cavities and top-knots were added only after the monument was erected. Recent discoveries have revealed that these concavities had inlaid eyes of white coral with a dark stone disk as pupil. From one to a dozen completed statues would stand in a row on a single *ahu*, always facing inland.

Experiments based on island traditions in 1955–56 showed that the numerous basalt picks left in the quarries were perfectly suitable for carving the hard tuff. Reenactments showed that 12 islanders were able to lift a 25-ton statue about 10 feet off the ground and to tilt it on end on top of an *ahu*; this work took 18 days with no tools other than two wooden logs that were used as levers. Stones of all sizes were wedged under the statue one by one to form a slowly rising cairn in order to lift the giant monoliths upright. Tradition claimed that the statues had "walked" across the terrain to their distant destinations, but in the experiment 180 islanders were able to pull a medium statue over the ground. A renewed experiment in 1986 revived the tradition and discovered that 15 men sufficed to move a medium-sized statue over the ground in upright position by jerking it ahead with a system of ropes.

The middle-period busts clearly evolved from a local prototype and have no counterpart elsewhere. Also peculiar to the middle period was a bird cult with attendant birdman rites that survived into the third, or late, period. Its ceremonial centre was the village of Orongo, on top of Rano Kao, which consisted of stone houses with roof vaults built as false arches. These houses and contiguous circular masonry dwellings with roof entrances are characteristic of the early and middle periods on the island; while unknown elsewhere in Polynesia they are common in the adjacent area of South America.

THOR HEYERDAHL AND THE *KON-TIKI*

The Norwegian ethnologist and adventurer Thor Heyerdahl (1914–2002) is best known for his celebrated voyage across the Pacific Ocean in the *Kon-Tiki*, a raft in which he and five companions sailed in 1947 from the western coast of South America to the islands east of Tahiti. Heyerdahl, who had earlier visited the Marquesas Islands, was interested in demonstrating the possibility that ancient people from the Americas could have colonized Polynesia. To do so, he constructed *Kon-Tiki* (named for a legendary Inca god) from locally available balsa logs at Callao, Peru, and in three and a half months traversed some 4,300 miles (6,900 km) of ocean. The story of the voyage was related in Heyerdahl's book *Kon-Tiki* (1950) and in a documentary motion picture of the same name. The *Kon-Tiki* has been preserved in a museum in Oslo, Nor.

Heyerdahl subsequently organized other transoceanic voyages to demonstrate how ancient civilizations could have influenced others and published *Early Man and the Ocean: A Search for the Beginnings of Navigation and Seaborne Civilizations* (1979), in which he synthesized the findings of these expeditions and provided additional evidence for his theory of cultural diffusion. For the most part, Heyerdahl's theories have not been accepted by anthropologists.

OLDUVAI GORGE

The world-famous Olduvai (or Olduwai) Gorge is a paleoanthropological site in the eastern Serengeti Plain within the boundaries of the Ngorongoro Conservation Area in northern Tanzania. It is a steep-sided ravine consisting of two branches that have a combined length of about 30 miles (48 km) and are 295 feet (90 metres) deep. Deposits exposed in the sides of the gorge cover a time span from about 2,100,000 to 15,000 years ago. The deposits have yielded the fossil remains of more than 60 hominins (members of the human lineage), providing the most continuous known record of human evolution during the past 2,000,000 years, as well as the longest known archaeological record of the development of stone-tool industries. Olduvai Gorge was designated part of a UNESCO World Heritage site in 1979. Although Olduvai Gorge has often

Rock formation at Olduvai Gorge, Tanzania. Cyril Toker/Photo Trends

been called the "Cradle of Mankind," a different World
Heritage site called the "Cradle of Humankind" is located
in South Africa.

The Olduvai fossil beds accumulated in a lake basin
between 4 and 9 miles (7 and 15 km) in diameter. The lake is
underlain by volcanic rocks of the Pliocene Epoch (5.3 to 1.8
million years ago) and, farther below, by metamorphic
deposits of Precambrian time (more than roughly 540 million years ago). Relatively continuous rift-valley fault
movements and volcanic action left Olduvai deeply incised.
Water flow through the gorge further eroded the rock,
exposing a delineated sequence of strata from which evolu-
tionary events could be traced. Seven major stratigraphic
units, or formations, have been distinguished. From the
oldest to the youngest they are: Bed I (about 1,700,000 to
2,100,000 years old), Bed II (1,150,000–1,700,000 years
old), Bed III (800,000–1,150,000 years old), Bed IV
(600,000–800,000 years old), the Masek Beds (400,000–
600,000 years old), the Ndutu Beds (32,000–400,000 years
old), and the Naisiusiu Beds (15,000–22,000 years old).

THE FOSSIL BEDS

Bed I is at most 197 feet (60 metres) thick. It consists
largely of lava flows, volcanic ash deposits, and detrital
sediments. The upper part of the bed (1.7 to 1.85 million
years old) contains a rich and varied fauna and archaeological sites of the Oldowan industry. It was there in 1959
that Mary Leakey discovered a skull fragment belonging
to an early hominin that her husband, Louis Leakey, named
Zinjanthropus boisei (later reclassified as *Paranthropus boisei*).
Officially labeled OH 5 (Olduvai Hominid 5) but dubbed
"Nutcracker Man" because of its huge molars (indicative
of a vegetarian diet), the skull was dated to about 1.75 million years ago. The discovery indicated that hominins

THE LEAKEY FAMILY

The Leakeys are a family of archaeologists and paleoanthropologists known for their discoveries of hominin and other fossil remains in eastern Africa. Louis S.B. Leakey (1903–72), born of British missionary parents, grew up in Kenya, was educated at Cambridge University, and eventually (1931) began field research at Olduvai Gorge in Tanzania. He was joined there by his wife, Mary D. Leakey (1913–96), who in 1959 uncovered remains of a form of *Australopithecus*. The couple later uncovered the first known remains of *Homo habilis*, as well as those of *Kenyapithecus*, a possible common ancestor of humans and apes that lived *c.* 14 million years ago. L.S.B. Leakey commissioned Jane Goodall, Biruté Galdikas, and Dian Fossey to undertake pioneering studies of chimpanzees, orangutans, and gorillas, respectively. Mary Leakey continued to make important discoveries, including the Laetoli footprints, after her husband's death. Their son, Richard Leakey (1944–), is known for his work at the Koobi Fora site on the shores of Lake Turkana in Kenya, where he uncovered evidence of *H. habilis* dated as early as 2.5 million years ago. His wife, zoologist Meave Leakey (1942–), discovered two new hominin species.

evolved in Africa. Specimens of *Homo habilis*, a more humanlike species, were also found at Olduvai. These included OH 24, a skull popularly known as "Twiggy" because it had to be reconstructed from a flattened state.

The remains of Bed I are found principally where streams from volcanic highlands brought fresh water to the southern margin of an alkaline lake that existed at Olduvai. Conditions for preservation were unusually favourable at these sites because ashfalls from nearby volcanoes and

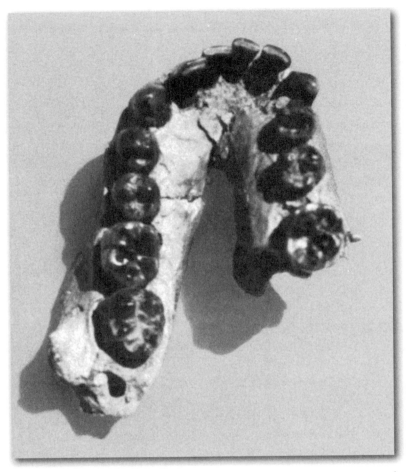

Lower jaw of OH 7, a specimen found in 1960 at Olduvai Gorge, Tanzania, and identified by Louis Leakey and others in 1964 as a fossil of Homo habilis. G. Philip Rightmire

fluctuations of the lake led to rapid burial of the hominin and associated remains. Other finds include Oldowan tools and the bones and teeth of various animals, notably medium-sized antelopes. Long animal bones and others containing marrow generally have been split and broken and often display bone-tool cut marks.

NATIONAL GEOGRAPHIC SOCIETY

The National Geographic Society was founded (1888) in Washington, D.C., by a small group of eminent explorers and scientists "for the increase and diffusion of geographic knowledge." With some nine million members, the organization is the world's largest scientific and educational society. Members receive the monthly *National Geographic Magazine*. The maps produced for the society and often issued to its members as supplements helped set cartographic standards.

Although overseen by a 24-person board, the society has been guided by a member of the Grosvenor family almost since its inception. Gilbert H. Grovesnor, appointed editor of the magazine by his father-in-law, Alexander Graham Bell, the society's second president, took over the presidency in 1898. He held that position until 1957, when he was succeeded by his son and eventually by his grandson. When the third Grosvenor retired in 1996, his successor was, for the first time in nearly a century, not a member of the family.

The National Geographic Society has supported more than 5,000 major scientific projects and expeditions, including the polar expeditions of the American explorers Robert E. Peary and Richard E. Byrd, the British archaeologist Howard Carter's discovery of the tomb of King Tutankhamen in Egypt, and the first American climb of Mount Everest. Other expeditions, often cosponsored with the Smithsonian Institution and other organizations, have studied volcanic eruptions and earthquakes, excavated Machu Picchu, and discovered in Mexico the oldest dated work of humans in the New World. In the 1960s the society funded research by the British anthropologists L.S.B. Leakey and Mary Leakey in the Olduvai Gorge of eastern Africa that produced remarkable fossil remains of early hominids. Society support also benefited the investigations of the French undersea explorer Jacques-Yves Cousteau, the work of the British ethologist Jane Goodall with chimpanzees and that of American zoologist Dian Fossey with gorillas, and the exploration of the wreck of the ocean liner *Titanic*.

In addition to the *National Geographic Magazine*, the society publishes books and atlases, issues weekly bulletins to educators, librarians, and students, and operates a news service and its own television channel. In one of its most successful endeavours, the society has created hundreds of documentary programs for television and has produced numerous educational video products, and interactive multimedia educational systems.

Richard E. Byrd in Antarctica, 1947. Navy Department/National Archives, Washington, D.C.

Living sites in Beds II, III, and IV generally are found in former river or stream channels. Bed II is 66–98 feet (20–30 metres) thick and consists of different rock formations separated by a disconformity, or erosional break. Only the Oldowan industry occurs below the disconformity; the so-called Developed Oldowan industry and the Acheulean industry occur above. *H. habilis* remains were found in the lower one-third of Bed II, and a cranium of *H. ergaster* (also called African *H. erectus*) was collected near the top of Bed II. *P. boisei* occurs both in upper and lower parts of Bed II.

Beds III and IV were deposited on an alluvial plain. These two units are distinct only in the eastern part of the gorge and are elsewhere combined into a single unit. The two beds have a maximum aggregate thickness of about 98 feet (30 metres) and consist almost entirely of stream-laid detrital sediment. Archaeological sites in Beds III and IV represent the Developed Oldowan and Acheulean industries. Hominin remains there are assigned to *H. erectus* and other species of *Homo*.

The Masek Beds accumulated during a period of major faulting and explosive volcanism. They are some 82 feet (25 metres) thick and consist of about equal amounts of stream-laid detrital sediment and aeolian (wind-worked) tuff. Only one archaeological site, of the Acheulean industry, is known in these beds. The Ndutu Beds were deposited during intermittent faulting, erosion, and partial filling of the gorge. They consist largely of aeolian tuffs, and their maximum thickness is 79 feet (24 metres). The Naisiusiu Beds were deposited on the sides and in the bottom of the gorge after it had been eroded to very near its present level. These deposits are as much as 33 feet (10 metres) thick and consist largely of aeolian tuff. They contain one archaeological site consisting of a microlithic tool assemblage and a *H. sapiens* skeleton, both of which have an age of about 17,000 years.

Glossary

acropolis The fortified height or citadel of an ancient Greek city.

acumen Quick and accurate judgment; keen insight.

adherent A supporter, as of a cause or individual.

ascribe To attribute to a specified cause, source, or origin.

autocratic Describes a ruler with absolute or unrestricted power.

chronometer An exceptionally precise watch, clock, or other timepiece.

citadel A fortress in a commanding position in or near a city.

confluence A flowing together of two or more streams.

couloir A deep mountainside, gorge, or gully.

equinoctial Pertaining to an equinox.

equinox Either of two points on the celestial sphere where the ecliptic intersects the celestial equator.

eschatology The branch of theology that is concerned with the ultimate or last things, such as death, judgment, heaven, and hell.

extant Still in existence; not destroyed, lost, or extinct.

griffin A beast in Greek mythology that has the head and wings of an eagle and the body of a lion.

hegemony Predominance; especially, preponderant influence of one state over others.

intrepid Resolutely courageous; fearless; bold.

laudatory Including, expressing, or bestowing praise.

perspicacious Acutely discerning, perceptive, or understanding.

promontory A high ridge of land or rock jutting out into a sea or other body of water.

recalcitrant Stubbornly resistant to authority, domination, or guidance.

sepulchre A burial vault.

sextant A navigational instrument used for measuring altitudes of celestial bodies.

sovereignty Supremacy of authority or rule, as exercised by a sovereign or sovereign state.

spurious Lacking authenticity or validity; counterfeit; false.

strata Horizontal layers of rock, especially parallel layers arranged on top of another.

subaltern Lower in position or rank; secondary.

subjugate To bring under dominion; conquer; subdue.

traversal Traveling across, over, or through.

usurp To seize and hold, as the power, position, or rights of another, by force and without legal rights or authority.

veracity Habitual adherence to the truth.

vicissitude Any change or variation in something.

For Further Reading

Amundsen, Roald. *Race to the South Pole* (The Great Adventures). Vercelli, Italy: White Star Publishing, 2007.

Bawlf, Samuel. *The Secret Voyage of Sir Francis Drake: 1577–1580*. New York, NY: Penguin, 2004.

Bergreen, Laurence. *Over the Edge of the World: Magellan's Terrifying Circumnavigation of the Globe*. New York, NY: Harper Perennial, 2004.

Brandt, Anthony, ed. *North Pole: A Narrative History*. Des Moines, IA: National Geographic, 2005.

Carter, Howard. *The Tomb of Tutankamen* (Abridged). Des Moines, IA: National Geographic, 2003.

Cremin, Aedeen. *The World Encyclopedia of Archaeology: The World's Most Significant Sites and Cultural Treasures*. Tonawanda, NY: Firefly Books, 2007.

Crosby, Alfred W. *The Columbian Exchange*. Westport, CT: Praeger Publishers, 2003.

Dale, Ronald J. *The Fall of New France: How the French Lost a North American Empire 1754–1763*. Toronto, Ont., Can.: Lorimer, 2004.

Deagan, Kathleen, and Jose Maria Cruxent. *Columbus's Outpost Among the Tainos: Spain and America at La Isabella, 1493–1498*. New Haven, CT: Yale University Press, 2002.

De Castro Tito Cusi Yupanqui, Diego. *History of How the Spaniards Arrived in Peru*. Indianapolis, IN: Hackett Publishing, 2006.

Fisher, David Hackett. *Champlain's Dream*. New York, NY: Simon & Schuster, 2008.

Fleming, Fergus. *Off the Map: Tales of Endurance and Exploration*. New York, NY: Grove Press, 2006.

Freedman, Paul. *Out of the East: Spices and the Medieval Imagination*. New Haven, CT: Yale University Press, 2009.

Fritze, Ronald H. *New Worlds: The Great Voyages of Discovery 1400–1600*. Westport, CT: Praeger Publishers, 2003.

Golay, Michael, and Bowman, John S. *North American Exploration*. Hoboken, NJ: John Wiley & Sons, 2003.

Howgego, Raymond John. *Encyclopedia of Exploration to 1800: A Comprehensive Reference Guide to the History and Literature of Exploration, Travel, and Colonization*. Sydney, Aus.: Hordren House, 2003.

Hunter, Douglas. *Half Moon: Henry Hudson and the Voyage That Redrew the Map of the New World*. New York, NY: Bloomsbury Press, 2009.

Levy, Buddy. *Conquistador: Hernan Cortes, King Montezuma, and the Last Stand of the Aztecs*. New York, NY: Bantam Books, 2008.

Malaurie, Jean. *Ultima Thule: Explorers and Natives in the Polar North*. New York, NY: W.W. Norton & Co., 2003.

Mancall, Peter C. (Editor). *Travel Narratives from the Age of Discovery: An Anthology*. New York, NY: Oxford University Press, 2006.

Obregon, Mauricio. *Beyond the Edge of the Sea: Sailing With Jason and the Argonauts, Ulysses, the Vikings, and Other Explorers of the Ancient World*. New York, NY: Modern Library (Random House), 2002.

Ortner, Sherry B. *Life and Death on Mt. Everest: Sherpas and Himalayan Mountaineering*. Princeton, NJ: Princeton University Press, 2001.

Paine, Lincoln P. *Ships of Discovery and Exploration*. New York, NY: Mariner Books, 2009.

Polo, Marco. *The Travels of Marco Polo*. Peter Harris, ed. New York, NY: Everyman's Library, 2008.

Russell, Sir Peter. *Prince Henry the Navigator*. New Haven, CT: Yale University Press, 2001.

Sale, Kirkpatrick. *Christopher Columbus and the Conquest of Paradise* (Second Edition). New York, NY: Tauris Parke Paperbacks, 2006.

Stirling, Stuart. *Pizarro: Conqueror of the Inca*. Charleston, SC: The History Press, 2006.

Thompson, David. *Scott, Shackleton, and Amundsen: Ambition and Tragedy in the Antarctic*. New York, NY: Basic Books, 2002.

Watkins, Ronald. *Unknown Seas: How Vasco da Gama Opened the East*. London, UK: John Murray Publishers, Ltd., 2004.

Wood, Francis. *The Silk Road: Two Thousand Years in the Heart of Asia*. Berkeley, CA: University of California Press, 2004.

*I*ndex